ENERGY ECONOMICS

ENERGY ECONOMICS

Edited by

Dr. Parag Diwan

Chirag Shah

PENTAGON ENERGY PRESS

ENERGY ECONOMICS

ISBN 978-81-8274-348-9

First Edition: 2009

First published in India by

PENTAGON ENERGY PRESS
An Imprint of
PENTAGON PRESS
206, Peacock Lane, Shahpur Jat,
New Delhi-110049
Phones: 011-64706243, 26491568
Telefax: 011-26490600
email: rajan@pentagon-press.com
website: www.pentagon-press.com

Printed at New Elegant Printers, New Delhi.

Preface

Energy economics is the field that studies human utilization of energy resources and energy commodities and the consequences of that utilization. Under the subject we essentially study Depletable Resource economics. Energy economics studies forces that lead economic agents – firms, individuals, governments – to supply energy resources, to convert those resources into other useful energy forms, to transport them to the users, to use them, and to dispose of the residuals. It studies roles of alternative market and regulatory structures on these activities, economic distributional impacts, and environmental consequences. It studies economically efficient provision and use of energy commodities and resources and factors that lead away from economic efficiency.

We further sub divide the subject into Oil and Natural Gas economics. Fossil fuels—coal, oil and natural gas—have satisfied most of the world's primary energy demand and it is anticipated that they will do so for the foreseeable future too. Products derived from oil such as petrol, aviation turbine fuel (henceforth referred to as ATF), diesel fuel, and heating oil, supply nearly 40 percent of the energy consumed by households, businesses, and manufacturers worldwide. Value of crude oil is driven by the demand for petroleum products, particularly in the transportation sector. Petroleum products power virtually all motor vehicles, aircraft, marine vessels, and trains around the globe. Natural gas and coal, by comparison, each supply less than 25 percent of the world's energy needs. Oil accounted for 8 percent of global trade in goods and services and about 2.5 percent of world activity in 2004—higher than any other commodity, although well below 1980 levels.

Despite a consistent fall in global oil intensity, crude oil remains an important commodity and events in the oil market continue to play a significant role in shaping global economic and political developments. Oil is the world economy's most important source of energy and is, therefore, critical to economic growth. Moreover, given the distribution of oil reserves and the structure of supply and demand, geopolitical factors play an important role in the oil market. Thus it is important to study the economics of Oil, that is the issues pertaining to the pricing, taxation and the regulatory framework for the sector.

Unlike oil and coal, there is no world gas market: 85% of the gas consumed in the world today is produced locally, and gas trade occurs largely on a regional scale. Thus, there is no world standard for gas pricing or marker price, such as WTI or Brent for crude oil. Small and remote gas discoveries are often hard to commercialise. As a result, there is a large amount of "stranded gas" in the world. The most significant difference is that, while investment in oil and coal production can be made independently from the conclusion of sales contracts, relying on selling the product on the world market, investment in gas production cannot proceed without long-term commitments between prospective producers and consumers.

In the last decade, natural gas has grown to become a truly global energy source. Increasingly, gas is seen as an essential fuel to meet the three important pillars on which energy policies are built: energy security, environmental sustainability, and economic competitiveness and growth. This thus makes it important to understand the economics and the policy framework for the Natural gas sector. The last section of the monograph on Energy economics accordingly deals with Natural Gas economics.

New Delhi
June 1, 2008

Dr. Parag Diwan
Chirag Shah

Contents

Chapter 1

Energy Economics: An Introduction

Energy economics is the field that studies human utilization of energy resources and energy commodities and the consequences of that utilization. In physical science terminology, "energy" is the capacity for doing work, e.g., lifting, accelerating, or heating material. In economic terminology, "energy" includes all energy commodities and energy resources, commodities or resources that embody significant amounts of physical energy and thus offer the ability to perform work. Energy commodities, e.g., gasoline, diesel fuel, natural gas, propane, coal, or electricity—can be used to provide energy services for human activities, such as lighting, space heating, water heating, cooking, motive power, electronic activity. Energy resources, e.g., crude oil, natural gas, coal, biomass, hydro, uranium, wind, sunlight, or geothermal deposits—can be harvested to produce energy commodities. Energy economics studies forces that lead economic agents—firms, individuals, governments—to supply energy resources, to convert those resources into other useful energy forms, to transport them to the users, to use them, and to dispose of the residuals. It studies roles of alternative market and regulatory structures on these activities, economic distributional impacts, and environmental consequences. It studies economically efficient provision and use of energy commodities and resources and factors that lead away from economic efficiency.

Other than all embodying significant amounts of physical energy, energy resources or commodities vary greatly. They may embody chemical energy (e.g., oil, natural gas, coal, biomass), mechanical energy (e.g., wind, falling water), thermal energy (geothermal deposits), radiation (sunlight, infrared radiation), electrical energy (electricity), or the potential to create energy through nuclear reactions (uranium, plutonium). They have differing physical forms. Crude oil, most refined petroleum products, and water are liquids. Of water includes available energy only through its motion. Coal, most biomass, and uranium are solids. Natural gas and wind are in gases, with wind including available energy based only on its movement. Geothermal energy is available through hot liquids (normally water) or solids (subterranean rock formations). Solar radiation is a pure form of energy. Electricity consists of electrons moving under an electrical potential. Resources can be viewed as renewable or depletable. Some renewable resources can be stored; others are not storable.

DEPLETABLE RESOURCES

Based on the speed of natural processes, one can classify primary energy resources as depletable or renewable. Renewable resources can be further subdivided into storable or non-storable resources. Renewable resources are self-renewing within a time scale important for economic decision-making. Storable renewable resources typically exist as a stock, which can be used or can be stored. Biomass, hydro power, and some geothermal, falls in this category. The amount used at one time influences the amount available in subsequent times. Non-storable renewable resources—wind, solar radiation, run-of-the-river hydro resources can be used or not, but the quantity used at a given time has no direct influence on the quantity available subsequently. Most energy commodities are storable (refined petroleum products, processed natural gas, coal, batteries), but electricity is not storable as electricity. Depletable resources are those whose renewal speeds are so slow that it is appropriate to view them as made available once and only once by nature. Crude oil, natural gas, coal, and uranium all fall in this category.

Initially all human energy use depended on renewable resources, in particular biomass resources used for food, heat, or light. In the United States, renewable energy—human, animal, water, wood, and wind power—dominated energy supply through the middle of the 19th century. Only during the second half of the 19th century did a depletable resource, coal, surpass renewable resource use. Crude oil and natural gas started supplying large quantities of energy only in the 1920s.

Now the dominant use of energy in developed nations is based on depletable resources, particularly fossil fuels. But depletable resource use cannot dominate forever. Once particular deposits have been used, they cannot be reused. Therefore, a future transition from depletable resources, particularly from fossil fuels, is inevitable. However, which renewable energy sources will dominate future consumption is not clear. And there is great uncertainty about the timing of a shift to renewable energy resources. Related is the unresolved question of future energy adequacy: will the renewable sources of energy be adequate to satisfy demands for energy, once the fossil fuel supplies move close to ultimate depletion?

DEPLETABLE RESOURCE ECONOMICS

The study of depletable resource economics began with articles by Lewis Grey and Harold Hotelling, which examined economically inter-temporal optimal extraction from a perfectly known stock of the resource, with perfectly predictable future prices of the extracted commodity. Many, but not all, subsequent articles maintained the perfect knowledge assumptions.

The essential result is that under optimal extraction paths the resource owner recognizes (explicitly or implicitly) an opportunity cost, or rent, in addition to the marginal extraction costs. All information about the role of future prices and costs would be embodied in this opportunity cost. The competitive firm would extract at a rate such that the marginal extraction cost plus opportunity cost would equal the selling price for the extracted commodity. Price would thus exceed marginal cost, even if the firm were operating perfectly competitively. This opportunity cost would evolve smoothly over time. As the resource neared depletion, the opportunity cost and the marginal extraction cost even at very low extraction rates would together have increased until they equaled the commodity price, at which time extraction would cease. In depletable resource theory, market prices would increase gradually to the cost of producing substitutes, reaching that cost only as the depletable resource were nearing depletion.

Substitutes would be produced only in small quantities until near the time of depletion. Market forces would automatically and optimally guide commodity prices upward so that when the depletable resources were nearing depletion, commodity prices would have risen to a point at which the demands could be fully satisfied by the substitutes. In reality, the economic cycle for depletable resources is far more complex and more prone to error and surprises. The cycle typically begins with innovations that allow the resource to be utilized. Technologies improve over time, partially guided by economic forces and public policy decisions, but often in somewhat unpredictable ways. Generally the magnitude and location of the resource base remains unknown and exploration is required to identify resource deposits. But exploration is costly. Therefore typically it is optimal for companies to explore only until they find sufficient resources to satisfy their expectations of near-term extraction.

These discovered resources—referred to as "reserves" —are typically only a fraction of the resource base and do not provide reliable estimates of the overall size of the resource stock. Firms may optimally extract from the proven reserves but cannot know with any certainty the quantity or extraction costs of the undiscovered resources. Opportunity cost would depend on the future prices of the extracted commodity, but future commodity prices will themselves depend on future demand and supply, which in turn depends on the uncertain future discoveries, and which therefore are very unpredictable.

With this additional complexity and uncertainty, although the opportunity cost concept remains important, it seems appropriate to focus more attention on responses of markets to random changes in technologies, reserves, and other market information. And it seems appropriate to abandon the notion that markets will automatically and optimally guide the system to a smooth transition to renewable resources. One central result does remain, however. If there is only a limited stock of a resource—undiscovered plus discovered—then there will be only a limited number of years during which the resource can be extracted. Here there is an important commonality between energy economics and ecological economics (see article on ecological economics). The typical pattern includes an initial period in which the resource is not used, before technology for extracting and/or using the resource is developed. Extraction rates rise over time, perhaps rapidly, as that technology develops and demand increases. Commodity prices would fall with falling extraction and finding costs. However, at some time, rising costs due to depletion of the resource start overtaking the decreasing costs due to technology advances. The extraction rate declines until ultimately all of the economical resource stocks are depleted. At that point, the consumers of the depletable resource must substitute some other means of satisfying energy service demand.

If markets work well, the renewable resources will then be available in sufficient quantities and at reasonable costs. A transition to renewable energy resources will have been successfully accomplished and there would always be an adequate energy supply to satisfy all demands at the prevailing market price. However, given the complexity and the uncertainty, it is not obvious that the transition will work as automatically, as smoothly, or as optimally as suggested above. It may be that fossil fuels saved for the future will ultimately never be needed because substitute forms of energy become available at a lower cost and at an earlier time than expected. Or it may be that fossil fuels are rapidly depleted but that costs of renewable resources remain well above expected levels or that quantities of renewable resources are more limited than expected. In either case, in retrospect everyone might wish to have made very different public policy decisions.

THE MARKETS

During the past few years, the prevailing perspective on the world energy markets has been thoroughly shaken-up. This turmoil is not confined to a single branch of the energy industry. On all fronts, business as usual has been truncated, as more-or-less unexpected events and phenomena have heralded a new era.

Within the oil market, a variety of political and economic factors drove up oil prices from 2004 onwards. On the demand side there was an unexpected strong growth in oil consumption by the US, India and China. The supply side has been simultaneously hampered by a greatly reduced surplus capacity in crude production and a weak and unbalanced processing and transport infrastructure, following years of rather meagre investment. Geopolitical tensions evolving from the Iraq situation and local instabilities in Nigeria and Venezuela have again made the world aware of its growing dependence on but a few net exporting countries, among which the Persian Gulf OPEC producers feature prominently. This situation of concentrated supplies is generally expected to worsen, when non-OPEC oil production declines in the near future. The role of Russia in this scenario is still uncertain and will depend primarily on national political and economic developments. In the main consumer countries in North America and Europe, during the 1990s, there was a growing expectation that foreign direct investments would strongly dilute state ownership of reserves and production assets when the new generation oil and gas fields would have to be developed.

To a large extent, liberalisation of energy markets in these consumer countries was founded on this premise. Such a development was seen as a logical continuation of the liberalisation of trade and finance during the 1980s and the difficulties some important producer countries experienced in generating domestic investment capital. With the expected shift of the investment market from North America and Europe to producer countries in Africa, the Middle East, Central Asia and Russia, increased 'private' flows of oil and gas were expected to reach the market.

Generally, globalisation was believed to have the effect of freeing up oil and gas reserves from government ownership. Contrary to expectations in the aforementioned consumer countries, producer countries have not privatised their oil and gas production sectors. For oil, only some offshore developments were opened to investment from major oil companies, while state-owned gas companies hold at least a 50% share for gas export projects in the main resource holding regions. Access to reserves of foreign capital generally has remained limited and has recently fuelled concerns about security of demand on the part of the producer governments (who must dedicate scarce capital to the gas industry and fear costly over-investment) and concerns about security of supply on the part of consumer governments (who fear underinvestment and politically motivated supply decisions).

The issue of ownership also impacts governance structure and compatibility of regulatory design along the various points of the value chain. Moreover, regulatory competition between producer and consumer governments over where rents can be captured is to be expected.

For the electricity sector, several supply interruptions and blackouts in the US, Italy and the UK have illustrated the need to start investing again in power plants, local networks and transmission lines, after years of asset sweating. Further, this industry sees its reserve margins dwindle rapidly, as is commonly argued. In China, demand for electricity is growing so quickly that despite large investment in new capacities, the country is frequently experiencing blackouts. Chinese consumers very often have to rely on oil-powered generators to overcome electricity shortages. The resulting additional demand for oil is translated into world crude pricing. A further factor of potentially large importance is increasing awareness and general acceptance of the dangers of global warming caused by carbon dioxide emissions from large-scale use of fossil fuels.

Step-by-step, there is gaining momentum towards implementing measures to reduce these emissions, by way of 'sustainable' sources of energy and enhancement of energy efficiency. In a number of countries, environmental concerns and emerging supply security considerations are also rekindling discussions to include nuclear energy in the energy mix.

A critical consequence of these developments has been a considerable increase in the average and peak level of prices. This is occurring, for all types of energy, against the backdrop of consumer country policymakers having underlined a decline in energy prices as one of the main benefits of liberalization for the consumers. Within the gas sector, the main issue is the growth of natural gas consumption in conditions of declining production in the main gas consuming areas, such as the US, Asia and the EU. This implies an increasing dependence of these markets on external supplies. The bulk of gas reserves are concentrated in but a few countries, although a rather large number of countries have possibilities to develop some limited indigenous supplies. Moreover, much of new gas supplies, in the form of LNG, will use the same marine trading routes as most crude oil transport, some of which are already considered to be logistical bottlenecks.

Liberalisation policies are confronting increased scepticism. Justified or not, this scepticism is rooted in incidences such as the Enron debacle and perceptions of decreasing security of electricity supply alongside decreasing reserve margins in generation capacity, blackouts and brownouts occurring in e.g. California, Italy, and the UK. Moreover, rising gas and electricity prices are often associated with the liberalisation of gas markets. Governments more often than not decided to immediately tax away most of the efficiency gains, while recent supply constraints have pushed prices further upwards. An increasing number of politicians are apparently losing confidence in the superiority of market mechanisms to provide sufficient energy at reasonable prices and instead seem to prefer more government coordination.

The general expectation of the early 1990s that economic liberalism and globalisation would be the guiding principles for development of international relations appears to be replaced by a world in which state interests play a more dominant role in international relations. In such a world, major consumers and power blocks increasingly compete for scarce resources, employing also non-economic means. This outlook has increased importing countries' fears that energy deliveries can be used as an instrument of political power in international relations. However, increasing import dependency on a particular producer country also implies that that the producer country is likely to become economically more dependent on the consumer country.

Nevertheless, there is still manoeuvring room to pick-off certain countries and to apply strong-arm politics.

These fundamental shifts in the determinants of energy systems all over the world are forcing a gradual re-evaluation of the prevailing market-based energy paradigm. Despite the fact that such a re-evaluation is taking place at a (geographically, ideologically and intellectually) very uneven rate, it is becoming obvious that new models for government-market interactions and their respective roles and responsibilities are necessary. With respect to security of energy supply and environmental concerns, for instance, the market should not be expected to yield the preferred long-term outcomes without clear government guidance. Considering the gas industry in a somewhat greater degree of detail, a number of important developments should be highlighted:

Natural gas consumption has grown rapidly over the past decade and will remain the fuel of choice for technical, environmental and—to a lesser extent—economic reasons.

The medium to long-term outlook for the oil supply and demand balance is very much under discussion. Such uncertainties translate via price linkages (direct or indirect) to the price outlook for natural gas. This unsure price outlook means that the future for natural gas is also uncertain—particularly for power generation. Hence, gas demand projections in general have become more difficult to make.

A growing share of gas consumption is used as fuel input for electricity generation. The consequences of this development for the overall supply and demand balance, for seasonal and daily patterns, and for price and cross elasticity of gas demand are still uncertain.

All three large regional consumer markets in the US, the EU and Asia, face the need to import increasing volumes of natural gas from sources outside their surrounding regions in the Middle East, Russia and Africa. The consequent dependence between suppliers and consumers, the imminent conflicts between their interests and the growing linkage of gas supply to the political economy of the world oil market imply the emergence of an increasingly politicised gas market.

Additionally, it is important to note that foreign private companies have direct access to only about one-third of remaining oil reserves. For gas, state control via large state-owned companies over gas reserves is about the same.

This in itself might impact industry structures, requiring large buyers with sufficient market leverage.

Geopolitics do indeed matter and energy and gas producing countries seem willing to use this strategic asset to their advantage as required. For example, Russia, facing a decline in military power, has turned to using its energy sources as an effective strategic tool for foreign relations.

Consequently, consumer governments have renewed their focus on (external) supply security. This inspires policies to underscore the growth in gas consumption with assurances and guarantees in supplies. Large consumer regions increasingly compete for the same gas sources. Regulatory models need to take this into account and be designed to stimulate required investments to facilitate increases of imported gas.

Issues are arising around the extent to which political circumstances and exploration and production (E&P) regimes allow for necessary investments and production levels. Distribution of incentives, rents and risks throughout the gas value chain is of fundamental importance, while geopolitical considerations and local socio-political conditions are essential determinants of supply security.

The long haul supply lines necessary to transport gas to consumer markets will increasingly confront transit issues, both in the US and EU contexts. Here a question arises about the adequacy of transit regimes and the positioning of transit markets. Should there be differences between regulatory rules for transit of gas and for gas imported into the markets crossed by these gases flows? What are appropriate connection rules when transit flows are entering the more integrated and connected gas networks and what are the appropriate transmission conditions for volumes of long haul gas once they have entered entry/exit transmission systems? Will (annual) adjustment of network codes and possible capacity reallocations affect transit flows to markets? The supply of long haul gas, via pipelines as well as LNG, generally implies large and constant throughput factors for the infrastructures in place. This requires that the seasonal, weekly and daily demand patterns may have to be satisfied via 'local' provision of storage and other forms of supply flexibility.

The need to construct additional supply infrastructure in the US, as well as in Europe and Asia, raises the question of who will invest and operate these pipelines, LNG terminals and storage and treatment facilities—and under what kinds of preconditions? How much market and how much 'essential facility' functionalities are to be respected, or to be allowed? Are partial exemptions to third party access (TPA) regimes necessary here and should they be the rule rather than the exception? How much ex ante regulatory policy would be necessary or achievable, in balancing investor requirements with the need to achieve effective and efficient use of infrastructure in support of the competitive markets?

The free gas market generally lacks mechanisms to coordinate timing and the amount of investment required to balance gas supply and demand under more-or-less extreme market circumstances, thus giving rise to volatile gas prices. As a consequence, regulatory systems will have to involve instruments to stimulate an efficient use of the infrastructure in place, while signalling the need for timely investments in additional facilities. Supplementary capacity generally contributes more to achieving a competitive market than to redistribution of existing capacity among shippers, through pro rata congestion management, auctions, or a shortening of the maximum duration of transportation reservations. The investment climate is served by a regulatory system that makes transparent choices and is clear in its objectives.

The traditional institutions for gas market coordination, such as long-term contracts with take or pay provisions, destination clauses and oil price parity pricing in captive markets, joint horizontal and vertical ownership over production facilities and pipelines, are under serious discussion or have already been removed to a varying extent in the various regional markets. Natural gas projects, given their high sunk costs and long repayment periods, are said to be suffering from a lack of certainty regarding future regulatory frameworks. Restructuring could lead to fragmentation of value chains and markets, creating noise in the information flows and delaying signals that invoke new investment. Is there a rationale for allowing 'alternative' structural coordination devices, such as large conglomerates and joint ventures in the market, or modernised forms of long-term contracts to provide for the necessary levels of predictability and reliability?

From primarily regional forms of organisation, increasing LNG flows are transforming the natural gas market into a world market, integrating the thus far separated regional gas markets in the US, EU, Asia and Latin America. From a regulatory perspective, relevant questions concern the regulatory regimes for the required infrastructures (pipelines, LNG plants and storage) and how to secure investor confidence in this new setting.

MINERAL TAXATION

Mining normally creates wealth or economic surpluses. This potential provides the incentive for private companies to explore for, develop, and then exploit mineral deposits. Although companies generally are driven by the pursuit of profits, the goals and objectives of the sovereign governments that control the terms and conditions under which private interests have access to mineral deposits are quite different. Their actions and policies, including the taxes they impose on the mineral sector, are designed to promote various social goals—economic development, for example—as determined through the prevailing political processes.

Policy Issues

All governments, in the process of determining the structure and nature of the taxes they impose on mining and on the mineral sector in general, encounter the following public policy issues.

Optimal Level of Taxation on Mining

The more the government taxes the mineral sector, the greater the share of wealth created by mining that flows to the government. This means, of course, that less of the wealth is fl owing to the companies. Therefore, rising tax rates undermine companies' incentive to carry out exploration, to develop new mines, and even, if the increases are sufficiently large, to remain in production at existing operations. Thus, one critical issue for public policy is determining the optimum level of mineral taxation. Clearly, a tax rate that takes all of the wealth is too high, because it kills the goose that lays the golden egg. On the other hand, a tax rate of zero is likely to be too low, leaving the state with only the non-tax benefits that flow from mining and mineral production. Somewhere between these two extremes is an optimal level of taxation that maximizes the net present value (NPV) of the tax revenues or, more appropriately, the NPV of all social benefits the country receives from its mineral sector.

Unfortunately, in practice it is not easy to determine the optimal level of taxation, which would require knowledge of how a firm's behavior is altered in the present and, more importantly, in the future by changing levels of taxation. In addition, estimating future tax revenues requires knowledge of the flow of future profits the domestic mineral sector is likely to generate, which depends on trends in metal prices and on production costs.

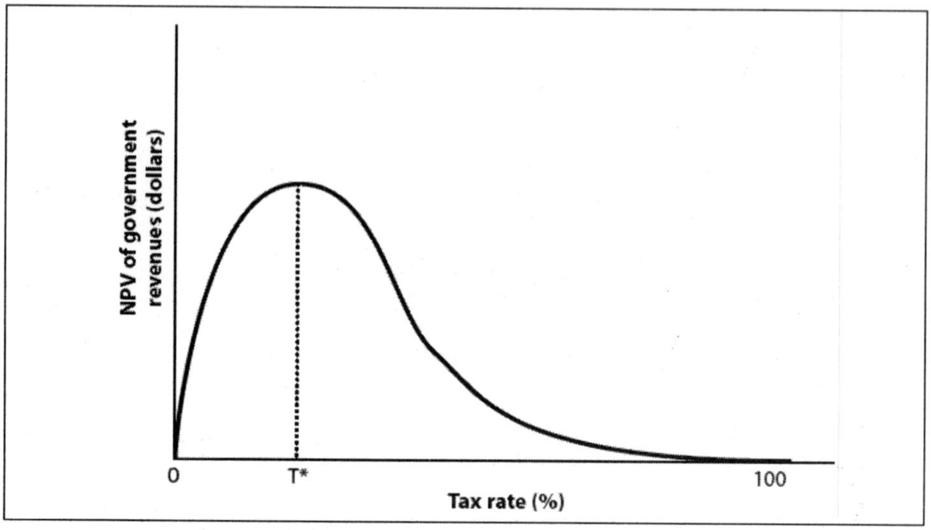

Source: Mining Royalties, A global study on their Impact on Investors, Government and Civil Society, World Bank, 2006.

Figure 1.1: Government Tax Revenue as a Function of Tax Rate

However, two things are known about the optimum level of taxation. First, the government can take its share of the wealth created by mining, either in the form of taxes or in the form of non-pecuniary benefits. The latter are government-imposed requirements on mining companies (or voluntary contributions) that raise production costs. For example, the government may require or pressure mining companies to build and maintain roads in remote regions that are used by the general public as well as for mining. It may force or otherwise encourage companies to provide schools, hospitals, and other social services in areas surrounding a mine. It may insist that companies use local suppliers or domestic workers, or that downstream processing be done domestically. The more such requirements increase production costs, the smaller the benefits the government can reap in the form of tax revenues, and hence the lower the optimal level of taxation. It is also clear that raising the level of taxation shifts toward the present the flow of benefits a country receives from its mineral sector over time. This is because a tax increase will almost always raise tax revenues over the first few years following its implementation. Over the longer run, however, the higher tax level is likely to discourage exploration and mine development, and so reduces tax revenues below what they would have been. As a result, raising the level of mineral taxation, such as imposing a new or higher royalty, almost always looks successful from the point of view of the government in the short run. It can take several years or longer for the negative effects on tax revenues to become apparent. Even then, the negative effects are hard to assess because they require comparing actual tax revenues with what revenues would have been in the absence of the tax increase.

Optimum Mix of Taxes

Many different types of taxes can be, and are, imposed on the mineral sector. Each, including the various forms of royalty, has its own set of advantages and disadvantages with respect to economic efficiency, the division of risks between the state and companies, ease of administration, and other considerations. Economists, for example, often fault royalties that impose a tax on each tonne of metal mined (or the market value of each tonne of metal produced) on the grounds that such taxes introduce inefficiencies in production decisions. For the firm, such a royalty is an additional cost of production. Low-grade ore, just economic enough to exploit without a royalty, may no longer be profitably extracted after a royalty is introduced.

In that regard, a tax on corporate income or profits is more efficient, because such a tax does not alter the optimal output of companies striving to maximize profits, and marginal ore will remain profitable to exploit. It would be wrong, however, to assume, as some have done, that corporate profit taxes and royalties based on profits have no distorting effects on firms' behavior. Such taxes do reduce firms' anticipated net present value and internal rate of return on both existing operations and potential new projects. As a result, high taxes on corporate profits and profit-based royalties encourage companies to close marginal operations sooner than would otherwise be the case and tend to reduce the economic attractiveness of new projects. However, their effect will be less than that of high levels of taxes that are not based on profitability.

The mix of taxes also influences the distribution of risks between the state and mining companies. Mining is a particularly risky activity. This is partly because of the long gestation period associated with the development of most new mines and the difficulty of anticipating prior to development all the potential technical, geological, economic, and political problems. In addition, most mineral commodity markets are highly volatile over the business cycle, with wide price fluctuations. When the world economy is booming, prices can be two to three times higher than during periods of slow or declining growth. As a result, profits vary greatly for individual mining companies over time. They also vary greatly at any point in time among mining companies. Some mines turn out to be bonanzas; others never return a profit, even during the years of high prices.

A corporate profits tax and royalties based on profitability tend to distribute the risk of mining evenly between the state and companies. When before-tax profits are down by 20 percent, both tax revenues flowing to the government and after-tax profits realized by companies are down by more or less the same amount. A unit- or value-based royalty shifts more of the risk to companies. Even when prices are depressed and companies are in the red, the government continues to receive a certain amount for each tonne of metal produced and sold. Conversely, a progressive income tax or "additional" profits tax tends to shift more of the risk to the government, because it merely imposes a tax on profits that rises with profits or, alternatively, with the internal rate of return or net present value realized by a mine.

Normally, companies are in a better position to assume risks and are less risk averse than governments. In such cases, the state may want to impose a mix of taxes that shifts more of the risks to companies; however, such a strategy has a cost. To compensate companies for assuming more risk, the government must be willing to allow firms to capture a large share of the expected profits, which means lower expected government revenues.

The mix of taxes also affects the flow of government revenues over time. An import duty, for example, on trucks, drills, ball mills, and other imported capital goods produces tax revenues during the development stage of a project. Revenues come from a unit- or value-based royalty at the time of production, from a corporate profits tax or profit-based royalty once the project is profitable, and from an additional profits tax only after the designated profit hurdle has been met. Moreover, with a corporate profits tax, provisions allowing the accelerated depreciation of capital equipment can postpone the flow of tax revenues for years.

Another important consideration in determining the mix of taxes is the difficulty of tax administration and the possibilities for evasion. Some taxes, including many types of royalties, are easy to administer and difficult to evade. Government officials simply need to know a company's total sales or production to determine its tax liability. This not only reduces administrative costs, it reduces the incentives firms have to devote resources to tax reduction efforts. Perhaps more importantly, it reduces the opportunities for corruption.

These advantages are less in evidence with the corporate profits tax and profit-based royalties. Assessing the appropriateness of costs, such as management fees paid to parent companies and other non-market transactions, is difficult, and companies that invest time and resources in efforts to reduce and avoid taxes may receive good returns.

Specificity or Uniformity

Another policy issue concerns the specificity of the tax code. For tax purposes, many countries consider the mining and the mineral sector special. This is in part because, for some countries, this sector plays a dominant role in the economy, accounting for a large share of all government revenues and foreign exchange earnings. In such instances, it is not unusual for the government to negotiate specific agreements covering a variety of issues, including taxation for individual large-scale, or "mega," projects. In addition, there is the widespread perception that the mineral sector is different, and so should be taxed differently, because it exploits a nonrenewable resource. In some instances that resource involves unusually rich and, hence, extremely profitable mineral deposits. This justification for tax specificity is also considered later in this section in the discussion of economic rent and user costs.

Other countries—Chile in recent years, for example—have taxed mining companies the same as all other companies. There are several benefits with this approach. It eliminates the ability of particular industries to obtain favourable tax legislation and so reduces the incentives for companies to lobby and plead for special favours. Uniformity also reduces the complexity of the tax codes, and makes them easier to administer. It eliminates or decreases the likelihood of one industry being singled out for special tax increases.

Regime Stability

Companies that are deciding whether to invest in a mineral project are largely influenced by the expected return after taxes and by risks. An important component of any assessment of risk is the perceived stability of the existing tax regime. Companies that plan to invest hundreds of millions of dollars or even billions of dollars in a new mine and mineral complex are very wary of possible changes in the tax burden after their investment is made and no longer mobile.

From the perspective of governments, the perception of tax regime stability is also important. Given the risk-return trade-off for firms, the greater the perception of stability, the lower the expected return investing firms require and, hence, the greater the share of wealth from mining the government can collect in the form of taxes or other benefits.

Unfortunately for both companies and governments, however, tax regime stability is hard to guarantee. One reason is the difficulty of binding future governments to the current promises and agreements. At some point, maybe 5 or 10 years after the decision to proceed, a new government may well be in power. Another reason is the shift in bargaining power that occurs over the life of a mineral project. Before a mineral project is developed, considerable uncertainty surrounds its future profitability for various reasons. As a result, companies are often reluctant to proceed without promises of favourable tax treatment. The host government, often keen for numerous reasons to see the project developed, tends to be accommodating. Once the project is completed, the invested capital is sunk and cannot be withdrawn from the country. Moreover the uncertainty regarding profitability dissipates. Some projects turn out to be unprofitable, whereas others are quite profitable.

In any case, unhappiness with the agreed-upon tax regime may arise whether a project is successful or unsuccessful. Unprofitable projects consume the country's nonrenewable resources but tend to return little or nothing to the state in the form of taxes. Moreover, the public may be suspicious that the lack of profitability reflects either company incompetence or, in the case of international companies, the export of profits abroad to avoid taxes. Profitable projects, on the other hand, do pay taxes, but they are consuming what are obviously valuable domestic resources, and often the public believes that too much of the wealth being generated is going to the companies, particularly in the case of highly successful projects.

These concerns may be accentuated by populism, in the case of the mineral sector, in which many multinational companies are likely to be operating. The public in general, often unaware of the possible negative implications in the long run, is quite likely to support higher taxes on the mineral sector, particularly taxes on large foreign companies. Politicians can easily frame the debate in terms of those who support the interests of the country and its citizens versus those who are more concerned about the interests of foreign companies and their wealthy shareholders. However, if the level of taxation is already at or above the optimal level, further increases are not only bad for mining companies, they are bad for the country. Moreover, changes in the tax regime undermine the investment community's perception of stability, raising the perceived risk of investment in the country. A higher perception of risk and uncertainty means that more of the expected wealth creation from any project must go to the company, as compensation for the higher risk, and less to the state. In short, changing the tax regime will likely reduce the optimum level of taxation as well.

Since changes in the tax regime can increase perceptions of risk and reduce the optimal level of taxation, how should countries respond when the perception of risk is falling over time? Indonesia, over several decades, offered mining companies different generations of contracts. The first generation was the most favourable from the viewpoint of foreign mining. The government was willing to provide companies with extra compensation for investing after a period of political and social unrest. When these investments proved attractive, and hence reduced the perceived risk of investing in the country, the government offered the next generation of investors slightly less attractive terms. This process continued through several generations. Once an agreement was reached, it was not changed, so companies knew before they invested what the tax regime would be. Most importantly, they knew that once they were in production, the likelihood of changes was slight.

Governments and companies may also enhance the stability of the tax regime by minimizing to the extent possible the likelihood that the government and the public will be unhappy once the project is in operation. This might be done by collecting the government's expected share of the wealth through a mix of taxes. A modest royalty on output would ensure that the state received something for its exploited resources even when the operation was unprofitable. Similarly, imposing some sort of additional or progressive profits tax when projects are highly successful would help protect the government from public accusations that it left too much money on the table to the detriment of the public interest. In the end, however, all parties have to realize that private companies need to be adequately compensated for the risks they take when projects are successful, and for the losses they suffer on unsuccessful projects.

Distribution and Use of Tax Revenues

Though much of the public debate over mineral taxes focuses on the appropriate division of wealth between companies and the state, as well as on other issues discussed above in this section, much more important is how the tax revenues are distributed and ultimately used. For a decade or so, economists, policy analysts, and others have been debating the positive and negative impacts of mineral production and exports for economic growth and development, particularly in developing countries. One of the conclusions emerging from what is called the resource curse debate is that mineral production can both foster and hinder economic growth, with the outcome being largely determined by how governments use the taxes and other funds they receive from the mineral sector.

Given the volatility of mineral prices and profits over the business cycle, one issue in the debate concerns the usefulness of a commodity stabilization fund. When mineral taxes are high, thanks to a boom in the mineral sector, the government deposits some of its mineral taxes into such funds. Revenues are then withdrawn when mineral prices and taxes are low. Such arrangements exist, or have existed, in Chile, Namibia, Nauru, Norway, Papua New Guinea, and other mineral-producing countries; they have worked well in some countries and not as well in others. An associated issue is what to do with the money while it is in the fund. Investing profits abroad, rather than domestically, helps insulate the domestic economy from the adverse microeconomic effects that a mineral boom can cause, thereby reducing the prospect of what is commonly called the Dutch disease from occurring. The government must also decide how to distribute mineral tax revenues. Historically, they have been largely retained by the central government with little going to provinces and the regions where mining occurs. In recent years, however, more of the revenues have been allocated to the provinces and mining districts in response to their increasing requests.

IDENTIFICATION OF TAX TYPES AND THEIR CLASSIFICATION

Governments have many options to choose from when designing fiscal systems, and various types and forms of taxation methods can be used. The methods applied to the mining sector usually fall into one of two main categories of tax: *in rem* or *in personam*.

In rem taxes are charges assessed against the mineral deposit or against the inputs and actions needed to exploit it. These charges can be divided into two groups: taxes that affect the variable costs of the project (such as unit-based royalties, ad valorem–based royalties, sales taxes, and excise taxes) and taxes that affect the fixed costs of the project (such as certain types of property taxes, import duties, registration fees, land rents, value-added tax, some types of stamp duties, and withholding taxes on loan interest and services). *In rem* taxes rarely take into account the concept of profitability. In contrast, *in personam* taxes are charges against some definition of net revenues, that is, revenues less qualifying costs. Examples include income tax, progressive or additional profits tax, withholding tax on remitted dividends, royalty based on some measure of profit, and royalty based on some measure of income.

Table 1.1: Taxes and their Basis

Tax Type	*Basis*
In rem taxes (unit or value based)	
Unit-based royalty	Set charge per unit
Ad Valorem-based royalty	% of mineral's value (definition of value may vary)
Sales and excise tax	% of value of sales
Property or capital tax	% of value of property or capital
Import duty	% of value of imports (usually)
Export duty	% of value of exports
Withholding on remitted loan interest	% of loan interest value
withholding on imported services	% of value of services
Value-added tax	% of the value of the good or service
Registration fees	Set charge per registration event
Rent or usage fees	Set charge per unit area
Stamp tax	Set charge per transaction or % of value of the transaction
In personam taxes (net revenue based)	
Income tax	% of income
Capital gains tax	% of profits on disposal of capital assets
Additional profits tax	% of additional profits
Excess profits tax	% of excess profits
Net profits royalty or net value royalty	% of mineral's value less allowable costs
Withholding on remitted profits or dividents	% of remitted value

Source: Mining Royalties, A Global Study on their Impact on Investors, *Government and Civil Society*, World Bank, 2006

Generally, *in rem* types of taxes have a greater likelihood of causing distortions in decision making pertaining to cutoff ore grades, mine life, and reserves than *in personam* types of taxes. When designing a tax system, policy makers should be aware of the cumulative effects that taxes can have on mine economics and potential levels of future investment. Such awareness must recognize the importance of each tax type in achieving specific objectives and the implications of their cumulative effects.

ENERGY PRICING

Energy pricing is fundamental for the operation of efficient energy markets. Energy prices perform the important role of balancing consumer energy demand with producer supply. However, energy prices can have many other provide the revenue basis for the owners of energy generating, transmission and distribution assets. Pricing trends, reflecting the interaction of demand and supply, can be used to evaluate the need for further investment and changes in the level of production.

Governments also have taken advantage of energy pricing as a tool to achieve policy objectives. Energy taxation has been used not only as a source of government revenue, but also to promote energy and environmental conservation, influence consumer choice, improve efficiency and improve energy security. In some instances, government revenues have been specifically tied to public energy infrastructure projects, such as the provision of rail or port facilities. Governments have also used subsidisation and tax relief measures as a means of encouraging infant energy industries, particularly for new energy sources such as renewables. A thorough understanding of the pricing mechanism could be considered more critical in energy markets due to the high capital intensity and long lead times associated with energy investments. Further, the essential nature of the service energy provides to all sectors of the economy requires that energy prices are set prudently and efficiently. If energy prices are held below the cost of production for social or industrial reasons, it can result in negative results in terms of over-consumption, environmental degradation and wasted national resources. Conversely, if prices are held artificially high, industrial competitiveness will suffer and some consumers would be deprived of an essential service.

As a result of the importance of energy, governments have traditionally maintained a close association with energy industries and, in some instances, these industries have been compulsorily nationalised—such as the nationalisation of the Mexican oil industry. More recently, although deregulation and privatisation initiatives have opened up energy markets, the industries have not been entirely emancipated as requirements for competition and free trade have often been legislated or referred to government monitoring agencies.

The energy pricing process is influenced by many factors; including government and private sector objectives, as well as external influences. Private sector objectives include the desire to increase market share, ensure financial viability and deliver profits to shareholders. Pricing may also differ as a result of the different cost structures of energy industries. Government objectives reflect a wide range of economic, social and political goals, which can be achieved through energy pricing policies. External influences, such as exchange rate variations, may also impact heavily in the energy pricing process.

The basic objectives of energy pricing are economic efficiency, social equity, and financial viability. The efficiency principle seeks to ensure the regulation of prices in such a manner that the allocation of the society's resources to the energy sector fully reflects their values in alternative uses. The equity principle relates to welfare and income distribution considerations. This may result in implementing differential pricing schemes on grounds of basic and essential needs, or the establishment of uniform prices to specific user groups regardless of the different costs of supply, justified on the basis of regional equity or similar concerns. The financial principle suggests that energy supply systems should be able to raise sufficient revenues to remain financially viable, so that continuity and quality of service is ensured, and future investment requirements are achieved. There are many different alternatives for pricing energy, often reflecting the energy policy framework determined by policy makers. The remainder of this section reviews some of the pricing alternatives available to energy industries.

Marginal Cost Pricing

The concept of marginal cost pricing aims to maximise social welfare by pricing energy commodities at a level where, theoretically, the additional benefit of additional units of energy is compensated by the additional cost (short run marginal cost) of providing the extra unit of energy. If more energy was provided beyond this point, net welfare would decline as the additional benefits associated with consuming more energy, would be outweighed by the higher costs of providing that energy.

Marginal cost pricing is most commonly provided in countries where the energy utilities are publicly owned, and the enterprise is run so that the revenue generated is sufficient to cover the operating costs of the utility. Alternatively, where enough private utilities exist to create a highly competitive market, prices tend to converge towards the marginal cost as competition ensures cost minimisation in the production and optimal investment decisions.

Determining the level of the short run marginal cost is problematic in practice. The short run marginal costs will include factors such as the cost of raw fuels and other materials, labour costs and maintenance. Capital costs are assumed to be fixed in the short-run, and therefore are not included in the short run calculation. In the long run, capital can also be varied so that the long run marginal cost includes the cost of increasing output by expanding capacity. Generally, it is agreed that when price is set equal to the long-run cost, it leads to efficient decisions in relation to the level of investment in productive capacity. Since the lifecycle of most energy projects are long, most economists agree that it is preferable to price energy according to the long run marginal cost. The Asian Development Bank strongly encourages this practice and it has successfully been used in France and, prior to privatisation of the electricity sector, the United Kingdom.

Marginal cost pricing has a number of attractive features in terms of allocative efficiency. By focusing on the future costs rather than previous sunk costs, consumers are provided with a more accurate reflection of the cost of their current decisions to consume an extra unit of electricity. Further, long run marginal cost pricing reduces pricing volatility by spreading the "one off" costs, such as a replacement power plant, over a longer period of time.

In practice the use of a long-run marginal-cost pricing scheme is problematic due to the difficulty of accurately estimating the marginal cost. Long run marginal costing attempts to estimate the cost of increasing production capacity in the future, rather than looking at costs already incurred. Long run marginal cost pricing also does not provide for periods of short-term market imbalances. For example, marginal cost pricing cannot incorporate short-term pricing variations so that consumption can be rationed in periods of high demand.

Pricing according to the short-run marginal cost solves some of these problems, and does lead to an efficient use of existing capacity, as well as providing efficient signals relating to the need for any additional production capacity in the future. Allocative efficiency is also assured when the available production capacity is distributed according to the short run marginal cost. Despite the advantages, problems arise because of the short-term market volatility, which makes it extremely difficult for regulators to adjust the price to match the short run marginal cost. Further, the constantly changing price is unpredictable for consumers, and makes long-term investment decisions difficult for the energy supplier.

Pure marginal cost pricing may also involve generic energy commodities being priced differently. This result is common in the electricity industry where are variety of different generators may rely on different methods to generate electricity at different costs. For example, nuclear and hydro electricity generation is characterised by low running costs and high capital costs, while fossil fuel fired generators tend to have higher running costs and lower capital costs.

Therefore marginal cost pricing will tend to create bias towards particular types of electricity generation. This problem is reduced when the long run marginal cost is used as a basis of pricing since the replacement cost (or depreciation) is taken into account as a running cost. On balance, most economists agree that the most practical system of marginal cost pricing involves some comparison with the long run marginal cost. However, this pricing mechanism may not be appropriate when the private sector is involved. For example, since long run marginal cost pricing takes no account of past sunk costs, it is difficult for suppliers to incorporate an ongoing interest component on borrowing used to finance the sunk costs. Some pricing mechanisms have been devised that overcome these problems, such as the "Ramsey" pricing mechanism that allows costs to be recovered by splitting a tariff into at least two parts and adding a mark-up to cover sunk investment costs.

Historical Cost Recovery Pricing

Historical cost recovery pricing involves energy suppliers pricing energy commodities at a level that permit an acceptable market rate of return to be earned and also allows recovery of past expenditures, such as the cost of oil exploration and the construction costs of a drilling rig. Historical cost recovery pricing is widely used around the world, in both highly regulated and loosely regulated economies. Depending on the level of market regulation, the price may be officially set by government or left to competitive market forces. In some countries, the government not only determines the level of price, but also determines the structure of tariff for different consumer groups. In the United States a formally developed system operates where the rate of return, which can be earned by energy producers, must be just and reasonable, and not result in any undue preference or discrimination. Producers are allowed to recover operational costs, plus a reasonable rate of return on capital investments. The rate of return is regulated on a state-by-state basis by various state utility commissions.

The historic cost recovery method of pricing has a number of positive attributes. The historical cost of production capacity is easily determined, allowing the rates of return to be accurately calculated. The system is relatively simple for consumers and producers, and also lowers the investment risk to energy suppliers. However, a historical cost recovery pricing mechanism can result in incorrect economic signals being sent, particularly when the price set does not equal the marginal cost. Also, it can lead to large fluctuations in energy charges if the flow of investment is not constant.

Further there is less incentive for producers to pursue efficiency measures since the rate of return in fixed, and there may be no facility to match risk with the return. Further, it is not clear how over capacity should be priced since it is of no immediate benefit to consumers. In the United States, regulators in some states prohibit so-called 'non useful' cost components, such as excess capacity, to be incorporated into the rate of return. There are a variety of measures that can be used to overcome the disadvantages associated with historic cost recovery pricing. For example market oriented pricing initiatives could be introduced or efficiency enhancement initiatives promoted to increase the rate of return. Under incentive ratemaking, the tariff is indexed to inflation so that it doesn't vary in real terms (often minus a percentage to allow for productivity increases). This gives an incentive to the energy producers to increase efficiency and therefore decrease their costs without impacting on the tariff they receive, thus increasing their rate of return. The system can be structured to allow for the benefit of increased production efficiency to be split between the producer and consumer.

Market Pricing

Market pricing involves the creation of a central market where bundles of energy can be traded between suppliers and consumers of energy at the nominated market price. Bids are accepted in the market from generators, and, in some markets, purchasers to produce or purchase electricity at a given price. Generally a merit order system is used to dispatch generation capacity. This leads to competition between producers and encourages efficiency in production since low cost producers are more likely to sell all of their production capacity.

In some electricity markets, producers receive the "system marginal price" for the electricity they supply to the system. The "system marginal price" is the price of the most expensive generating offer accepted. This system provides an incentive for the producer to increase efficiency since cheaper production methods translate to greater producer profits. However, the consumer surplus is lower since consumers are forced to pay an inefficiency tariff' on electricity production.

In theory, competitive free market prices will approximate the marginal cost of supply, promote the efficient use of capacity in the short-term and provide the correct market signals in relation to future investment capacity requirements. However, in practice other problems exist such as market dominance by large players who can remove competition and lower the economic efficiency of the system. Further, free market mechanisms are prone to periods of instability, and high levels of natural variability that can increase the uncertainty of investments in the long-term. Supporters of market pricing argue that the problems of market pricing are solvable if the efficiency impediment can be removed.

Oligopolistic Pricing

A market is said to be oligopolistic if there are only a few sellers in the market with one or two major sellers controlling over a large share of the market. The remaining sellers may have the remaining of the market, but on an individual basis each controls a relatively small market share. In such a situation, the smaller sellers individually do not have enough power to have a significant impact on market behaviour affecting critical parameters like pricing, production or sales levels.

An oligopolistic market becomes a cartel if there exist arrangements amongst at least a few larger sellers, on key decisions in such areas as pricing, level of production and market shares. Other features, which tend to sustain an oligopolistic market appear to be associated with the oil sector. These interrelated features include vertical integration and the existence of both fiscal and non-fiscal barriers to entry.

Most of the oil firms operating in developing economies are vertically integrated both internally and internationally. Economic theory associating oligopolistic markets with a number of pricing behaviours, one of which—price leadership—has been adopted by the oil sector in developing economies since the deregulation. Price leadership is a practice in which one of the leading sellers ('price leader') takes a lead in determining and announcing price changes, with the immediately, with the remaining 'wait and see' sellers following immediately, or almost immediately, and announcing prices in line with the price leader's adjustment. Price leadership is said to be the most commonly practised pricing behaviour in an oligopolistic market.

The oil sector in many developing economies is characterised by a number of barriers, which tend to restrain free entry into the market, thereby sustaining the oligopolistic structure of the sector.

Discriminatory Pricing

Suppliers can use Price discrimination as a means of extracting higher revenues by differentiating prices according to the consumer groups preferences. Discriminatory pricing only refers to instances where different prices are charged relative to a single marginal cost of supply. It should be noted that differential pricing structures do not necessarily mean discriminatory pricing since differences in the quantity, timing, and location of deliveries will result in variations in the marginal cost of supply.

Price discrimination is often practised whenever it is possible to differentiate between user groups—such as residential, commercial and industrial customers. It is common in pricing schedules for electricity and natural gas systems, which can easily discriminate between customers through individually metered connections. Discrimination is less common for other types of energy supplies because of the difficulties of preventing resales and arbitrage, such as in petroleum products.

Price discrimination permits income redistribution, attempts to foster economic developments through low energy pricing to specific sectors, and can also be used as a tool for encouraging economically efficient development. It may also facilitate the operation of a plant with excess capacity since discriminatory pricing schedules may raise enough total revenue to cover the long-run marginal costs. This situation is common in developing economies where, for example, the construction of a new power plant is unlikely to reach full capacity until further economic development has taken place. To avoid the higher average cost of operating at lower capacity, the utility may use discriminatory pricing as a means of increasing revenue. Alternatively, the utility may search for additional markets and off load the surplus capacity at lower prices—implying that the primary market subsidises the secondary market.

Promotional Pricing

Promotional pricing refers to the temporary under-pricing of energy supplies to selected customer groups at levels below the long-run marginal cost. The aim of promotional pricing is to increase market share, and thereby expand project utilisation at a faster rate. Promotional pricing, sometimes referred to as 'predatory pricing' is sometimes also used as a means of reducing the consumption of alternative energy sources.

In some instances, it may be reasonable and economically more efficient to price energy supplies not at the present low volume, high value, long run marginal costs, but at the expected average lifetime long run marginal cost that is based on a more rapid, immediate load build-up. An important consideration in adopting such a pricing scheme is that the financial resources of the supplier need to be sufficiently large to cover the initial financial losses incurred. It is also imperative that demand forecasts are realistic, since massive losses can be accrued if consumers do not switch products.

Government Price Intervention

The principal reason for government intervention in energy markets is to fulfil community service responsibilities and obligations. In relation to energy markets, these responsibilities and obligations range from improving social equity by providing low-income concessions on energy commodities, to encouraging industry development and the creation of competitive markets. Governments may also have an interest in enforcing uniform tariffs so that all consumers have access to reasonably priced energy regardless of the cost of supply and ensuring that domestic energy users are not exploited by overseas energy utilities. The framework for accomplishing government responsibilities and obligations to the community is reflected in the energy policies that are adopted. In terms of energy pricing, government objectives can generally be classified according to one of three groups; improving resource allocation efficiency, improving social equity and ensuring the financial viability of the energy sector. In some circumstances, conflicts may arise between these objectives and compromises will be required.

Traditionally most public and private enterprises in the energy industry have been required to undertake non-commercial activities to satisfy a range of government policies and social goals of an essentially non-commercial nature. Implementing price adjustment mechanisms is widely considered by governments as an effective policy tool. Policy makers argue that the benefits of applying these mechanisms, in terms of distributional welfare adjustments, outweigh the efficiency loss from the free market environment.

There are a range of policy available to governments to influence energy prices. Most of the mechanisms introduce economic and welfare costs on the community, which are often hidden. From an economic perspective, approaches that promote transparency and minimise inefficient distortions are preferred. These measures include direct subsidies paid by governments or industry levies. Some of the policy tools available to governments, and the implications are discussed in the remainder of this section.

Energy Taxation

Governments have used taxation of energy as a cost-effective method of raising revenues in situations where the demand for energy resources is relatively inelastic, that is, the higher energy price does not lead to a significant decrease in consumption. Taxing relatively inelastic goods, such as energy, also has the benefit that the distortionary effects of taxation, in terms of economic efficiency losses, are minimised. Taxation is also used by governments to cover specific government energy related expenditure, such as facilitating transport networks and funding environmental programmes (effectively internalising the externality cost into the energy price), influence consumer behaviour, for example discouraging energy imports by implementing an import tariff (and thereby promote domestic energy sources).

Cross Subsidies

Cross subsidies involve excess charges (prices greater than the cost of supply) being paid by some users in order to subsidise other users of the same product (who face prices that are less than the cost of supply). In effect cross subsidies represent a consumption tax and consumption subsidy for different energy consumers. Cross-subsidies can arise either as a result of different prices being paid for the same product by different users, or from the application of uniform prices paid for a product regardless of differences in the cost of supply.

Cross subsidies result in allocative inefficiency. Consumers whose consumption is taxed restrict their energy usage, even though they may value the consumption of additional units above the cost of supply. Conversely, subsidised consumers are encouraged to expand their energy use to the extent that the benefit they derived from increased usage is offset by higher costs of supply. The result is a decrease in allocative efficiency and a loss in welfare. Industrial resource use is also altered by cross subsidies. Firms utilising subsidised energy more intensively gain an increase in competitiveness at the expense of other firms that are funding the subsidy through higher energy prices. Other inefficiencies may also result as the subsidised firms are subject to less competitive pressure. Nevertheless, governments have used cross subsidies as a means of encouraging economic development in specific sectors of the economy.

Concessional Domestic Tariffs

Concessional domestic tariffs transfer income from a small number of high volume, low cost, industrial and commercial energy users to numerous small volume, high cost, domestic users. The aim of concessional domestic tariffs is to transfer income between tariff classes, such that higher income business owners and shareholders income is transferred to lower income domestic energy users. Governments to encourage industry development in certain sectors of the economy can also use concessional tariffs. The funding of concessional tariffs can also be accomplished through cross-subsidisation, resulting in similar decreases in allocative efficiency levels.

Uniform Tariffs and Connection Subsidies

In many economies legislation has been passed requiring that all consumers are able to access energy at a 'reasonable' price. In the electricity industry for example, utilities may be prohibited from charging rural electricity users a higher tariff than consumers in urban areas. This requirement is despite the higher cost of providing electricity to few users in less populated areas, and reflects the equity concerns that all consumers should have equal access to essential goods. There are a number of advantages and disadvantages associated with uniform pricing initiatives. Particularly, when implementing uniform tariffs, no account is taken of the income levels of the consumers and producers. Unless careful analysis is conducted on the welfare implications of the scheme, unexpected adverse impacts may arise and create vertical and horizontal inequity.

Similarly connection subsidies, where all consumers have equal access to supply regardless of location and cost, can result in economically inefficiency if more cost effective supply alternatives exist. For example, a requirement that all consumers are able to access a national electricity grid ignores a situation in rural areas where individual generation alternative, such as solar power generators, prove more cost effective.

Setting Lower Rates of Return

Publicly owned energy utilities, particularly in the electricity sector, are sometime required to maintain lower rates of return and not exploit their producer surplus. Lowering the rate of return of public utilities is analogous to the public subsidising the consumers who benefit from the lower energy prices. This approach shares the problems of funding a cross subsidy in terms of cost transparency and accountability. For example, confusion may arise over the degree to which the rate of return has been lowered to directly benefit consumer, and to what extent it may indirectly benefit or disadvantage other parties.

Direct Subsidies

Direct budget subsidisation involves government funding for selected beneficiaries directly from taxation revenue. In contrast to cross-subsidies, direct budget funding avoids the distortionary effects associated with incorrect pricing of services. Prices can be maintained at levels that reflect costs, so that efficient resource allocation results. Additionally, direct budget funding improves transparency and removes the multiple objective problems characteristic of cross subsidies. Direct budget funding can be implemented through two approaches: a producer subsidy paid to the energy enterprise for providing low cost energy services to the intended recipient, or alternatively a consumer subsidy paid directly to the energy consumer.

Levies on Users

Governments to generate revenue for specific purposes can impose energy consumption levies. The explicit nature of levies increases transparency, and funds received can be explicitly directed to the purpose or reimbursed to selected recipients rather than hidden by a system of indirect cross subsidies.

Environmental Energy Pricing

Incorporating an environmental component in to the final energy price charged to energy consumers has increasingly become common practice among developed economies. Adding an environmental component to energy prices recognises the significant costs associated with the production of energy, such as air pollution, land degradation and water contamination, and that these costs are not subject to the internal cost structure of the polluter. The additional environmental component to energy prices can be applied directly or indirectly through taxes, price controls and the use of direct or indirect subsidies. By enforcing an environmental component in their energy prices, such as an environment levy, policy makers aim to compensate society for the environmental degradation by charging an energy cost reflective of the 'real' cost of energy.

These external costs, known as 'externalities', are incorporated into a polluting utility's operational management structure—effectively 'internalising' the external cost. This approach is also referred to as the 'polluter pays' principle.

Generally speaking, environmental costs associated with energy production can be of three forms:

1. Costs that are economically significant, but not to the decision-makers. For example, water purification costs are more likely to be met by the water user rather than the polluter.
2. Costs that, although quantifiable, cannot be easily priced. For example, pricing for greenhouse gas emissions where no market for the emissions currently exists.
3. Costs that cannot be measured or quantified. Examples include prices for aesthetic goods, such as a view obscured by a power station.

By introducing environmental pricing practices, policy makers are effectively internalizing these external costs so that they form part of the polluters decision making process.

There are a number of different ways that externalities can be internalised. These include:

- Legislative control
- Tradable permits
- Offset programmes
- Taxes

Regulatory Aspects to Pricing

Energy prices are an integral part of energy policies throughout the APEC region. Energy prices are often used as an indicator of market performance, and also as a tool for modifying market behaviour, through controls, taxes and subsidies. It is commonly agreed that government regulation is required in some instances to control the operation of imperfect markets. The IEA provide examples of instances where some form of government regulatory intervention is justified. These include:

Natural Monopoly—In energy market containing natural monopolies, such as in the case of local electricity distribution for many economies, prices charged for services often need to be closely monitored to prevent the monopoly service provider exploiting the excessive profits potential. In many instances, governments directly regulate, or impose operating controls, over energy prices imposed by non-government monopoly energy suppliers.

Supply Security—Energy supply security can generally be divided into three risk categories; the risk associated with short-term supply disruptions from supply and demand imbalances, the long-term risk that market failure will result in inadequate investment to secure future supplies, and the risk of inadequate supply diversity in the event of major disruption. Energy prices offer one policy option to manage these risks, such as through regulatory provisions guaranteeing prices and eliminating market driven price variability.

Anti-Competitive behaviour—Regulatory control of energy prices also limits the opportunity for dominant market participants to engage in anticompetitive market strategies, such as through predatory pricing initiatives to discourage new market participants.

Consumer welfare protection—Most governments in the APEC region seek to provide consumer welfare protection to household customers, particularly the disadvantaged and charity organisations. In some instances, governments regulate prices to these consumer groups to negligible levels.

The degree of regulation, light-handed or heavy-handed, varies between economies depending on the objectives of the regulation. Relatively light-handed approaches exist in Australia and New Zealand, where the existence of anti-competitive institutions arguably acts as a deterrent to competitive market behaviour. Conversely, more detailed heavy-handed regulation in the United States natural gas sector aims to reinforce the fundamentals of competition law through explicit mechanisms designed to control the behaviour of natural monopoly transporters—including controls on pricing, handling of network access, and financial and operational performance regulations.

ENERGY SUBSIDIES

There is enormous confusion about what is meant by an energy subsidy and limited information about the size of such subsidies. The narrowest and perhaps most commonly used definition is a direct cash payment by a government to an energy producer or consumer. But this is just one way in which governments can stimulate the production or use of a particular fuel or form of energy, including oil. Broader definitions attempt to capture other types of government interventions that affect prices or costs, either directly or indirectly. The IEA has defined energy subsidies as any government action that concerns primarily the energy sector that lowers the cost of energy production, raises the price received by energy producers or lowers the price paid by energy consumers. This definition has been widely adopted.

There are many different types of energy subsidies. Some have a direct effect on price, like grants and tax exemptions, while others act indirectly, such as regulations that skew the market in favour of a particular fuel or government-sponsored technology research and development. How governments choose to go about subsidising energy depends on a number of factors, including the overall cost of the programme and the impact—financial and otherwise—on different social groups. A simple per unit cash payment to producers or consumers is the simplest and most transparent form of subsidy, but can involve considerable accounting and transaction costs and puts a direct financial burden on the national treasury. Governments like to keep subsidies 'off-budget' for political reasons; on-budget subsidies are an easy target for pressure groups interested in reducing the overall tax burden. For this reason, subsidies often take the form of price controls that keep set prices below full cost, especially where the energy company is state-owned, or the form of requirements on energy buyers to take minimum volumes from a specific, usually indigenous, supply source. Subsidies may be aimed at producers, such as a grant paid for each unit of production, or to consumers, such as a rebate or exemption on the normal sales tax. Both types of subsidy tend to lower the final price to consumers.

Taxes have the opposite effect on prices to subsidies, so one needs to make a distinction between gross and net subsidies. In some cases, subsidies are more than offset by special taxes and duties that raise the final end-use price to above free market levels (taking account of normal sales taxes applied to all goods and services). This is often the case with oil products, which are usually heavily taxed. By contrast, subsidies often exceed taxes on non-oil forms of energy—especially in non-OECD countries. What matters in practice is the overall impact of all subsidies and taxes on the absolute level of prices and costs and the competitiveness of each fuel or technology.

The Size of Energy Subsidies

Most countries subsidises (and tax) oil in one way or another, but they vary greatly in size—in absolute terms and relative to taxes. Estimating their size depends heavily on definitions and methodologies. Differences in definitions make comparisons of individual studies of the size and impact of oil and other energy subsidies in specific countries or regions difficult. For example, some studies include even the cost of defending oil supplies from the Arabian Gulf, which greatly adds to the overall size of subsidies.

Hard data on energy subsidies is extremely patchy. Few studies have attempted to quantify subsidies for the world as a whole, because of data deficiencies and the sheer scale of the exercise. The most comprehensive studies are now somewhat dated. What is clear from the evidence available, however, is that subsidies are much higher in non-OECD countries than in the OECD. A major study carried out by the World Bank in 1997 put fossil-fuel consumption subsidies alone at $48 billion in twenty of the largest countries outside the OECD and $10 billion in the OECD. The 1999 *World Energy Outlook*, which examined eight of the largest non-OECD countries covering almost 60% of total non-OECD energy demand, put the total value of energy subsidies in those countries—as measured by the difference between actual and estimated market prices—at around $95 billion. The bulk of these subsidies went to electricity and coal. End-use prices were found to be on average about one-fifth below market levels in those countries. A subsequent IEA/EAD review of OECD subsidies in 2000 estimated total OECD energy subsidies at $20-30 billion. Subsidies, both in gross terms and net of taxes, have fallen over the last two decades in most OECD and non-OECD countries in aggregate. Global consumption subsidies dropped by more than half in the five years to 1996 according to the World Bank. The biggest reduction has occurred in the transition economies and in China, where coal subsidies have been largely phased out.

OECD countries mainly subsidise energy production. OECD subsidy policies take various forms, from direct grants to cover losses in coal production and tax allowances for fuel producers to price support and loans at low interest rates or favourable conditions to domestic producers. Publicly funded R&D accounts for $10 billion. The bulk of OECD subsidies go to fossil fuels and most of the rest to nuclear (mainly through R&D). Coal subsidies, as estimated using the IEA's PSE, amounted to around $7 billion in 2001 (the last year available), but are thought to have declined since. EU state aid to the coal industry was €6.3 billion in the same year. Germany still accounts for the bulk of these subsidies. Around 7% of OECD coal production was subsidised at the start of the current decade. A 2000 DOE study put US federal energy subsidies at $6 billion, with half going to fossil fuels and only 5% to renewables. But another study by Koplow and Martin, commissioned by Greenpeace, puts oil industry subsidies alone at between $5 billion and $12 billion. An earlier Greenpeace study estimated total European Union energy subsidies during the first half of the 1990s at $16 billion, of which 63% went to fossil fuels, 28% to nuclear and a mere 9% to renewables. The share of renewables in total OECD energy subsidies has undoubtedly increased sharply in recent years, but comprehensive figures are not available.

In non-OECD countries, most energy subsidies go to consumers—usually through price controls that hold end-user prices below the full cost of supply. Electricity is thought to be the most heavily subsidised form of energy. Oil is heavily subsidised in some countries, notably Iran and Indonesia. As quantified in WEO-2005, Iran subsidies oil product sales to the tune of $11 billion in 2003, with a further $3 billion going to electricity and almost the same amount to natural gas. In 2003, energy subsidies in Iran were equal to 10% of GDP—by far the highest share in the world. Oil subsidies in Indonesia averaged $6 billion per year between 2000 and 2005 according to a recent study by the Asian Development Bank. With the recent increase in world prices, Indonesian oil subsidies are thought to have ballooned to over $7 billion in 2004 and more than $12 billion in 2005—equal to 5% of GDP and almost a third of total government spending. Iranian and Indonesian subsidies to oil alone are equivalent to perhaps all energy subsidies in OECD countries as a whole.

China is an exception among developing countries, in that oil subsidies go mainly to production. These were running at $4 billion per year in the 1990s. While wholesale and retail oil product prices remain regulated, retail taxes more than offset any embedded subsidies: retail gasoline and diesel prices including taxes are currently close to US levels. Wholesale prices have recently

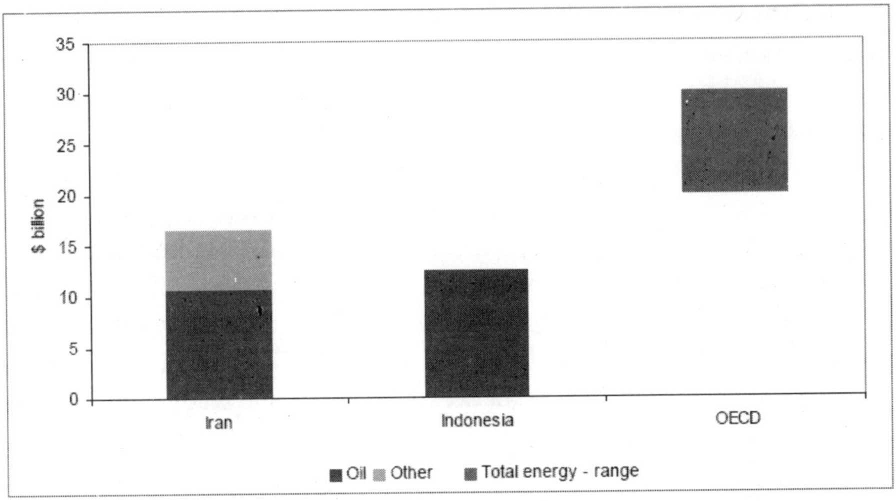

Source: Carrots and Sticks: Taxing and Subsidizing Energy, International Energy Agency, 2006.

Figure 1.2: Energy Subsidies in Iran, Indonesia and the OECD

been held below import cost levels, causing refiners to make large losses. The pump prices of motor fuels in India are also above supply costs, but some oil products—notably LPG and kerosene—remain subsidised for social reasons. The total cost of these subsidies reached almost $5 billion in FY2004. Electricity subsidies are also very large in India.

Economic, Social and Environmental Effects

A subsidy by its very nature involves a complex set of changes in economic resource allocation through its effect on costs and/or prices. These shifts inevitably have economic, social and environmental implications. Indeed, the reason any subsidy exists at all is to support some economic, social or environmental goal. Quantifying these different effects, in terms of costs and benefits, is extremely difficult and judgemental. This is especially true when measuring the social and environmental benefits. But there are many examples from different countries and regions of the high economic costs associated with energy subsidies. The IEA, for example, estimates the net present value of the loss of economic growth due to consumer energy subsidies in the eight largest non-OECD countries at $257 billion per year using a discount rate of 7 per cent. The overall social and environmental benefits of those subsidies are unlikely to be higher and could, in any case, be achieved at lower cost in ways that do not involve subsidizing energy. Depending on the type of subsidy, the loss of economic efficiency is manifested in one or more of the following ways:

> Subsidies to consumption and/or production, by lowering end-use prices, lead to higher energy use and reduced incentives to conserve or use energy more efficiently. An extreme example is the disregard for energy efficiency in housing blocks in Russia and other transition economies during the Soviet era, which resulted from a failure to price heating services properly—in some cases, not at all. The situation has improved in the past decade. In Hungary, for instance, spending on energy efficiency jumped from $5–10 million to $80 million per year after consumer price subsidies were removed in 1997. But subsidies and waste persist in most other transition economies.

By reducing the price received by producers, a subsidy may undermine energy providers' return on investment and, consequently, their ability and incentive to invest in new infrastructure. As a result, the subsidy may encourage reliance on out-of-date and dirtier technologies. The dire financial straits of energy companies and the resulting under-investment in several developing countries, such as the state electricity boards in India, are largely due to under-pricing.

Subsidies to producers, by cushioning them from competitive market pressures, tend to reduce incentives to minimize costs, resulting in less efficient plant operation and investments that may otherwise not be economic. Subsidies on coal production in several OECD countries have hampered efforts to improve productivity in past decades.

Direct subsidies in the form of grants or tax exemptions act as a drain on government finances. For example, the IMF estimates that the Iranian Government's direct spending on energy subsidies amounted to $4 billion in 1997-98 per cent of its budget. Direct subsidies on oil products can lead to acute pressure on the government budget during periods of rising prices. In the long run, indirect subsidies that reduce economic growth also lead to lower tax revenues.

Price caps or ceilings below market-clearing levels may lead to physical shortages and a need for administratively costly rationing arrangements. This is the case in India, where subsidized oil products are rationed. By increasing energy use, consumption subsidies boost demand for imports or reduce the amount of energy available for export. This harms the balance of payments and energy supply security by increasing the country's dependence on imports. The Indonesian Government, for example, estimates that energy subsidies will cost the country $16 billion in lost export earnings over the five years to 2005 if they are left as they are.

Subsidies to specific energy technologies inevitably undermine the development and commercialization of other technologies that might ultimately become more economically and environmentally attractive. In this way, subsidies can 'lock in' technologies to the exclusion of other, more promising ones. Some of these costs are ultimately borne, at least in part, by the intended beneficiaries of the subsidies as well as the rest of society. And not all of these costs disappear straight away with the removal of subsidies because it can take a long time to replace the stock of energy-supply and combustion equipment.

Social Implications

The social implications of energy subsidies vary according to the type of subsidy. Subsidies to modern cooking and heating fuels, such as kerosene, LPG and natural gas, as well as electricity are common in developing countries. They are aimed at improving poor households' living conditions by making those fuels more affordable and accessible. Where they result in switching from traditional fuels and improved access to electricity, those subsidies can bring considerable benefits to poor communities. These include less indoor pollution and a reduction in the time women and children spend gathering fuel and, therefore, more time they can spend on productive activities, like farming, and education. In reality, however, these subsidies often benefit mainly the energy companies, equipment suppliers and the better-off households, especially in the towns and cities, and, in some cases, may not even reach the poor at all. As a result, many energy-subsidy programmes intended to boost poor households' purchasing power or rural communities' access to modern energy through lower prices can, paradoxically, leave the poor worse off, since the costs are shared by the entire population including the poor. There are three main reasons for this:

1. The poorest households may be unable to afford even subsidized energy or may have no physical access to it, for example when a rural community is not connected to the electricity grid.
2. Even if the poor are able to benefit from an energy subsidy, the financial value to them may be small since their consumption is

generally modest. Higher income households tend to benefit much more in nominal terms since they consume more of the subsidized fuel.

3. Consumption subsidies that involve the imposition of caps on prices below market levels may lead to a need for rationing. Middle and higher income households tend to get hold of the bulk of subsidized energy in countries where it is rationed, through petty corruption and favouritism. Price caps, where they have led to big differences in prices with neighbouring countries, have also encouraged smuggling in some parts of Africa and Asia.

Subsidies can hurt the interests of poor people in other ways too. In practice, energy subsidies often go to large capital-intensive projects, such as hydroelectric dams, at the expense of local, small-scale labour-intensive alternatives, such as biomass burners. The construction of dams usually involves displacing communities, although the improved availability of electric power and water for irrigation can bring important social benefits as well. Subsidies to large-scale thermal power plants, oil refineries and gas-processing plants affect poor households close to those facilities most, since they are usually less able to move to avoid local pollution and safety risks.

Environmental Effects

The environmental effects of introducing and maintaining energy subsidies are complex. They can be positive and negative, depending on the precise nature of the subsidy and energy source. Subsidies that encourage the production and use of fossil fuels inevitably have some harmful consequences for the environment. Consumer subsidies that lower the price paid for those fuels or the cost of using them, mean more gets used, which can lead to higher airborne emissions of noxious and/or greenhouse gases. Higher fossil-fuel production can also damage the environment directly, by polluting water supplies and spoiling the landscape. For example, subsidies on biofuels, used by several OECD countries, usually result in greater use of fertilizers and pesticides, which can damage local ecosystems and cause both soil and water pollution.

A number of studies have demonstrated the harmful effects of various types of fossil-fuel subsidies. A recent study by the OECD, for example, shows that global carbon dioxide emissions would be reduced by more than 6 per cent and real income increased by 0.1 per cent by 2010 if all subsidies on fossil fuels used in industry and the power sector were removed everywhere in the world. The IEA's 1999 study shows that the removal of consumption subsidies in eight of the largest non-OECD countries would reduce primary energy use by 13 per cent, lower carbon dioxide emissions by 16 per cent and raise GDP by almost 1 per cent in those countries as a whole. Because coal is the 'dirtiest fuel', the removal of coal subsidies generally yields the biggest environmental benefits.

But the overall impact of fossil-fuel and other energy subsidies on the environment is not always negative. For example, encouraging the use of oil products can reduce deforestation in developing countries as poor rural households switch from firewood. This is a major reason for maintaining subsidies to kerosene and LPG in many cases. Public funding of fossil-fuel research and development can also yield positive environmental effects if it results in the use of more efficient, cleaner-burning technologies in the long-term.

And subsidies to indigenous fossil-fuel production do not systematically lead to higher consumption if they result in a switch from imported to indigenously produced fuel on a one-for-one basis. This has been a strong argument to defend coal-production subsidies in Germany and the United Kingdom, because they now cover the difference between actual production costs and import prices and do not involve lower prices and, therefore, higher consumption. Nonetheless, the financial and economic cost of keeping inefficient mines open is very high. Past agreements that mandated the burning of minimum amounts of coal in German power stations undoubtedly held back the use of cleaner fuels such as natural gas. Subsidies on oil products and electricity in poor countries can also reduce indoor pollution, if they encourage switching away from traditional energy like wood, straw, crop residues and dung. Recent evidence from India suggests that indoor pollution caused by burning these fuels accounts for about half-a-million premature deaths a year in women and children under five years old. Given that India contains about one-quarter of the world's solid fuel cooking stoves, the global impact could be expected to be about four times larger, or about 2 million premature deaths per year. The World Health Organization has come up with an estimate of 2.5 million by extrapolating industrialized country studies to developing countries.

Subsidies to support renewables and energy-efficient technologies may help to reduce harmful emissions depending on how they are structured and market conditions. If renewables replace fossil fuels and the amount of fossil-fuel-based energy consumed in building the plants and equipment is not too high, then the net effect on emissions will generally be positive—although other environmental or aesthetic effects may be significant. Denmark's long-standing commitment to subsidizing wind, as described in, is driven by the goal of reducing carbon dioxide emissions through switching from coal. Most industrialized countries have introduced and increased subsidies to renewables or energy-efficient combustion technologies for environmental and energy-security reasons. These include grants for producing electricity or transport fuels based on renewables and for buying energy-efficient combustion plant and equipment, preferential power tariffs and spending on research and development projects. In some cases, these subsidies need to be big to make those technologies competitive with existing ones based on fossil fuels.

Quantifying Energy Subsidies

Energy consumption subsidies—government measures that result in an end user price that is below the price that would prevail in a truly competitive market including all the costs of supply—are large in some countries. Energy is most commonly subsidised through price controls, often through state owned companies. Consumption subsidies have been largely eliminated in the OECD, but remain large in some non-OECD countries, both in gross terms and net of any taxes. Electricity and household heating and cooking fuels are usually most heavily subsidised, though several countries still subsidise road transport fuels. Remaining energy subsidies in OECD countries are mainly directed to production and do not necessarily reduce end-user prices below market levels.

Analysis carried out for IEA World Energy Outlook 2006 confirms the prevalence of consumption subsidies in non-OECD countries. Total subsidies (net of taxes on each fuel) in the 20 countries assessed, which collectively make up 81% of total non-OECD primary energy use, amount to around $220 billion per year, according to 2005 data. On the assumption that subsidies per unit of energy consumed are of the same magnitude in other non-OECD countries, world subsidies might amount to well over $250 billion per year. That is equal to all the investment needed in the power sector every year on average in non-OECD countries in the Reference Scenario. Total subsidies to oil products amount to over $90 billion.

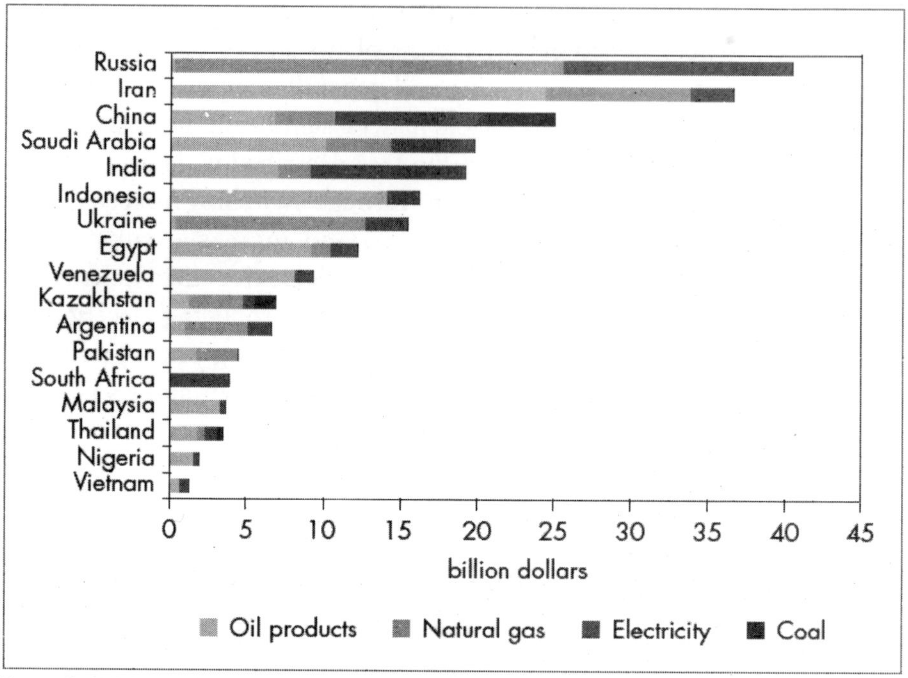

Note: Subsidies in Brazil, the Philippines and Chinese Taipei are not shown, as they amount to less than $1 billion in each case.

Source: World Energy Outlook 2006, International Energy Agency.

Figure 1.3: Economic Value of Energy Subsidies in Non-OECD Countries

Russia has the largest subsidies in dollar terms, amounting to about $40 billion per year. Most of these subsidies go to natural gas and the rest to electricity (which includes the underpricing of gas delivered to power stations). Subsidies of $25 billion per year to final consumption of gas are alone more than twice the annual investment projected for the entire Russian gas industry. Iranian energy subsidies are almost as large, at an estimated $37 billion per year. Six other countries—China, Saudi Arabia, India, Indonesia, Ukraine and Egypt—have subsidies in excess of $10 billion per year each. In terms of fuels, the biggest subsidies overall go to oil products. Most of the countries included in this analysis were found to subsidise at least one oil product.

Industrial and residential fuels other than gasoline and automotive diesels—notably kerosene and liquefied petroleum gas—and other forms of energy are generally subsidised more than road fuels. Subsidies to gasoline and diesel have fallen sharply in percentage terms in recent years in many countries—despite rising international prices. This has not been the case in Iran, which continues to subsidise transport fuels heavily. In fact, Iran had the highest rate of oil subsidisation in 2005. Oil subsidies were also large in Indonesia, but have since fallen sharply following a government decision to double the pump price of road fuels in October 2005. Several other developing Asian countries have announced their intention to bring domestic prices more into line with international prices in 2006 and 2007, partly because of the rising fiscal cost of subsidies or, as in the case of China and India, losses incurred by refiners. China, Indonesia and Malaysia raised oil-product prices in March 2006.

Under pricing is biggest for natural gas. On average, consumers in the countries analysed pay less than half the true economic value of the gas they use. Gas subsidies are biggest in the transition economies, Saudi Arabia and Egypt. Electricity subsidies are less prevalent, but are large in some countries, including Saudi Arabia.

Chapter 2

Oil Economics

Fossil fuels—coal, oil and natural gas—have satisfied most of the world's primary energy demand and it is anticipated that they will do so for the foreseeable future too. Products derived from oil such as petrol, aviation turbine fuel (henceforth referred to as ATF), diesel fuel, and heating oil, supply nearly 40 percent of the energy consumed by households, businesses, and manufacturers worldwide. Value of crude oil is driven by the demand for petroleum products, particularly in the transportation sector. Petroleum products power virtually all motor vehicles, aircraft, marine vessels, and trains around the globe. Natural gas and coal, by comparison, each supply less than 25 percent of the world's energy needs. Oil accounted for 8 percent of global trade in goods and services and about 2.5 percent of world activity in 2004—higher than any other commodity, although well below 1980 levels.

Despite a consistent fall in global oil intensity, crude oil remains an important commodity and events in the oil market continue to play a significant role in shaping global economic and political developments. Oil is the world economy's most important source of energy and is, therefore, critical to economic growth. Moreover, given the distribution of oil reserves and the structure of supply and demand, geopolitical factors play an important role in the oil market.

Oil will continue to be the single largest fuel in the global primary energy mix, with oil and coal together accounting for over 60 percent of energy supply. The past century has seen a steadily growing role for oil and gas in fuelling development around the globe. All the studies on energy's future point out that oil and gas will remain dominant in world energy supply well into this century (See Figure 1A). Primary oil demand is expected to grow by 1.3 percent per year over 2005-2030, reaching 99 million barrels/day (henceforth million barrels/day would be referred to as MB/D and million barrels as MB) in 2015 and going upto 116 MB/D in 2030, up from 84 MB/D in 2005. More than 70 percent of the increase in oil demand comes from developing countries which see average annual demand growth rates of 2.5 percent. Demand in the Organisation for Economic Cooperation and Development (henceforth referred to as OECD) countries is expected to rise only by 0.6 percent per year. On the other hand, oil supply has traditionally been concentrated in the hands of a small number of major producers in whose countries oil resources are mostly located. The Organisation of Petroleum Exporting Countries (henceforth referred to as OPEC) share of global supply is expected to grow from the current 40 percent to 42 percent in 2015 and 48 percent by 2030. Non-OPEC conventional crude oil output will peak by the middle of the next decade, though natural gas liquids production continues to rise (IEA, 2006a).

The world currently consumes more than 85 MB/D of oil. This supply comes from oil fields (or reserves) located all around the world produced by thousands of companies. The largest sources of supply are Saudi Arabia, Russia, the United States (henceforth referred to as U.S.), Iran, Mexico, China, and Europe's North Sea. Within the U.S., the largest areas of production are the Gulf Coast—including the Gulf of Mexico, West Texas, California, and Alaska.

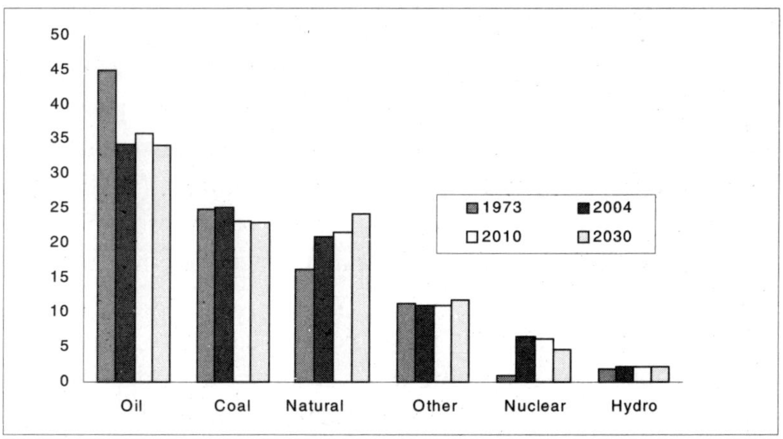

Source: IEA (2006b)

Figure 2.1: Fuel Share in Total Primary Energy Supply (percent)

OPEC, an international cartel of oil-producing countries, is the single most important production-related entity. It produces about 40 percent of the world's daily consumption of crude oil. In contrast to companies operating from these OPEC member countries, many major private oil companies, which operate outside the OPEC countries, compete individually in the world crude oil market. The major oil companies, despite being large, have relatively small shares of global oil reserves and production. These small shares ensure that private oil companies must behave competitively in the world oil market and cannot individually cut output and influence world oil prices (Grant et. al., 2006).

Hydrocarbons

Crude oil is a complex mixture of a large number of organic compounds that vary in appearance and composition from one oil field to another. Crude oil is classified as paraffinic, naphthenic, aromatic or asphaltic based on the predominant proportion of hydrocarbon series molecules which dictate their physical and chemical properties. Theories vary regarding the origin of crude oil though the general consensus is that most of the deposits have resulted from the burial and transformation of biomass over geological periods during the last 200 million years or so. In terms of quantities, therefore, the total amount of oil and gas residing in the earth's subsurface is certainly finite. While it is recognised that some of these resources have yet to be found, there is considerable uncertainty about the magnitude of the "undiscovered resources". The most widely used estimates of total amounts of crude oil to be found in the earth's subsurface are those of the U.S. Geological Survey 2000 (IEA, 2004) which deals primarily with conventional oil and gas.

Crude oil is not distributed uniformly around the globe. Some regions and countries are well endowed, while others are not. Most of the proven reserves of conventional oil are to be found in the Middle East countries, namely, Iran, Iraq, Kuwait, Saudi Arabia and the United Arab Emirates (UAE). Similarly, conventional gas is located primarily in Russia and other Former Soviet Union (FSU) countries, Iran, Qatar and Saudi Arabia. Since these reserves are often not in the same regions as the markets they serve, considerations of security and diversity of supply are among the important factors to be placed in the balance in decisions over squeezing more crude oil from deposits in other regions closer to home or over developing non-conventional crude oil.

Crude oil differs in two important respects: the quality of crude and the

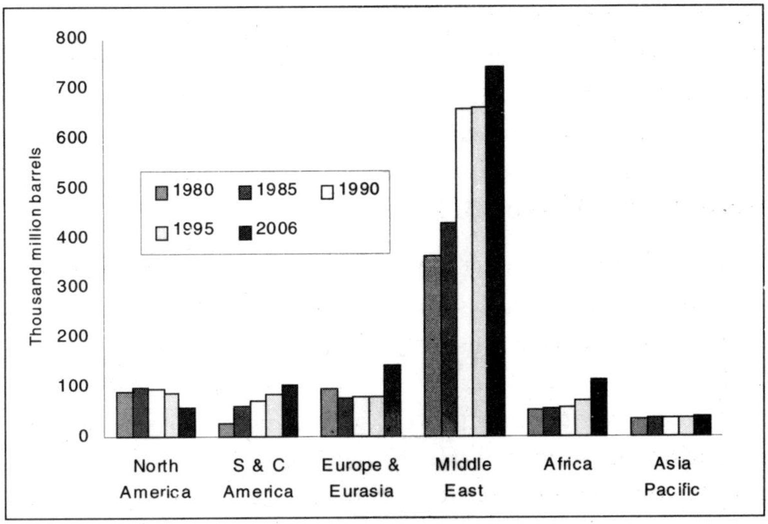

Source: BP (2007) & Historic data sheet

Figure 2.2: Distribution and Growth in World Proved Oil Reserves

location of the production. The exact composition of the mixture will determine the mix of the products that can be obtained from crude oil by refining and the ease at which it is refined. Hence, the crude oil, which yields a large proportion of more valuable products and which can be treated by a large number of the world's refineries, will command a premium over those which produce a larger proportion of lower value products or which can be processed by only a limited number of refineries. Similarly, on the aspects of location of production, oil produced close to major markets for refining will require less transportation and therefore will be more attractive and command a premium over oil produced further from the market and which has to incur larger transportation costs to get to the market (World Bank, 2005). Historically analysts have focused on two key qualities of crude oil, namely, the API gravity and sulphur content, to explain inter-crude price differentials.

The types of crude oil that are traded on the international market have steadily increased over the past years, partly as a response to the desire to diversify sources of supply and partly because increasing global demand has encouraged production in less well-known oil producing areas. Currently, more than 150 grades are described in the International Crude Oil Market Handbook (World Bank, 2005). Many players are involved in the oil and gas production chain, from the owners of the subsurface resources to financing organisations and on to operators, drillers, equipment manufacturers, facility constructors, service providers and engineering companies. The producing companies are generally classified into the following three main groups: the international majors, the independents and the major resources holders.

The International Perspective

Oil is world economy's most important source of energy and is, therefore, critical to economic growth. Its value is driven by demand for petroleum products, particularly in the transportation sector. Petroleum products power virtually all motor vehicles, aircraft, marine vessels, and trains around the globe. In total, products derived from oil, such as motor gasoline, jet fuel, diesel fuel, and heating oil, supply nearly 40 percent of the energy consumed by households, businesses, and manufacturers worldwide. Natural gas and coal, by comparison, each supply less than 25 percent of the world's energy needs.

The world consumes more than 85 million barrels of oil per day. This supply comes from oil fields (or reserves) located around the world, produced by thousands of companies. The largest sources of supply are Saudi Arabia, Russia, the United States, Iran, Mexico, China, and Europe's North Sea. Within the United States, the largest areas of production are the Gulf Coast —including the Gulf of Mexico, West Texas, California, and Alaska.

The Organization of Petroleum Exporting Countries (OPEC), an international cartel of oil-producing countries, is the single most important production-related entity. It produces about 40 percent of the world's daily consumption of crude oil. OPEC's objective has been to manage its members' collective supply through individual producer quotas in order to influence world oil prices. While OPEC has sought to limit supply to the marketplace, its policies have also recognized that it is not in the organization's interest for crude prices to rise above levels that would harm global economic growth. Moreover, despite its large share of reserves and global production, OPEC's ability to influence crude oil prices has varied over time, as evidenced by the significant changes in world prices for crude oil over the last 25 years. These price changes highlight the fact that global supply-and-demand forces in the global oil market can limit OPEC's effectiveness in influencing world prices.

In contrast to OPEC members, the major private oil companies compete individually in the world crude oil market. The major oil companies, despite being large, have relatively small shares of global oil reserves and production. These small shares ensure that private oil companies must behave competitively in the world oil market and cannot individually cut output and influence world oil prices. Eight largest companies by reserves are all OPEC members, collectively representing 65 percent of the world's oil reserves. Saudi Aramco, Saudi Arabia's state-owned production company, alone owns over 21 percent of the world's oil reserves. In contrast, none of the multinational companies has more than 1.1 percent of world's oil reserves. These small percentages speak directly to the inability of the major oil companies to influence the world price of crude oil.

The World Petroleum Market

At the beginning of 2007 the world oil proved reserves were 1,208 thousand million barrels. Proved reserves have thus increased significantly from around 877 thousand million barrels in 1986. The growth, distribution and production of proved oil reserves help to understand the current and future market dynamics.

But perhaps the most important indicator of market power of any company or country would be the extent of exports market it satisfies. This explains to what extent it can control the market supply if need be. Interestingly, the exports constituted close to 38,810 thousand barrels of oil daily in 2006. Former Soviet Union and Middle East supplied close to 60 per

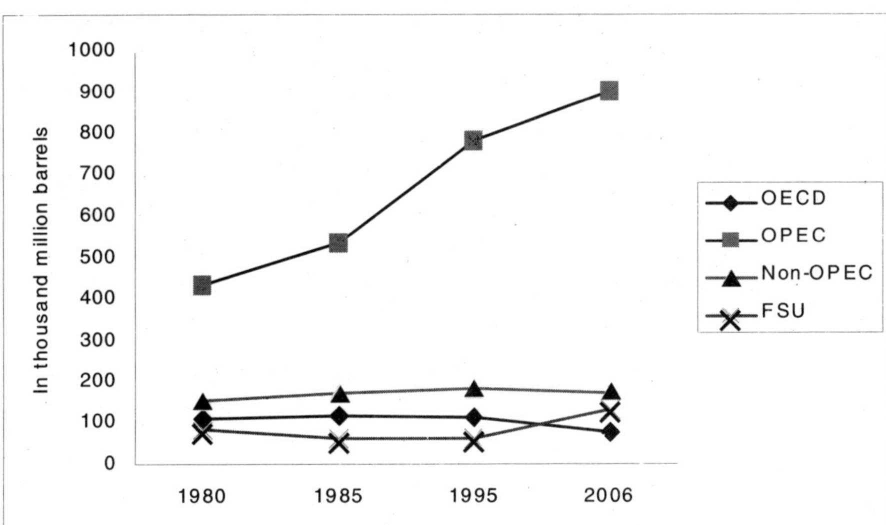

Note: Figures are for Year Beginning, 2007.

Source: *BP Statistical Review of World Energy*, 2007.

Figure 2.3: Growth in Proved Reserves at Beginning, 2007

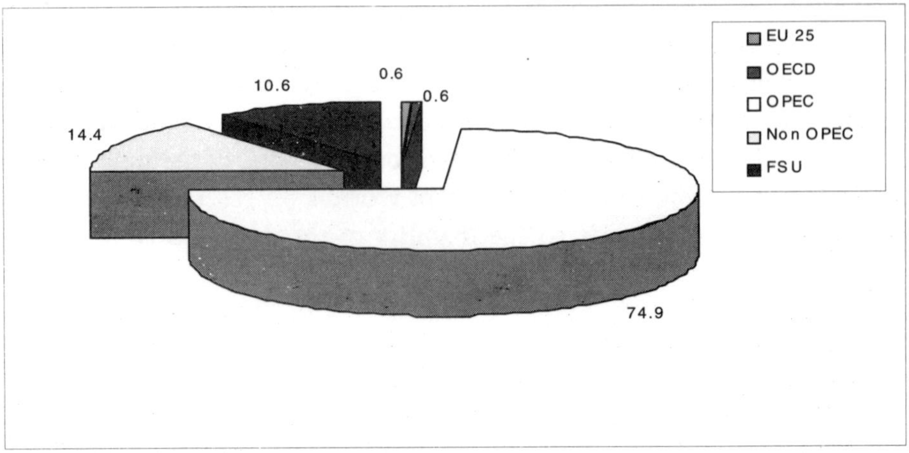

Note: Figures are for Year Beginning, 2007.

Source: BP Statistical Review of World Energy, 2007.

Figure 2.4: Distribution of Proved Reserves Beginning, 2007 (per cent)

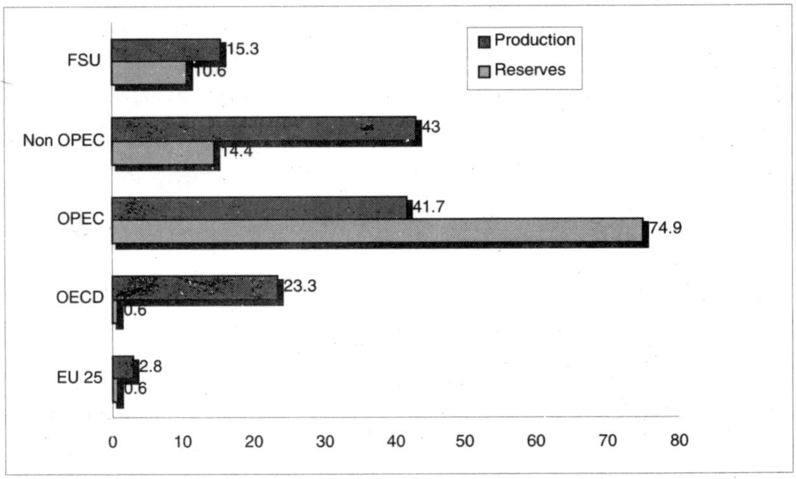

Note: Figures are for Year Beginning, 2007.

Source: *BP Statistical Review of World Energy,* 2007.

Figure 2.5: The Future Uncertainty (per cent share)

cent of these exports; thus making the market vulnerable.

The OECD is the key consumption market for oil, constituting around 58.1 per cent of the total. Other Emerging market economies like the South and Central America, Africa, Middle East, non-OECD Asia, non-OECD Europe constituted close to 37.1 per cent of the market, with the rest accounted for by EU 25 and Former Soviet Union.

The Big Five

The five major integrated oil companies are usually regarded as ExxonMobil Corporation (ExxonMobil), BP p.l.c. (BP), Royal Dutch Shell p.l.c. (Shell), Chevron Corporation (Chevron), and ConocoPhillips. All five of the companies produce crude oil. Over the period 2004-2006, ExxonMobil produced an average of 2.6 million barrels per day (b/d), and was the leading producer among the five companies. Shell averaged 2.1 million b/d, BP averaged 2.5 million b/d, Chevron averaged 1.7 million b/d, and ConocoPhillips averaged 1.0 million b/d. Higher world prices for crude oil increased the revenue from this production in proportion to the increase in prices. In addition to the increasing price of crude oil, tightness in the refining industry contributed to the increase in petroleum product prices, notably gasoline. All five of the selected companies are active in the refining industry.

Table 2.1: Refining Capacity of Major Integrated Oil Companies (mb/d)

	2000	*2001*	*2002*	*2003*	*2004*	*2005*	*2006*
ExxonMobil	1.77	1.79	1.80	1.84	1.81	1.86	1.86
BP	1.66	1.56	1.50	1.50	1.50	1.47	1.47
Shell				.59	.59	.53	.57
Chevron	1.04	1.05	1.08	1.00	1.00	1.01	1.01
ConcoPhillips	.938	2.25	2.27	2.19	2.19	2.29	2.22

Although, historically, refining margins and profitability have tended to be volatile over time, profit margins have remained at or near historic highs since 2004 as a result of the tightening balance between the growth of demand outpacing the growth in supply, as well as the damage and disruption caused by hurricanes Katrina and Rita. For the five companies, operating in both the upstream (exploration and production) and downstream (refining, distribution, and marketing) segments of the oil market has led to growing profitability.

Table 2.2: Net Income of Major Integrated Companies (billion dollars)

	2000	*2001*	*2002*	*2003*	*2004*	*2005*	*2006*
ExxonMobil	17.7	15.3	11.4	21.5	25.3	36.1	39.5
BP	9.3	8.4	5.6	12.4	15.4	19.3	22.2
Shell	12.7	10.5	9.4	12.7	19.2	26.2	25.4
Chevron	5.1	3.2	1.1	7.2	13.3	14.1	17.1
ConcoPhillips	1.8	1.6	-0.29	4.7	8.1	13.5	13.5

Profits declined for the five companies from 2000 through 2002, then doubled in 2003. Profits rose by 39% in 2004, 34% in 2005, and 8% in 2006. Profits continued to increase in 2007, with three of the five companies gaining more than 10% compared to the first quarter of 2006, ConocoPhillips gaining 7.7%, and only BP experiencing a decline in net income. The magnitude of the profits earned, as well as the rapidity with which they accrued, has created a challenge for the oil companies: how to best utilize these resources and meet the varied demands of shareholders and the public.

The National Oil Companies (NOCs)

But clearly the NOCs are the market makers in the world petroleum market. In the United States, the term "big oil companies" is likely to be taken to mean the major private international oil companies, largely based in Europe or America. However, while some of those companies are indeed among the largest in the world, by many important measures, a majority of the largest oil companies are state-owned, national oil companies. By conventional definitions, national oil companies hold the majority of petroleum reserves and produce the majority of the world's supply of crude oil. Since national oil companies generally hold exclusive rights to exploration and development of petroleum resources within the home country, they also can decide on the degree to which they require participation by private companies in those activities.

Rankings of companies can be accomplished using a number of different criteria. In the oil industry, based as it is on current production to generate current earnings and on reserve positions to ensure the future viability of the enterprise, several standards need to be applied to assess the evolving nature of the companies in the industry. Additionally, investment, in the form of exploration and development expenditures, serves as a link between the present and the future, ensuring an ongoing continuity for the company so that reserves are not unduly depleted by current activities.

Table 2.3 shows a ranking of the top ten world oil companies on the basis of a composite criterion. In 2006, five of the top ten companies could be classified as state owned and operated. In 2000, six of the top ten companies were state owned and operated. On the surface, these rankings appear to show a decline in the importance of state-owned firms in the world oil market. However, these rankings may give an unclear picture of the underlying relative strengths of the private and state-owned companies in the world oil market.

Table 2.3: Comparative Ranking of Top 10 Oil Companies

Rank in 2006	*Company*	*Ownership*
1	Saudi Aramco	State
2	ExxonMobil	Private
3	NIOC	State
4	PDV	State
5	BP	Private
6	Shell	Private
7	PetroChina	90% State
8	Chevron	Private
9	Total	Private
10	Pemex	State

Table 2.4: World Liquid Petroleum Reserves Holdings (millions of barrels)

Rank in 2006	*Company*	*Reserves*
1	Saudi Aramco	264,200
2	NIOC	137,500
3	INOC	115,000
4	KPC	101,500
5	PDV	79,700
6	Adnoc	56,920
7	Libya NOC	33,235
8	NNPC	21,540
9	Lukoil	16,114
10	QP	15,200

Every firm in the top ten reserve holders, with the exception of Lukoil, in both 2006 and 2000 was state owned. Among the major international oil companies, ExxonMobil is ranked fourteenth, BP seventeenth, Chevron nineteenth, ConocoPhillips, twenty-third, and Shell is ranked twenty-fifth in 2006. These five firms hold only 3.8% of world liquid reserves, and their major holdings are in the United States and Canada. In contrast, the top ten firms listed in Table 2.4 hold 80.6% of the total world liquid reserves. The top ten companies in 2006 have an average reserve to production ratio of 78 years, with INOC, the Iraqi National Oil Company, the highest at 173 years and Lukoil, a privately held Russian company, the lowest at 24 years. The five large international oil companies have reserve to production ratios of 11 years.

These values suggest that the ten largest reserve holding companies, largely state owned, will be major forces in the world oil market about seven times as long as the five major international oil companies. In a market where reserve position is likely to translate into production and pricing power, the state oil companies are in a dominant position, and the international oil companies are likely to continue to play a lesser role.

Recognition of national oil companies' growing dominance of the world oil market has led some experts to view this as an energy security issue. The growing strength of the national oil companies implies, at least in a relative sense, the diminished importance of the private international oil companies. This dynamic could transform the reaction of the market to demand and supply signals. Since a major thread of current policy toward oil is "let the market take care of it," a change in the way the market works might call for significant adjustments in the policies of oil-consuming nations. Some of the policy options presented below have been extensively debated in the past as features of broadly based energy strategies, while others are controversial and would likely be difficult to implement. Others, such as the creation of a U.S. national oil company are extremely unlikely to be considered while the world oil market continues to function as a viable market.

International and National Oil Companies

The increasing importance of national oil companies (NOCs) has brought new challenges and potential opportunities for international oil companies (IOCs). The relationship is changing between IOCs and NOCs; improved partnership between the two—taking better advantage of each other's strengths and needs—would strengthen prospects for increasing investment in the oil sector as a whole. The structure of NOCs and their governance and partnership arrangements with IOCs vary considerably. Oil production growth in 2000–05 has generally been higher in countries where IOCs' presence is greater. The bulk of world reserves are in countries with majority NOC control. However, the regulatory quality of the government is lower in this group of countries.

The global oil industry continues to have an oligopolistic structure, but the importance of NOCs in the control of production has risen dramatically. Twenty national and international oil companies own almost 80 percent of the world's proven reserves. Significantly, the top four—which own 60 percent of the world's reserves—are NOCs from Saudi Arabia, the Islamic Republic of Iran, Iraq, and Kuwait with full ownership and control of their oil wells. Moreover, some NOCs are quickly expanding outside their borders.

Companies like PetroChina, Petronas, and Petrobras, formerly exclusively involved in domestic production, have won lucrative international contracts. NOCs from oil-importing countries such as China, Japan, and India have been very active in forging foreign upstream ventures and acquiring foreign assets, a behavior akin to traditional major IOCs.

Most NOCs are fully publicly owned, although some NOCs (such as Brazil's Petrobras, China's Sinopec, and Oman's PDO) have some private ownership. When oil companies forge joint ventures, typically a new company or subsidiary is created with equal ownership rights of each partner.

The difference is that these strategies are often driven by their countries' energy security policies. The distinction between types of companies is also becoming blurred. It is not uncommon to have a project run as a joint venture where the partners are a subsidiary of the host NOC, an IOC, and a foreign NOC. Partnerships among different types of companies should, in theory, allow each side to contribute its strengths, but in practice differences between major IOCs and large NOCs make such unions rare. Part of the explanation may have to do with fundamentally different and clashing objectives between the two. IOCs want access to equity, acceptable rates of return, and incentives for enhanced recovery. NOCs, for their part, want access to the managerial, technical, and financial expertise of IOCs without having to give up ownership and control of their national reserves. NOC managers sometimes express concern that IOCs have a tendency to over produce fields in a quest to satisfy the short-term expectations of their shareholders, and that in the past they have not received the full benefits of production-sharing agreements. A number of governments have recently altered contracting laws and production-sharing rules with foreign investors so as to increase control over their resources to varying degrees (as in Bolivia, Ecuador, Venezuela, and Russia). For their part, IOCs have expressed frustration about changing "rules of the game," project delays, and dealing with the bureaucratic structures of NOCs. They believe the host governments do not always adequately factor in the risks associated with unpredictable political and tax environments. Well-designed partnerships could lead to increasing investment levels in the oil industry as a whole, especially if the risks and returns from the production venture are appropriately distributed. Given that NOCs today own the majority of the world's reserves, IOCs are coming to terms with the reality that their future activity may have to increasingly take place in partnerships in which profits and control must be shared. In turn, governments of NOCs will have to work to provide a more stable and transparent investment environment and stronger governance of NOCs. Once these frictions are worked out, global investment in the sector would be better placed to respond to price incentives.

Investment and International Oil Companies

It is often argued that IOCs are not doing enough to increase investment—and thus capacity—to mitigate upward pressures on oil prices. According to data on companies listed on stock exchanges in the Group of Seven (G-7) countries, oil and gas companies have posted record profits in the past two years—well above the rest of the non-financial corporate sector—largely owing to the increase in energy prices. In the United States, the oil and gas corporate sector has almost doubled in valuation since mid-2000, well above the increase in the total S&P index, while oil service companies, which supply equipment and related services, have done even better. However, notwithstanding a significant increase in real investment since 2000, investment levels are still below the levels in the early 1990s, when spare capacity was much higher, and a large share of profits has gone toward paying higher dividends and acquiring new assets.

A number of specific factors have impeded higher investment by IOCs. First, investment opportunities are constrained by limited access to reserves in some oil-rich countries, while changes in regulatory regimes and risks of nationalization in some countries have made returns on new investments more uncertain. Second, in OECD countries and in others where IOCs dominate production, existing conventional fields are going into decline, and it has become more difficult and costly to extend their production life. Third, following the extensive downsizings of the 1990s, the IOCs are constrained by the availability of qualified staff and are facing higher short-term investment costs. As a result, an increasing share of earnings has been used to acquire other oil companies as a less risky alternative to greenfield investments. The median share of oil and gas companies' cash earnings spent on domestic and foreign asset acquisitions increased from 13 percent in the 1990s to 20 percent during 2001–04. Such acquisitions imply an increase in capital expenditures and production capacity for an individual IOC, but not for the global economy as a whole. Faced by limited opportunities in conventional fields, the IOCs have become active in developing alternative production sources (such as fields in new areas or new technologies). In these areas too, the IOCs face competition from NOCs—including from oil-importing countries—which in recent years have become just as active as IOCs in acquiring foreign assets, as well as in forging downstream and upstream ventures abroad, creating new challenges and opportunities for IOCs.

Investment and National Oil Companies

NOCs in a number of major oil producers—particularly where financial constraints are less binding or there is flexibility in attracting private capital—have ratcheted up plans for investment in the past year. Large companies—such as Saudi Arabia's Aramco, UAE's ADNOC, and Kuwait's KPC, which can self-finance projects and have maintained their human and productive capital base during the lean years of the 1990s—have developed ambitious capacity expansion plans at all levels of the production chain. Some NOCs in more fiscally strapped countries have recently sought new ways of accessing private sector financing and know-how, while at the same time abiding by the constitutionally mandated prohibition of foreign ownership.

NOCs such as Mexico's Pemex, Algeria's Sonatrach, and the Islamic Republic of Iran's INOC set up "build-operate-transfer" projects with IOCs, and have seen investment in these projects take off very rapidly, although overall investment has lagged.

Real investment of most other NOCs does not appear to have recovered from the decline in the 1990s despite a slight pickup since 2000, although data are limited. Investment has been constrained by numerous explicit and implicit restrictions imposed by their own governments. NOCs in many low-income, but oil-rich, countries are often short of financial resources, because cash flow is siphoned off to the budget—for example, through high implicit fuel subsidies (when the domestic fuel price for consumers is kept artificially low) and in some cases as a result of corruption. Even where the intentions of the government are benign, competing objectives can lead to politically difficult trade-offs. For example, if the government needs to undertake fiscal adjustment, it may do so at the cost of reducing resources available to the NOC. Analysts have shown that budgetary allocations to NOCs are a significant determinant of NOCs' investment the following year. Consequently, the lack of investment in oil production infrastructure over a number of years can imply that NOCs are not in a position to take full advantage of potential gains from current price levels.

Demand-Based Policy

The success of many economic policy measures designed to alter market outcomes requires consideration of likely actions by both those who demand the product as well as those who supply it. As a result, if oil-importing countries believe that the growing importance of national oil companies are a potential threat to their ability to gain access to desired supplies, not only should importers seek to change the behavior of national oil companies, but they might also change their own energy strategies. The key elements in such a demand-side policy are well known. They include diversifying the supply base, so that potential political problems are less likely to result in economic damage through reduced oil supply. In addition, conservation that reduces demand, or at least reduces the growth in demand, perhaps through taxes on imported oil or petroleum products, for example, might serve to reduce the potential influence that oil-based actions have on the domestic economy.

Supply-Based Policy

Oil importing nations might also use their political influence to try to encourage the national oil companies and their governments to alter their behaviors. The companies might be encouraged to improve their efficiency and respond to market signals more like privately owned firms. If the national oil companies find a need to access international capital markets more regularly, this result might be achieved as a natural result of exposure to the requirements of lenders. On a more political level, governments might try to encourage the governments of national oil companies to reduce their intervention in the operational decisions of the companies. This might be difficult to achieve in countries like Venezuela under the Chavez government, but progress likely can be made in more democratic environments. The clearest example might be Statoil and Norway, which operates largely on market principles.

As the world oil market changes its structure to include the growing importance of national oil companies, recognition of the likely consequences of this trend is an important first step in helping to secure oil supply. If the national oil companies hold the title to ever-greater portions of actual and potential oil reserves, production, and exploration and development activities, and if they are relatively less capable of utilizing those resources, oil supplies are likely to be relatively constrained in the future. Given projections of demand growth of about 50% by 2030, constrained supply might imply sharply rising oil prices.

Venezuela provides an early example of how the political influence of a government can affect the supply of oil, disturb existing market partnerships, both with companies and with the United States, and forward the interests of U.S. competitors. The private international oil companies are unlikely to be able to counter national oil companies to preserve their own profit-seeking interests as well as those of the U.S. market, which requires adequate physical supply at moderate prices. Various policy directions are available to counter the effects of national oil companies, but the recognition that a potential problem exists, as well as a long-term commitment to any chosen policy direction, will likely be needed to minimize the threat to U.S. oil market stability and energy security.

Mergers and Acquisitions

Depending on the relative prices of known oil resources and exploration, and existing facilities and construction, it has, on occasion, in the past, been cheaper for a company that wishes to expand to acquire assets financially, rather than through exploration and/or construction. This, along with other reasons, like scaling the company to an appropriate size for international competition, has led to periods of merger and acquisition activity in the oil industry. Many of the major oil companies were involved in merger activity from 1998 to 2002. In 1999, Exxon and Mobil merged. BP followed its 1998 acquisition of Amoco with a takeover of Arco in 2000. Conoco and Phillips merged in 2002, and Chevron and Texaco combined in 2001.

Recent years have seen few transactions on the scale of 1998-2002. Chevron acquired Unocal in 2005 in a deal that was reported to cost $18 billion. ConocoPhillips acquired Burlington Resources in 2006 for a reported $35.5 billion.

The Changing Market Structures

Over the last 25 years, the global oil industry has seen a transformation in the contractual structures used to purchase and sell crude oil. A market structure formerly based on rigid long-term, commercial arrangements has been replaced by a more efficient one that allows buyers and sellers greater flexibility in establishing commercial relationships that better meet their respective needs.

Whereas "spot" and "futures" markets have been long established institutional structures for many commodities, they are relatively new to the oil industry. Their uses, however, have grown rapidly and are now a well-developed part of the market. Today it is from the spot and futures markets that the global oil market – producers, refiners, marketers, traders, consumers, investment banks, hedge funds, and so forth – receives competitively determined market signals that inform buyers and sellers on current and future supply and demand conditions. In sum, the interactions of well-informed traders on spot and futures markets assure that the global price of crude properly reflects its market value.

International Petroleum Fiscal Regimes

Fiscal regimes in oil deal essentially with the upstream, that is exploration and production, they may, or may not, be defined in a single law. More often than not, the components of fiscal regimes in oil are actually found dispersed in different laws and rulings, and their beneficiaries may include municipalities, provincial administration and the central government. In order to be entitled to explore a plot of land and to exploit the reservoirs that might be discovered the oil company will enter in some kind of legal arrangements with the natural resource owner. These arrangements—a licence, concession, lease, service contract, profit or production-sharing agreement—normally also include besides royalties and taxes some specific payments and several other conditions.

These conditions will be considered as part of fiscal regimes even when the natural resource is privately owned and, therefore, the oil companies have to acquire private leases. The reason is that from the lessee's standpoint it is the total payment, whether made to the government and or the private owners, that matters. Private ownership of reservoirs still survives in the United States where private land property generally extends to the subsoil. In the rest of the world and, of course, on public lands in the USA (including, most importantly, waters), reservoirs are publicly owned, Yet to bring the exceptional case of the USA into the picture is not only of practical importance as this country has been the cradle of the petroleum industry, but is also theoretically appropriate. Indeed, looking at the theoretical side of fiscal regimes in oil, it turns out that the relevant issues were originally developed and discussed under the assumption of private landed property.

Fiscal terms for upstream investment refer to the agreement between a local government and an oil and gas exploration company to explore, develop and produce hydrocarbons. The objective of a host government is to maximize wealth from its natural resources by encouraging appropriate levels of exploration and development activity. In order to accomplish this, governments must design fiscal systems. The objectives of the oil companies are to build equity and maximize wealth by finding and producing oil and gas reserves at the lowest possible cost and highest possible profit margin.

In a competitive world, areas with the least favourable geology, the highest costs, and the lowest prices at the wellhead would offer the best fiscal terms, while areas with the best geology, the lowest costs, and the highest prices at the wellhead would offer the toughest fiscal terms. The objective of the host government is to design a fiscal system where exploration and development rights are acquired by those companies who place the highest value on these rights. In an efficient market, competitive bidding can help achieve this objective. The hallmark of an efficient market is availability of information. Yet exploration is dominated by numerous unknowns and uncertainty. With sufficient competition the industry will help determine what the market can bear, and profit will be allocated accordingly. In the absence of competition, efficiency must be designed into the fiscal terms. This is not easy to do.

Regardless of what fiscal system is used, the bottom line is the financial issue of how costs are recovered and profits divided. In order to accomplish this, governments must design fiscal systems that:

- Provide a fair return to the state and to the industry.
- Avoid undue speculation.
- Limit undue administrative burden.
- Provide flexibility.
- Create healthy competition and market efficiency.

The design of an efficient fiscal system must take into consideration the political and geological risks as well as the potential rewards. Detailed economic modeling using cash flow analysis is the best way to evaluate division of profits. Factors that limit a company's profits in a contract, such as cost recovery allowance, a government's right to back-in for an extra share of production, or an additional tax, can be modeled for the purposes of contract negotiation or project evaluation. Division of profits is commonly referred as *contractor take* and *government take.*

There are two main types of petroleum fiscal arrangements: concessionary systems and contractual systems. In concessionary systems private ownership is allowed whereas in contractual systems the state retains ownership. In contractual systems companies have the right to receive a share of production or revenues from the sale of oil or gas in accordance with a production sharing contract (PSC) or a service contract.

Contractual Systems

To calculate the contractor take, the first item to be deducted from the gross revenues from oil and gas production are the royalties. Gross revenues less royalty equals net revenue. The next item are deductions, which include operating costs, depreciation, and amortization; and intangible drilling costs. These are deducted from net revenue to arrive at taxable income. The third item is taxation. Revenue remaining after royalty and deductions is called taxable income. Taxable income might be taxed in two layers: provincial and federal. The remaining revenue after taxation is the contractors take. Concessionary contracts are a relatively simple and are not as widely used as the more complex production sharing contracts. Royalties are regressive because they are levied on gross revenues. For less profitable ventures, the relative percentage of royalty increases. The further from gross revenues that taxes are levied, the more progressive the system becomes.

Production Sharing Contracts

In most contractual systems, the facilities put in place by the contractor within the host government domain become the property of the state either the moment they are landed in the country or upon startup or commissioning. Sometimes, the title to the assets or facilities does not pass to the government until the attendant costs have been recovered. Contractual systems are divided into service contracts and production sharing contracts. The difference between them depends on whether or not the contractor receives compensation in cash or in kind (crude).

Basic Features of Production Sharing Contracts

- The title of the hydrocarbons remains with the state.
- The State maintains management control and the contractor is responsible for the execution of petroleum operations in accordance to the terms of the contract.
- The contractor is required to submit annual work programs and budgets for scrutiny and approval the State Company.
- The contract is based on production sharing and not profit-sharing basis.

- The contractor provides all financing and technology required for the operations and bore the risks.
- During the term of the contract, after allowance for up to a specified percentage of annual production for recovery of costs, the remaining production is split between the contractor and State.
- Equipment purchased and imported by the contractor become property of the State.
- Service company equipment and leased equipment are exempt.

Deductions Stages

Royalty: Royalties are the first deduction.

Cost Recovery

Before sharing of production, the contractor is allowed to recover costs out of net revenues. Most PSCs place a limit on cost recovery. If operating costs and DD&A amounts to more than the allowed limit, the balance would be carried forward and recovered later. From the mechanical point of view, the cost recovery limit is the only true distinction between concessionary systems and PSCs.

Profit Oil Split

Revenues remaining after royalty and cost recovery are referred to as profit oil or profit gas. The analog in a concessionary system would be taxable income. The contractor share of profit oil or gas is a specified percentage. If this were a service agreement, the contractor's share would be called service fee-not profit oil.

Taxes

The contractor's share of profit oil and gas is subject to taxation.

The Basic Elements

The basic elements of a production sharing system are categorized in Table below. These elements are also found in concessionary systems with the exception of the cost recovery limit and production sharing. Many aspects of the government/contractor relationship may be negotiated but some are normally determined by legislation. Those elements not determined by legislation must be negotiated. Usually, it is better to have more aspects that are subject to negotiation. This is true for the government agency responsible for negotiations as well as for the oil companies. Flexibility is required to offset differences between basins, regions, and license areas within a country.

Table 2.5: The Elements

	National Legislation	*Contract Negotiation*
Operational Aspects	Government participation Ownership transfer Arbitration Insurance	Work commitment Relinquishment Commerciality
Revenue or Production Sharing Elements	Royalties Taxation Depreciation rates Investment credits Domestic obligation Ringfencing	Bonus payments Cost recovery limits Production sharing

Source: Fiscal terms for Upstream Projects—An Overview, Center for Energy Economics, University of Texas at Austin.

Work Commitment

The work commitment refers to the obligations an exploration company incurs once a PSC is formalized. Work commitments are generally measured in kilometers of seismic data and the number of wells to be drilled in the exploration phase.

Bonus Payments

Cash bonuses are lump sums paid by the contractor to acquire a particular license. These cash bonuses are the main element in bidding rounds of very prospective acreage. Production bonuses are paid when production from a given contract area or field reaches a specified level.

Royalties

Royalties are taken right off the gross revenues. Royalties range as high as 15%, although many PSCs do not have a royalty. A specific rate royalty is relatively rare, but it may also go by another name, such as "export tariff', like in the former Soviet Union or the War Tax levy in Colombia. Another aspect of royalties that contributes to their lack of popularity with the industry is that they can cause production to become uneconomic prematurely. This works to the disadvantage of both the industry and government. One remedy that has become popular is to scale royalties and other fiscal elements to accommodate marginal situations.

Sliding Scales: A feature found in many petroleum fiscal systems is the sliding scale used for royalties, taxes and various other items. The most common approach is an incremental sliding scale based on average daily production.

Cost Recovery

Cost recovery is the means by which the contractor recoups costs of exploration, development, and operations out of gross revenues. Most PSCs have a limit to the amount of revenues the contractor may claim for cost recovery but will allow unrecovered costs to be carried forward and recovered in succeeding years. Cost recovery limits or cost recovery ceilings, as they are also known, if they exist typically range from 30% to 60%. Sometimes the hierarchy of cost recovery can make a difference in cash flow calculations. This is particularly the case if certain cost recovery items are taxable. Cost recovery of *cost oil* normally includes the following items listed in this order:

1. Unrecovered costs carried over from previous years.
2. Operating costs.
3. Expensed capital costs.
4. Current year DD&A.
5. Interest on financing (usually with limitations).
6. Investment credit (uplift).
7. Abandonment cost recovery fund.

In most respects, cost recovery is similar to deductions in calculating taxable income under a concessionary system. There are some exceptions. For example, some PSCs have no limit to cost recovery and some have no cost recovery.

Tangible vs Intangible Capital Costs: Sometimes a distinction is made between depreciation of fixed capital assets and amortization of intangible capital costs. Under some concession agreements, intangible exploration and development costs are not amortized. They are expensed in the year they are incurred and treated as ordinary operating expenses. Those rare cases where intangible capital costs are written off immediately can be an important financial incentive. Most systems will force intangible systems to be amortized. Therefore, recovery of these costs takes longer, with more revenues subject to taxation in the early stages of production.

Interest Cost Recovery: Sometimes interest expense is allowed as a deduction. Some systems limit the amount of interest expense by using a theoretical capitalization structure such as a maximum 70% debt.

General and Administrative Costs: Many systems allow the contractor to recover some office administrative and overhead expenses. Non operators are normally not allowed to recover such costs.

Unrecovered Costs Carried Forward: Most unrecovered costs are carried forward and are available for recovery in subsequent periods. The same is true for unused deductions. The term "*sunk cost*" is applied to past costs that have not been recovered. There are four classes of sunk cost: tax loss carry forward, unrecovered depreciation balance, unrecovered amortization balance and cost recovery carry forward. These items are typically held in abeyance (inactive) prior to the beginning of production. Many PSCs do not allow preproduction costs to begin depreciation or amortization prior to the beginning of production. Exploration sunk costs can have a significant impact on field development economics and can strongly affect the development decision. The importance of sunk costs and development feasibility centers on an important concept called *commerciality*. The financial impact of a sunk cost position on the development position can be easily determined with discounted cash flow analysis. The field development cash flow projection should be run once with sunk costs and one without.

Abandonment Costs: Under most PSCs the contractor cedes ownership rights to the government for equipment, platforms, pipelines and facilities upon commissioning or startup. The government as owner is theoretically responsible for the cost of abandonment. Anticipated cost of abandonment is accumulated through a sinking fund that matures at the time of abandonment. The costs are recovered prior to abandonment so that funds are available when needed.

Profit Oil Split Taxation: Profit oil and gas is split between the contractor and the government, according to the terms of the PSC. Sometimes it is negotiable. The contractor's share is usually subject to taxation.

COMMERCIALITY

Commerciality deals with who determines whether or not a discovery is economically feasible and should be developed. Some regimes allow the contractor to decide whether or not to commence development operations. Other systems have a commerciality requirement where the contractor has to prove that the development of a discovery is economically beneficial for both the contractor and the government. The benchmark for obtaining commercial status for a discovery cannot be developed unless it is granted commercial status by the host government. The grant of the commercial status marks the end of the exploration phase and the beginning of the development phase of a contract.

GOVERNMENT PARTICIPATION (JOINT VENTURES)

Many systems provide an option for the national oil company to participate in development projects. Under most government participation arrangements, the contractor bears the cost and risk of exploration. If there is a discovery, the government backs-in for a percentage, the government is carried through exploration.

The key aspects of government participation are:

- What percentage participation? (most range from 10% to 51%)
- When does the government back in? (usually once a discoveries made)
- How much participation in management? (large range of degree of participation)
- What costs will the government bear? (usually only their prorated share of development costs)
- How does government fund its portion of costs? (often out of production)

The financial effect of a government partner is similar to that of any working-interest partner with a few exceptions:

1. The government is usually carried through the exploration phase, and may or may not reimburse the contractor for past exploration costs.
2. The government's contribution to capital and operating costs is normally paid out of production.
3. The government is seldom a silent partner.

Contractors prefer no government participation. This stems from a desire for efficiency as well as economy. Joint operations of any sort, especially between diverse cultures, can have a negative impact on operational efficiency. This is particularly true when the interests of government and an oil company can be so polarized.

Investment Credits and Uplifts

Uplift allows the contractor to recover an additional percentage of capital costs through cost recovery. For example, an uplift of 20% on capital expenditures of $100 million would allow the contractor to recover $120 million. Uplifts can create incentives for the industry. Uplifts are the key of rate of return contracts.

Domestic Obligation

Many contracts specify that a certain percentage of the contractor's profit oil be sold to the government. The sales price to the government is usually at a discount to world prices.

Ring Fencing

Ordinarily all costs associated with a given block or license must be recovered from revenues generated within that block. The block is *ring fenced.* This element of a system can have a huge impact on the recovery costs of exploration and development. From the government perspective, any consideration for costs to cross a ring fence means that the government may in effect subsidize unsuccessful operations. However, allowing exploration costs to *cross the fence* can be a strong financial incentive for the industry.

Reinvestment Obligations

Some contracts require the contractor to set aside a specified percentage of income for further exploratory work within the license.

Tax and Royalty Holidays

The purpose of tax and royalty holidays is to attract additional investment.

Risk Service Contracts

In service contracts the contractor provides all capital associated with exploration and development of petroleum resources. In return, if exploration efforts are successful, the government allows the contractor to recover costs through sale of the oil or gas and pays the contractor a fee based on a percentage of the remaining revenues. The fee is often subject to taxes. The net importing countries are the ones most likely to use this approach. The distinction between PSCs and risk service contracts is minute. The nature of the payment of the contractor's services is the point of distinction.

Rate of Return Contracts

Contracts with flexible terms are becoming standard. There are many advantages for both the host government and the contractor with contracts that encompass a range of economic conditions. The most common method used for creating a flexible system is with *sliding scale terms.* Most sliding-scale systems trigger on production rates. As production rates increase, government take increases. This theoretically allows equitable terms for development of both large and small fields. Some contracts will provide flexibility through a progressive tax rate, others will tie more than one variable to a sliding scale such as cost recovery, profit oil split and royalty. The most common contract terms subject to sliding scale are profit oil split, royalty and bonuses. Less common are cost recovery limits and taxes. The most common factors and conditions used to trigger sliding scales are production rates, water depth, cumulative production, oil prices, age or depth of the reservoir, onshore vs offshore, R factors and the remoteness of locations. Less common are oil vs gas, crude quality, time period (history), distance from shore and rate of return.

The objective with sliding scale systems is to create an environment where the government take flexes upward as with increased profitability. The result of most fiscal structures is that project profitability is a function of government take. In general, it is better for both parties when government take is a function of profitability. Some countries have developed progressive taxes or sharing arrangements based on project rate of return (ROR). The effective government take increases as the project ROR increases. In order to be truly progressive, the sliding-scale taxes and other attempts at flexibility should be based on profitability, not production rates. Some contracts use what is called an R factor. The R factor = Accrued net earnings / Accrued total expenditures. R factors deal with all variables that affect project economics. Contractor potential upside from price increase is diminished, but the downside is also protected.

Technical Assistance Contracts (TACs)

TACs are often referred to as rehabilitation, redevelopment or enhanced oil recovery projects. They are associated with existing fields of production and sometimes, but to a lesser extent, abandoned fields. The contractor takes over operations including equipment and personnel if applicable. The assistance that includes capital provided by the contractor is principally based on special know-how such as steam or water flood expertise.

Fiscal Terms for Gas

Only a few nations specifically support gas development through the fiscal system.

However, most nations that provide support have seen a strong development of the natural gas sector. Since most gas projects will typically have a relatively low rate of return compared with oil, ROR-based scales typically favour gas development. The higher the ROR benchmark, the more gas is being favoured. The same applies to contracts that have R-factor sliding scales being used in production sharing, royalties or taxes. R-factor scales help gas economics because gas requires more investment and results often in lower prices at the wellhead on an energy basis. This means lower R factors. Jurisdictions that make use of uplifts or depletion allowances in calculations that apply to oil and gas usually also favour gas with a few percentage points government take.

OPEC and the world Crude Oil Market

Since the 1973 oil price shock, the history and behaviour of the Organization of Petroleum Exporting Countries (OPEC) have received considerable attention both in the academic literature and in the media. Many conflicting theoretical and empirical interpretations about the nature of OPEC and its influence on world oil markets have been proposed. The debate is not centred on whether OPEC restricts output, but the reasons behind these restrictions. Some studies emphasize that production decisions are made with reference to budgetary needs, which in turn depend on the absorptive capacity of the domestic economies. Others explain production cuts in the 1970s in terms of the transfer of property rights from international oil companies to governments, which tend to have lower discount rates. Others explain output restrictions in terms of coordinated actions of OPEC members. Within the literature, OPEC behaviour ranges from classic textbook cartel to two block cartel, to clumsy cartel, to dominant firm, to loosely co-operating oligopoly, to residual firm monopolist and most recently to bureaucratic cartel. Others have suggested that OPEC oscillates between various positions but always acts as a vacillating federation of producers. The existing empirical evidence has not helped narrow these different views. Some analysts have observed in the mid-1980s that the empirical studies tend to "reach onto the shelf of economic models to select one, to validate its choice by pointing to selected events not inconsistent with model's prediction" still dominates the empirical approach to studying OPEC behaviour and its pricing power.

At first sight, it may seem that OPEC plays a very limited role in the formation of oil prices. OPEC countries, like other oil exporters, just take the marker price from the spot market (and, more recently, from the futures market) and plug it in the pricing formula to arrive at the price at which they sell their oil. But this simple description does not provide a realistic portrayal of OPEC's role in price formation. By changing production quotas, the organization and its dominant player Saudi Arabia are bound to have an influence on oil prices. OPEC sets production quotas based on its assessment of the market's call on its supply. Oil prices fluctuate in part according to how well OPEC performs this calculation. Through the process of adjusting its production quotas, OPEC can only hope to influence price movements towards a target level or target zone. In a supply– demand framework, the oil price is determined by OPEC and non-OPEC supplies as well as oil arriving to the market from OPEC members who do not abide by the assigned quotas. Since these supplies cannot be predicted with accuracy and are influenced by factors other than prices, OPEC can only hope that the resulting oil price is close to its preferred price. In this context, models that consider OPEC simply as a price setter to maximize the net present value (NPV) of oil receipts over time are of limited usefulness.

Achieving the desired price level to acquire 'more' revenues has become more difficult in the current context in which prices are increasingly being determined in the futures market. OPEC's influence on prices is now dependent on the expectations of participants in the futures markets. In principle, quota decisions can be viewed as signals to the market about OPEC's preferred range of prices. It is important to stress that this signalling mechanism may or may not succeed, depending on how the market interprets these signals. Specifically, the effectiveness of the signal will depend on whether the market believes that OPEC is able to undertake the necessary output adjustment in different market conditions.

Although OPEC has on many occasions succeeded in defending the oil price, adjusting output downward has sometimes proven to be unsuccessful. If global demand for oil falls, non-OPEC suppliers will continue to produce at their maximum potential. In their attempt to defend a target price, OPEC members would call for production cuts. However, because of the different features, needs and bargaining power and the divergent interests of member countries, OPEC cannot usually reach agreements on allocation of production cuts. Even when agreements are reached, each member has the incentive to go against these decisions. Because of the absence of a monitoring mechanism, these violations are not usually detected and even if they are, the organization does not have the power to punish and force member countries to abide by the agreed production cuts. These problems become more acute when the required cuts are significant as the small OPEC members usually find it difficult to reduce their production on a pro-rata basis: the usual system adopted by OPEC over the years.

In these circumstances, market participants would doubt the credibility of OPEC's decision to cut production and may decide to ignore the signal. This is particularly true if there are deep divisions and political rivalries among member countries, which will jeopardize the success of any coordination efforts. Lack of transparency about the decision-making processes and lack of information about production and investment reduces the credibility of the signal. Adjusting output in the face of growing global oil demand can also be problematic, although for different reasons. Although agreements to increase quotas are easier to reach and implement when global demand is rising, OPEC may not respond quickly to this upward trend in an environment of imperfect information and uncertainty about future demand. After all, the decision to wait and not increase output is more profitable than to increase output when the trend may turn out to be false. Expecting that, market participants may ignore the signal of an output increase, considering such a move as not being credible.

Loosing Pricing Power?

OPEC's pricing power is not straightforward. Any theoretical and empirical model should take into account the following three features. First,

OPEC behaviour is not constant and can exhibit variation in conduct with important implications on price dynamics in the oil market. In this respect a 1987 study represents an important but lonely contribution. Using quarterly data from 1966 to 1981, they find evidence, which is consistent with variation in conduct. Second, OPEC's influence is asymmetrical depending on whether it is responding to rising or falling global oil demand. In fact, a large literature developed on whether firms find it more difficult to collude during booms or recessions. The main intuition within the literature is that changes in demand conditions affect the one-shot deviation gains, the losses of future collusive profits and the future cost of being punished, which directly affect the sustainability of collusive outcomes. Analysts have also found that under certain assumptions of constant and symmetrical marginal costs, a firm's incentives to deviate are stronger when future demand is falling. This is due to the fact that the value of the foregone collusive profits is smaller when demand is falling than when demand is rising. Thus, according to their model, it becomes more difficult to sustain collusion under decreasing demand. However, this clear-cut result is less so if capacity constraints are introduced into the picture. For instance, analysts have shown that when firms face severe capacity constraints, demand fluctuations can also have an impact on the future cost of being punished. When firms are operating close to their maximum capacity, the future costs of being punished are lower while the large excess capacity in face of decline in global demand implies that the future cost of being punished is high. This can make collusion more difficult during booms rather than recessions. Incorporating these and similar insights into OPEC models can prove quite useful.

Third, the shift to the futures markets for price determination has introduced a large number of players and the large variety of participants (floor traders, fund managers, refiners, producers, financial institutions and speculators) has certainly complicated the process of decision-making within OPEC. OPEC's influence on prices has become dependent on the expectations of these participants and how they interpret OPEC signals. In standard signalling models, informed agents communicate private information indirectly via choices of observable actions. Because the choices made are costly, signalling becomes credible. The signalling hypothesis has been successfully applied to a large number of issues including banking, corporate finance, macroeconomic and monetary policy and industrial organization. However, these traditional models of signalling may not be appropriate in this context. First, OPEC communication with the market is directly through public announcements. Second, different from traditional models of signalling, OPEC signals are without cost. This raises the question whether any information can be credibly transmitted when signalling is without cost and direct. This issue has been extensively analysed within the context of 'cheap talk' in game theory. The insights from this literature can be very useful in studying OPEC relationship with the market. The main shortcoming however is that 'cheap talk' models are characterized by a multiplicity of equilibria ranging from the 'babbling' equilibrium in which recipients consider all signals to be meaningless to the more informative equilibrium. However, analysts show that informative equilibria still entail a significant loss of information. The literature examines some of the measures that can be used to limit information loss.

Oil Pricing Regime and the Shift

From the discovery of oil in the Middle East at the beginning of the twentieth century until the early 1970s, OPEC member countries played no role in the production or pricing of crude oil. Governments simply received a stream of income calculated on the basis of 'posted' price. Being a fiscal parameter, the posted price did not respond to the usual market forces of supply and demand and hence did not play any signalling role. Other prices such as spot and long-term contract prices played a very limited role in price discovery due to the vertically and horizontally integrated industrial structure dominated by the large multinational oil companies known as the Seven Sisters. This meant that oil trading became, to a large extent, a question of inter-company exchange with no free market operating outside the control of these companies. Multinational oil companies used to balance their positions on the basis of long-term contracts, but the prices in these contracts were never disclosed. By the late 1950s, changes in the oil market, such as the arrival of independent oil companies that were able to obtain access to crude oil outside the control of the Seven Sisters and the arrival of crude oil from the former USSR, started to challenge the dominance of the multinational oil companies.

However, these changes never posed a serious threat to the Seven Sisters or to the posted price system. At the same time, OPEC countries were too weak to change the existing pricing regime. Thus, the multinational oil companies maintained their dominance both in the upstream and downstream parts of the industry for most of the 1960s. It was not until the early 1970s that the oil pricing system witnessed a major transformation, which saw the price setting power shift from the multinational oil companies to OPEC. This transformation was driven by an array of factors, the most important of which is the tight supply–demand conditions that emerged in the early 1970s. Between 1970 and 1973, global demand for oil increased at a fast rate with most of the increase in demand met by OPEC countries. This enhanced the power of OPEC governments relative to the multinational oil companies, and governments began seeking higher stakes on their oil sales. In October 1973, after negotiations with multinational oil companies to increase oil prices failed, the six Gulf members of OPEC unilaterally announced an immediate increase in the posted price of the Arab light crude from $3.65 to $5.119. In December 1973, OPEC raised the posted price of the Arab light further to $11.651. These events represented a dramatic change in the pricing system. For the first time in its history, OPEC assumed a unilateral role in setting posted prices while previously it had only been able to prevent oil companies from reducing them. At the centre of the new pricing system was the marker or reference price with individual member countries setting their prices in relation to the price of the Arab light, which became the marker crude.

Another important development in the early 1970s that had direct implications on the pricing system was the decision of OPEC governments to stop granting new concessions and claim equity participation in the existing concessions, with a few of them opting for full nationalization (Algeria, Iraq and Libya). Equity participation gave OPEC governments a share of the oil produced which they had to sell to thirdparty buyers on the basis of official selling price (OSP) or government selling price (GSP). However, for reasons of convenience, lack of marketing experience and inability to integrate downwards into refining and marketing in oil importing countries, as part of the equity participation agreements governments made it compulsory to sell the oil at buyback prices to the companies that had originally held the concessions.

Equity participation and nationalization of oil resources profoundly affected the structure of the oil industry. During the late 1970s, multinational oil companies lost large reserves of crude oil and became increasingly dependent on OPEC supplies. The degree of vertical integration between upstream and downstream weakened considerably as companies no longer had enough access to crude oil to meet their downstream requirements. This encouraged the development of an oil market outside the inter-multinational oil companies trade and pushed companies to diversify their sources of oil supply by gaining access to and developing reserves outside OPEC. In the early

1980s, new discoveries in non-OPEC countries responding to higher oil prices and taking advantage of new technologies meant that significant amounts of oil began to reach the international market from outside OPEC. According to the EIA, between 1975 and 1985 non-OPEC countries increased their share of world total oil production from 48% to 71% with most of the increase coming from Mexico, the North Sea and the Soviet Union. The increase in non-OPEC supply had two main effects. First, non-OPEC countries were setting their own prices which were more responsive to market conditions and hence more competitive. Second, the number of crude oil producers increased dramatically. The new suppliers of oil who ended up with more crude oil than required by contract buyers secured the sale of all their production by undercutting OPEC prices in the spot market. Buyers who became more diverse were attracted by the competitive prices on offer, which were below the long-term contract prices.

It became clear by the mid-1980s that the OPEC-administered oil-pricing regime was unlikely to survive these competitive pressures for long. OPEC's, or more precisely Saudi Arabia's, attempts to defend the marker price would only result in a dramatic reduction in its oil exports and loss of market share as other producers could offer to sell their oil at a discount to the Arab light. As a result of these pressures, OPEC saw its own market share in the world's oil production fall from 52% in 1973 to less than 30% in 1985 with Saudi Arabia's share being the most affected. In an attempt to restore the country's market share, Saudi Arabia adopted the netback pricing system in 1986. The netback pricing system provided oil companies with a guaranteed refining margin since it was based on a general formula in which the price of crude oil was set equal to the *ex post* product realization minus refining and transport costs. The netback pricing system resulted in the 1986 price collapse, from $26 per barrel in 1985 to less than $10 per barrel in mid-1986. Out of the 1986 crisis, the current 'market-related' oil-pricing regime was born. The adoption of the current market-related pricing system represented a new chapter in the history of oil price determination since it resulted in the abandonment of the administered oil pricing system that had dominated the oil market from the 1950s until the mid-1980s.

Formula pricing constitutes the basis of the current international oil pricing regime. The formula used in pricing oil is straightforward: the price of a certain variety of crude oil is set as a differential to a certain marker or reference price. Specifically, for crude oil variety X, the formula pricing is: $PX = PR \pm D$ where PX is the price of crude X, PR is the reference or marker price and *D* is the value of the price differential. The most important element of formula pricing is the identification of the reference or benchmark crude. Brent, WTI and Dubai-Oman are the main crude oil benchmarks of the current oil pricing system. Nearly all oil traded outside America and the Far East is priced using Brent as a benchmark. WTI is the main benchmark used for pricing oil imports into the USA. Dubai-Oman is used as a benchmark for Gulf crudes (Saudi Arabia, Iran, Iraq, the UAE, Qatar and Kuwait) sold in the Asia-Pacific market.

In the early stages of the current oil pricing system which emerged in the period 1986-88, crude oil was priced off the spot market quotations of these benchmarks (namely dated Brent, spot WTI and Dubai) as assessed by oil reporting agencies such as Platts and Petroleum Argus. In the last few years however, there have been some serious doubts about the ability of the spot physical market to generate a price that reflects accurately the margin of the physical barrel of oil. One of the main problems is that these markets have become very thin i.e. very little actual trading occurs in these crudes which makes the process of price discovery very difficult. This has been the direct consequence of a rapid decline in the volumes of production of the benchmark crudes. The Brent system witnessed a dramatic decline in production in the early 1990s. The co-mingling of the Brent system with the Ninian system at the end of 1990 alleviated this problem and the combined production from the Ninian and Brent systems (still known as Brent) increased to around 900,000 barrels per day in 1992. Thereafter, the production of Brent fell to around 350,000 barrels per day in 2002. To avoid potential distortions and squeezing in the thin Brent market, Platts broadened its definition of Brent to include Forties (UK North Sea) and Oseberg (Norway) as of 10 July 2002. This new benchmark has been given the name BFO. The inclusion of these two grades increased the number of cargoes to around 60-70 cargoes per month.

The WTI has also witnessed a similar decline, with production reaching less than 400,000 barrels per day in 2002. This decline reflects a sharp fall in US crude oil production in the past few years. US total oil production in 2003 declined sharply from 10.6 mb/d in 1985. During 2003, the United States produced around 7.8 million barrels per day of hydrocarbon liquid of which 5.7 mb/d was crude oil. The bulk of oil exported from the Middle East to Asia Pacific is priced using a combination of Dubai and Oman spot quotations as a benchmark. Initially, the benchmark only included crude oil produced in Dubai. Dubai became the main price marker for the region by default as it was one of the few Gulf crudes available for sale on the spot market. However, the volume of Dubai crude production has dropped from a peak of 400,000 b/d in the period 1990-95 to under 120,000 b/d in 2004, with production hovering around 100,000 b/d in 2005. In 2006, Dubai crude continued to fall and according to Petroleum Argus (10 July, 2006) Dubai is currently producing about 90,000 bpd i.e. around five cargoes each month, with only four of these cargoes traded on the spot market (the remaining cargo is shipped by the producer ConocoPhillips to its refineries).

Due to this rapid fall in Dubai's oil production, in 2001 Platts introduced Oman into the assessment mechanism. This counteracted the problem of low liquidity and effectively doubled the volume of crude oil in the Dubai-Oman benchmark for price assessment. The addition of Oman in the assessment of Dubai however has created problems of its own. Oman crude has lower sulphur content and higher gravity than the Dubai crude. The increase in demand for lower sulphur and higher gravity crude oil relative to heavier sour crude has widened the price gap between the two types of crude. Since September 2004, the Dubai-Oman markets have diverged with the spread between the two grades reaching $2.30 per barrel in October 2004. As a result of this divergence, sellers have not been willing to supply the more expensive Omani crude into the Dubai contract. To counteract this problem, Platts decides to include Oman and Upper Zakum as alternative delivery into the Dubai bids with effect from February 1, 2006.

In March 2004, Platts introduced another innovation, the partials mechanism, to counteract the problem of Dubai's low trading activity caused by the rapid fall in Dubai's production. The partials mechanism has the effect of cutting the cargo into small parcels that can be traded. In the Dubai context, the smallest trading unit was set at 25,000 barrels. Since operators do not allow sale of cargoes of that volume, it meant that a seller of a partial contract would not have been able to meet his contractual obligation. Thus, delivery will only occur if both buyer and sellers trade 19 partials totalling 475,000 barrels. Any traded amount less than 475,000 barrels is not deliverable and should be cash settled. Trading however in the partials contracts have been in decline in recent months.

The Shift to the Futures Market

The declining liquidity of the physical base of the reference crudes and the narrowness of the spot market has caused many oil-exporting and oil-consuming countries to look for an alternative market to derive the price of the reference crude. The alternative was found in the futures market. For instance, instead of using dated Brent for its exports to Europe, several major oil-producing countries such as Saudi Arabia, Kuwait and Iran rely on the IPE Brent Weighted Average (BWAVE) as the basis of pricing crude exports to Europe. The BWAVE is the weighted average of all futures price quotations that arise for a given contract of the futures exchange (IPE) during a trading day. The weights are the shares of the relevant volume of transactions on that day. This shift is quite important since it places the futures market, which is a market for financial contracts, at the heart of the current pricing system. The shift to this new stage was justified by the perceived inadequacies of the spot market. Many have argued that the natural decline in oil production in Brent reduced overall market liquidity and hence increased the crude market's vulnerability to manipulation, distortions and squeezes. Another reason for shifting to the futures market for price determination is that a futures price is, after all, determined by actual transactions in the futures exchanges and not on the basis of some assessed prices by oil reporting agencies. Furthermore, the timely availability of futures prices enhances price transparency. At any time, a seller or a buyer, can look at the prevailing price and use it in spot and term contracts. The volume of daily transactions and open positions is additional useful information to gauge the liquidity of the market. Thus, the move towards establishing an oil futures contract for pricing Middle East sour crudes can be seen as part of a more general shift in the international pricing system to the futures market for crude oil price discovery. This shift is seen by many observers as necessary to deal with the shortcomings of the spot Dubai market for price discovery.

But why not rely on the highly liquid WTI and Brent futures markets for price discovery and pricing Gulf oil exports to Asia? The answer is that neither of these two comes close to representing the type of crude oil in the region which is mainly sour. More generally, it is often argued that WTI and Brent no longer represent the marginal barrel of oil. For instance, according to a recent report by ENI, almost all of last year's increase in crude oil supply is of the heavy to medium sour variety and despite the fact that sweet grades will make their way to the market in the coming years, this trend towards sourer heavier slate is likely to continue. Furthermore, marginal refining capacity in the world cannot process heavy, sour crudes. The conversion of existing refining capacity to deal with this new reality is expensive and slow. Faced with this refining bottleneck and the increasing trend towards sourer and heavier slate, the relative demand for sweet oil continues to rise creating a large wedge between sweet crude and sour crude prices. This represents a fundamental change in oil markets; and pressures to change the world benchmarks to heavier more sour crudes have become paramount.

Sour Pricing

Even as we are witnessing a shift in the oil pricing regime under which the futures market is gaining more importance, and is been deciding the actual price of oil, at the heart of the debate on crude oil pricing lies a paradox: as sour crudes grow in importance, the debate about pricing benchmarks has continued to focus on light crudes such as Brent and WTI, which have been the markers for the last 20 years.

But as the world becomes critically reliant on heavier and higher-sulfur streams, the emphasis needs to be increasingly on sour crudes since these grades are assuming more importance in the price discovery process. Producers and consumers face not only extreme volatility in the price of oil but also in the relationship between light sweet and heavy sour streams as the incremental heavy barrel behaves in line with its own fundamentals. Over half of the world's oil supply nowadays is heavy sour. More significantly, incremental production is primarily of sour crude from the Middle East as OPEC members with spare production capacity modify their output levels to meet the requirements of growing economies across many regions. So what is the dilemma in sour crude pricing? In the world of Middle Eastern sour, production is high and benchmarking is pegged essentially to the price of Dubai, a medium sour crude from the United Arab Emirates, which has low output. The Dubai benchmark allows producers and consumers to determine a competitive price for other sour crudes in the region, with prices set at a differential to physical Dubai. The system therefore allows buyers and sellers to measure the price of one physical crude against the value of another.

But the pricing system needs to be constructed well and updated regularly as physical benchmarks are vulnerable to production declines, which create the potential for distortions in price. Derivatives are also prone to the same vulnerabilities as derivative instruments such as swaps derive their value from the root physical commodity. If the root is infected, it will affect the whole tree. The challenge then is to keep the existing physical benchmarks healthy.

Rising Oil Prices

Why have oil prices been rising? In the 1970s, for example, price rises were due primarily to disruptions in supply. But recently, in a period when supplies have been tight, the increases have been due more to strong demand. At the same time, prices have also been pushed up by rises in marginal costs. In the OPEC region, for example, more of the output is coming from smaller oilfields, which have higher unit costs, while in the non-OPEC countries more output is coming from mature basins, which tend to have higher marginal costs. Geopolitical tensions and conflicts in some major oil producing regions, especially the Middle East, are another potential cause of price increases, because they are raising the prospect of supply disruptions and adding a 'risk premium' to prices.

Growth in Oil Demand

The rise in crude prices in recent years has been driven partly by the conspicuous growth in demand. According to the International Energy Agency, between 2002 and 2005 world oil demand expanded by 7 percent, to 84 million barrels per day. Much of this growth in demand came from the United States and from Asian developing countries, notably China, which over the period 2002-2005 accounted for 30 percent of total demand growth. This prompted many oil producers to increase their production. It also absorbed much of OPEC's surplus capacity, making the oil market more vulnerable to supply or demand fluctuations. Demand has been consistently ahead of supply. Before 2003 the gaps were due not to a real shortfall but mainly to the OPEC cartel's control of production to fix prices. In recent years, growth in demand is straining physical supply, so the supply gap is more real and market determined.

An important feature of this rising demand is that much of it has been for gasoline and diesel. The United States continues to be a major user of gasoline for cars, but developing countries like Brazil, China and India are also consuming more gasoline for personal transportation. European countries, on the other hand, have been switching more to diesel for cars. Asian developing countries are also using more diesel though in this case it is used to fuel the many backup generators, as well as to replace coal in large-scale electricity generating plants in efforts.

Shrinking Buffers

In the past, three main buffers have dampened fluctuations in supply and demand: surplus production capacity among OPEC members, large oil inventories and surplus refining capacity in consuming countries. All three buffers have, however, been shrinking. As a result, the world oil market has become more vulnerable to price volatility and supply disruptions. In the past, OPEC provided much of the surplus production capacity. This has now decreased: between 2000 and 2004, it fell from around 7.0 to 0.6 million barrels per day. Subsequently it rose, reaching 2.2 million barrels per day by May 2005, but is still relatively small. Moreover, this surplus comes from just a few countries, notably Saudi Arabia and Iraq, so any problems with their exports will have major repercussions for the world oil market.

A further cause of tightening oil markets is shrinking oil inventories. To rationalize their production and cut costs, oil companies, particularly in the United States, have been holding lower stocks of both oil and gasoline. Refineries too are working with less slack. Despite rising demand, the oil companies have not been building many new refineries, preferring instead to reduce their surplus refining capacity. The combination of tighter supplies and changing demand – or speculation about such changes – has made prices much more volatile and increased vulnerability to disruptions in supply, particularly in oil-importing developing countries.

Oil Supply Insecurity

Security issues, linked primarily to the unstable situation in the Middle East, have also affected oil prices. In May 2004, for example, oil facilities in Saudi Arabia, the world's largest oil producer, suffered two attacks. These did not reduce Saudi production, but they did have a psychological impact, raising doubts about the country's security and causing price hikes in the market for crude-oil futures. Added to this is the uncertainty created by the situation in Iraq. Around the time of the Iraq War, oil production fluctuated wildly before returning in March 2004 to the pre-war level of 2.4 million barrels per day. Since then, deteriorating public security and attacks by insurgents on oil facilities have again undermined production, which has been as low as 1.8 million barrels per day.

Oil supply problems also have occurred in other parts of the world. In 2004, legal problems with the government led to the collapse of Russia's largest oil company, Yukos; in Mexico, devastating hurricanes hit the oil-producing Mexican Gulf coast; and in Nigeria, intermittent militant attacks on facilities have made it more difficult to maintain supplies. The situation is further aggravated by the possibility of structural changes in countries like Bolivia and Venezuela, which are nationalizing their oil and gas industries. Furthermore, in some parts of the world, notably Mexico and OECD Europe, production prospects are deteriorating because of low levels of investment in exploration. All these factors are heightening oil supply insecurity. They have also raised questions as to whether world oil production has already peaked.

Speculation in the Market

Oil supply-demand imbalances and uncertainties have been exacerbated by a massive influx of speculative money into the market for crude oil futures. Speculators, reacting to vulnerabilities in supply, fluctuations in demand and external shocks, have expanded their trading, often basing their judgments on media reports. In so doing, they have heightened the price volatility. Speculative activity can push oil prices higher, since this unstable situation adds a larger 'risk premium.' Over the short-term, futures prices thus may be subject to excessive hikes that bear no direct relation to current supply or demand fundamentals. However, these prices can themselves trigger further changes in supply or demand, leading to another round of wild fluctuations The oil price hikes also incorporate an element of 'geopolitical risk premium.' Buyers who fear the prospect of damage to oil facilities in the Middle East are prepared to pay more to secure supplies. This is thought to be contributing to between 20 and 25 percent of the current oil price.

Under Investment in Exploration and Refining

Prices have also been higher because of under investment. The key players in the global energy industry, OPEC national companies and the large multinational companies, failed to anticipate the growth in demand and did not sufficiently expand their output. Indeed, at the end of the 20th Century, following the collapse of the price, they had often reduced or even stopped investment and then did not subsequently step up production as prices rose. Some people argue that the recent price rises, particularly for sweet-light crudes such as WTI, have actually served a useful purpose in stimulating investment across the oil supply chain. This is also often seen as a 'justification' for the oil price rise. However, under investment in the oil sector may not be simply an inadequate response to rising demand but also may reflect a general situation of uncertainty and price volatility, leading to a vicious circle whereby the lack of investment could once again propel prices upward. Added to under investment in exploration is inadequate investment in refining capacity, particularly for the lighter products that have to be processed out of heavy-sour crudes, mainly gasoline, diesel and ATF.

Dollar Depreciation

According to IMF World Economic Outlook 2008, over the past few years, dollar depreciation has coincided with soaring commodity prices. In March 2008, both crude oil and gold reached fresh highs within a short period after the U.S. dollar set new record lows against some other major currencies. These co-movements are no coincidence. Over the past 20 years, commodity prices have generally been negatively correlated with the U.S. dollar—both in nominal and real effective terms—with the notable exception of crude oil during the 1980s. However, dollar depreciation has been only one factor affecting commodity prices in recent years.

There are a number of channels through which a fall in the nominal effective value of the U.S. dollar can raise commodity prices in dollars.

The purchasing power and cost channel: Most commodities—notably crude oil, precious metals, industrial metals, and grains such as wheat and corn—are priced in U.S. dollars. Dollar depreciation makes commodities less expensive for consumers in non-dollar regions, thereby increasing their demand. On the supply side, price pressures arise from declining profits in local currency for producers outside the dollar area.

The asset channel: Given the purchasing power and cost channel, a falling U.S. dollar reduces the returns on dollar-denominated financial assets in foreign currencies, which can make commodities a more attractive class of alternative assets to foreign investors. Moreover, dollar depreciation raises risks of inflationary pressure in the United States, prompting investors to move toward real assets—such as commodities—to hedge against inflation. For example, commodity markets rallied in the 1970s amid high inflation.

Other channels: Dollar depreciation could lead to monetary policy easing in other economies, especially in countries with currencies pegged to the dollar. This could result in lower interest rates and increased liquidity, thereby stimulating demand for commodities and other assets.

Based on the IMF World Economic Outlook 2008 estimates, the nominal U.S. dollar exchange rate has a significant impact in both the long run and the short run on crude oil and gold prices. In the long run, a 1 percent depreciation of the U.S. dollar is associated with increases for gold and oil prices of more than 1 percent. In the short run, the elasticity is close to 1, but higher for gold than for crude oil. For other non-fuel commodities, as measured by the IMF's index, the U.S. dollar impact is significant but smaller in magnitude over both the short and long runs. For metals,

U.S. dollar movements also have a significant impact. In contrast, the impact on grains is not significant. The long-run impact of the real exchange rate is stronger than that of its nominal counterpart across most commodities. Specifically, a 1 percent real depreciation of the dollar would result in an increase of greater than 1 percent in the real prices of gold, crude oil, aluminum, and copper in the long run. The real exchange rate also has a significant impact on corn prices, which do not respond strongly to the nominal exchange rate. The stronger impact of real effective exchange rates likely captures that the importance of the purchasing power and cost channel over the long run is better reflected in real variables.

Macroeconomic Impacts of Higher Energy Prices

An increase in the price of oil and other traded forms of energy leads to a transfer of income from importing to exporting countries through a shift in the terms of trade. For oil-importing countries, the immediate magnitude of the direct effect of a given oil-price increase on national income depends on the ratio of oil imports to GDP. This, in turn, is a function of the amount of oil consumed for a given level of national income (oil intensity) and the degree of dependence on imported oil (import dependence). It also depends on the extent to which gas and other energy prices rise in response to an oil-price increase and the gas-import intensity of the economy. Naturally, the bigger the initial oil-price increase and the longer higher prices are sustained, the bigger the macroeconomic impact. In the longer term, however, the impact will be reduced according to how much end users reduce their energy consumption and switch away from oil and how much domestic production of oil and other fuels increases in response to sustained higher prices. For net oil-exporting countries, a price increase directly increases real national income through higher export earnings. However, part of this gain would be later offset by losses from lower demand for their exports, generally due to the decline in GDP suffered by trading partners and possibly to a fall in non-oil exports caused by a rise in the exchange rate – a phenomenon known as "Dutch disease".

An oil-price increase leads to a reduction in the purchasing power of the export earnings of importing countries. If an importer continues to import the same value of non-oil goods and services while the cost of oil imports increases, the balance of payments will deteriorate, putting downward pressure on exchange rates. As a result, imports become more expensive, leading to a drop in real national income and lower domestic consumption. The dollar will also tend to rise, if oil-producing countries' demand for dollar denominated international reserve assets grows, aggravating the downward adjustment in real income for economies other than the United States and others with a currency linked to the US dollar.

Domestic output is not directly affected by higher oil prices. But adjustment, or second-round effects, which result from nominal wage, price and structural rigidities in the economy, typically lead to a fall in GDP in practice in net oil importing countries. Higher oil prices push up inflation, increasing input costs for businesses, reducing non-oil demand and lowering investment. Unless firms are able to pass through all of the increase in energy costs to higher prices for their final goods and services, profits fall, dragging down investment further. Tax revenues fall and the budget deficit increases, due to rigidities in government expenditure. If oil-product prices are directly subsidised by the government such that not all of the increase in bulk prices feeds through into final prices, as in many Asian countries, spending on subsidies rises. This leads either to a reduction in other forms of government spending, cutting overall demand, or a deterioration in the fiscal balance. Because of resistance to any real decline in wages, an oil-price increase may lead to upward pressure on nominal wage levels, which, together with reduced demand, tends to lead to higher unemployment. These effects are greater if the price increase is sudden (for example, if it results from a serious supply disruption) and sustained, and are magnified by the negative impact of higher prices on consumer and business confidence.

The fiscal and monetary policy measures chosen in response to higher energy prices also affect the overall impact on the economy over the longer term. Government policy cannot eliminate the adverse effects described above but it can minimise them; inappropriate policies can worsen them. The reaction of the monetary authorities to the threat of inflation and, perhaps more importantly, their *ex-ante* credibility in fighting inflationary pressures are critical. The quicker the authorities respond to inflation by raising interest rates, the bigger the short-term dip in GDP growth will be but the more likely it is that inflationary pressures will be squeezed out of the economy before expectations of higher rates of price and wage increases become entrenched. In practice, the monetary authorities need to strike a balance between dampening inflationary expectations and limiting the fall in GDP growth. Contractionary monetary and fiscal policies which are too severe could exacerbate the recessionary effects on income and employment. But unduly expansionary policies may simply delay the fall in real income necessitated by the increase in oil prices, stoke up inflationary pressures and worsen the impact of higher prices in the long run.

A fall in oil prices affects the macro economy of oil-importing countries in a reverse manner, but as in the case of a price rise, the magnitude of the impact does not match the full extent of the price change because of the offsetting costs of structural change. Similarly, the boost to economic growth in oil *exporting* countries provided by higher oil prices has, in the past, always been less than the loss of economic growth in importing countries, such that the net global effect has always been negative. This is explained both by the cost of structural change and by the fact that the fall in spending in net importing countries is typically bigger than the stimulus to spending in the exporting countries in the first few years following a price increase. Demand in the latter countries tends to rise only gradually, so that net global demand tends to fall in the short-term.

The Recent Implications

Following a decade of fluctuation within a relatively narrow range in the 1990s, and a low point of US$13 per barrel in 1998, the price of oil has increased sharply. Between 2002 and July 2006 the price nearly tripled, from US$25 to US$74 per barrel, and in mid-2007 remained around US$70.

An important feature of recent trends in oil prices is the gradual reduction in the difference between nominal prices and real prices. Nominal prices are converted to real prices using a 'GDP deflator,' in this case using 2000 as a base year with a value of 100. In 1980, for example, the deflator, based on year 2000 dollars, fell as low as 87, while in the 1990s it fluctuated in a narrow band between 90 and 110. One reason for the convergence in real and nominal prices in the 1990s and the early 2000s has been the general stability of prices. Since 2004, there has been some divergence between nominal and real prices, though not on the same scale as in the 1990s. Increases in prices for crude oil have been matched by increases in the prices of petroleum and other oil products, with differing rates of increase.

The main products of interest for households are kerosene and LPG; for industry, they are naphtha, fuel oil and diesel; and for the transport sector, they are gasoline, diesel and aviation turbine fuel (ATF). The uses of these products are summarized in Table 2.6. For consumers, some of these products have been subsidized, typically those such as kerosene, which is used by the poor, or diesel, which affects the price of transport. But recently, in efforts to balance their budgets, governments have been cutting down on subsidies, resulting in steep price increases for consumers.

It should also be noted that recent increases have been greater for certain types of oil: higher for light-sweet crudes, such as WTI, than for heavy-sour crudes, such as those in the OPEC basket. The price differential between WTI and the OPEC basket was around US$1.9 early in 2002, but by various quarters in 2004 and 2005, it had increased to between US$6 and US$9.5. This was due to a number of factors: rising demand for light-oil products, particularly gasoline for transportation; stronger regulations on the quality of petroleum products; bottlenecks in refining capacity for processing heavy or high-sulphur crude oil; and changes in the supply mix, with a falling proportion of light sweet crude. Oil prices have also been affected by the falling value of the US

Table 2.6

	Diesel	*Kerosene*	*LPG*	*Naphtha*	*Gasoline*
Major user sectors	Transportation, agriculture, power generation	Households: for lighting and cooking Transportation: used by some vehicles instead of diesel if the price is lower	Households: for cooking Transportation: limited use in some countries	Agricultural sector: for fertilizers, and also by some industries	Transportation
Relevance for poor households	Used directly by poor farmers and indirectly by poor households through public transport	Important for lighting in non-electrified households and during power outages; also used for cooking	Used for cooking and heating; Usually sold in large cylinders that are expensive for poor households	Only relevant indirectly, e.g. through the price of fertilizers	Not widely used in public transport; Not an important fuel for poor households

dollar. As the US dollar has lost value, the oil price rises have been higher in US dollars than in euros or yen, which has created problems for certain countries. Moreover, the depreciating US dollar combined with low interest rates may itself have contributed to increasing oil demand and thus to the rise in oil prices.

High Oil Prices and Supply

Markets and analysts alike increasingly expect high oil prices to endure. An important factor behind the firming of these expectations has been weaker-than-expected prospects for an expansion in supply. Indeed, the increase in long-dated futures prices over the past three years has coincided with steady downward revisions to projections for non-OPEC supply. Although initial uncertainty about how long high oil prices would last was plausibly an important reason for oil producers not to rapidly ratchet up their investment, the sluggish supply response has become increasingly puzzling in light of persistently high prices.

The sluggish response to higher oil prices is clearly not the result of a lack of investment. During 2004–06, nominal oil investment grew by about 70 percent. However, soaring prices for investment meant that this did not translate into large real investment increases. The higher investment costs were due to a global scarcity both of equipment such as rigs and of services such as skilled engineers and project managers and to higher average exploration and development costs.

Many of the factors contributing to higher costs are cyclical in nature and should moderate as input supplies adjust to the increased demand. However, based on evidence presented below, a significant component of these costs is the result of geological constraints—a more permanent rigidity—implying that the responsiveness of supply to high prices is likely to remain low for some time.

Investment Lags

IMF analysis suggests that oil companies' investment—in particular that of major international firms—was slower to respond to the price signals in the current boom than in earlier periods. Using a panel of company data for investment between 1993 and 2006, IMF staff estimates show that the lag between spare capacity (a proxy for the price signal) and investment is about three years. However, this lag increased in recent years. For international oil companies, this may reflect limited given oil sector foreign direct investment restrictions in an increasing number of countries, as well as a reluctance to quickly switch to a risk-taking mode following the consolidation and cost-cutting strategies implemented during the 1990s, when oil prices remained low.

Comparing investment across companies suggests that the largest companies are also those that take on the greatest technical risks, even after controlling for higher costs. Indeed, regression estimates using company-level data suggest that increased technical risk significantly raises real investment. Political variables in the host country were somewhat important in explaining investment. Political stability and the fiscal balance of the host country had positive coefficients in the regressions, as expected, but they were not always statistically significant. It is possible that fears of "resource nationalism" have increased uncertainty about investment in a less-tangible way that is not yet being captured by the data. There could also be some self-selection: the strong positive correlation between exploration and production costs and political stability may suggest that oil companies would prefer to gamble on difficult geology than to take the necessary steps to hedge against political uncertainties. Increased tax assessments by governments have raised the costs of international joint venture projects. In 2007, payments to governments (including royalties) represented more than half the cost of a barrel of oil. It was not possible to isolate the specific effect of higher taxes, but after-tax profits were found to have a positive and very significant effect on investment. In other words, to the extent that high tax rates affect companies' bottom lines, they adversely affect investment.

Comparing investment behavior across companies, there is no evidence that national oil companies were investing less than international oil companies. On the contrary, some emerging, outwardly oriented national oil companies are increasing foreign and domestic investment very rapidly, in some cases with strong political and financial support from their governments. However, traditional national oil companies—which are typically smaller—have been struggling with high costs and aging infrastructure. Smaller oil companies are investing more as a share of revenues than larger ones, but they are much less likely to embark on technically risky projects. Soaring costs have been particularly taxing for smaller, independent companies with limited cash flow, which are less diversified than larger ones. In some cases, an important consequence of rising investment costs is that some projects have become unviable.

Turning to results obtained from analyzing field-level investment data, the analysis found that the amount of time it takes, on average, for investment to translate into output has also increased, as more complex projects have become the norm. The projects attracting most of the marginal investment—such as deep-water offshore drilling in Brazil, the Gulf of Mexico, and West Africa; Canadian oil sands projects; and Siberian projects—take longer to explore and develop than more traditional projects. According to estimates based on field-level investment data of about 150 projects during 2003–07, these projects showed roughly twice the lag before the start of production as conventional projects. The lags likely reflect the complexities of working with emerging technology and are intrinsically related to soaring exploration and development costs. In some cases, projects have been delayed because governments have refused to renew some contracts in their current form in the face of higher-than expected cost overruns. In sum, the evidence suggests that although investment eventually does respond to prices, it does so with a greater lag and more slowly than in the past.

Geological Factors

In addition to slow investment responses, there are two other factors that suggest that capacity growth will be more constrained by geology than in the past. First, although peak production rates in major fields are attained earlier—because extraction methods have become more efficient—"decline rates" are also higher in major fields. The International Energy Agency suggests that almost two-thirds of the additional gross capacity needed over the next eight years will be required just to replace declines in output from existing fields.

Second, oil will increasingly come from unconventional sources, because output has declined from peak levels at conventional fields in many countries, and the size of oil fields is getting smaller on average. This does not mean that the world is about to run out of oil, but it suggests that higher oil prices are needed to induce the additional investment required to balance the market over the medium term. The rigidities that are currently preventing an adjustment toward greater supply growth suggest that the current cycle will be different from the major oil boom of the late 1970s. The table shows many of the underlying oil market factors associated with both episodes: in the late 1970s oil companies had ample opportunity to expand geographically, more oil fields were conventional, and production was located close to the main consuming centers. Ultimately, policy and technology will determine the size of the supply and demand responses to high prices this time around. Although both demand and supply will eventually adjust, a policy-induced demand response can be implemented faster and is likely to have a more immediate impact than a supply response, because many of the output constraints are geological and technological. Specifically, policies that lead to higher vehicle fuel-efficiency standards and the elimination of domestic fuel subsidies in some countries have the greatest potential to ease market tightness. It will also be important to remove investment obstacles and foster efficient and stable tax policies for companies.

Indian Upstream Sector

The Ministry of Petroleum and Natural Gas (MOP & NG) is entrusted with the responsibility of exploration and production of oil and natural gas (including import of Liquefied Natural Gas), their refining, distribution and marketing. The Indian Oil Sector can be divided into three sub-sectors:

(i) Oil and Gas Exploration and Production;
(ii) Oil Refining; and
(iii) Marketing (Gas and Refined Products)

Oil and Natural Gas Corporation Limited (ONGC) and Oil India Limited (OIL), the two National Oil Companies (NOCs), and private and joint-venture companies are engaged in the Exploration and Production (E&P) of oil and natural gas in the country.

Oil and natural gas also known as hydrocarbons are some of the most important fossil fuels to meet the energy requirements of the country and support economic growth. Currently, in India, the share of oil and gas in the primary energy is about 45 percent. In spite of several advances in technology, exploration of oil and gas has been stated, till today, to be a probabilistic discipline with a high degree of risk of failure. The habitat for oil and natural gas having been determined by geological events of the remote past, any estimation of resources is based on various possible hypotheses and models constructed thereon. Exploration is undertaken based on the same hypotheses and geological models constructed on the basis of data acquired by exploration companies. India has 26 sedimentary basins, comprising both on land and offshore areas. Only 19 of the 26 sedimentary basins in India have been taken up for exploration so far, with acquisition of seismic data and carrying out exploratory drilling. Of the total sedimentary basin area of India of 3.14 million sq. km., about 1.39 million sq. km area is in the onshore area and 0.39 million sq. km in the offshore area (up to 200 m isobath water depth). The deep water area is about 1.35-million sq. km. Most of the basins are under various stages of active and/or reconnoitory exploration. The sedimentary basins of India have been classified into four categories as a function of geological knowledge of the basin, presence and/or indication of hydrocarbons and current status of exploration.

In the early days after independence, very little petroleum was produced in India. Digboi, the only source in early 1950s, yielded about 60 million gallons annually which was about 7 percent of India's then requirement. Around 1950s, mineral exploration and their utilization in the country received little attention. Except for coal, iron ore and petroleum required for internal use, a majority of the minerals were raised in India for the purpose of bulk export without any dressing, processing and fabrication. These exports brought about only a small return for the country. The search for oii in the country had commenced as far back as 1866 in Upper Assam. Oil in commercial quantities was discovered for the first time in 1889 at Digboi. The move towards shifting the crude oil production from Assam was marked by the Indo-Stanvac Petroleum Project. It was the first project that marked a major effort at exploration for oil outside the known oil bearing regions of Assam.

In view of the great need to establish indigenous sources of oil, the nucleus of an organization for oil exploration was set up by GOI towards the end of the First Plan period. With limited equipment and technical personnel available, investigations were started in the Jaisalmer area of Rajasthan. The Second Plan provided for an intensification of the effort and enlargement of the organization therefore. The Oil and Natural Gas Commission (now Corporation) was set up in 1956 by an Act of Parliament to explore and exploit hydrocarbon reserves in the Indian sedimentary basins. The Commission undertook geological surveys, geophysical investigations and exploratory drilling for oil in Punjab and later in the region of Cambay and in the Brahmaputra valley in Assam. In 1958, Burmah Oil also transferred bulk of its share to the GOI, and accordingly a joint venture company named OIL was formed.

In April 1956, the GOI adopted the Industrial Policy Resolution, which placed the mineral oil industry among schedule 'A' industries, the future development of which was to be the sole and exclusive responsibility of the state. The Indian upstream sector, thus, historically, has been under the dominance of PSUs. ONGC and OIL—the National Oil Companies (henceforth referred to as NOCs) and more recently private and joint venture companies are engaged in E&P of oil and natural gas in the country.

Exploration Regimes

Exploration of oil and gas in spite of several advances in technology has been stated, till today to be a probabilistic discipline with a high degree or risk of failure. The habitat for oil and natural gas having been determined by geological events of the remote past, any estimation of resources is based on various possible hypotheses and models constructed thereon. Exploration is undertaken based on the same hypotheses and geological models constructed on the basis of data acquired by exploration companies.

At present, the following regimes are in place for exploration and production of oil and gas in the country:

Exploration areas allocated to ONGC and OIL on nomination basis: ONGC and OIL have been given certain areas on nomination basis for exploration of oil and gas. As on 1st August, 2004, ONGC has 117 Petroleum Exploration Licenses (PELs) and OIL has 18 PELs on nomination basis. Each PEL now has an agreed and committed exploration work programme.

Production Sharing Contracts (PSCs) signed before New Exploration Licensing Policy (pre-NELP PSCs): At present, 19 PSCs are in place against pre-NELP rounds in which exploration activities are being undertaken by private companies.

PSCs signed under NELP: The Government has signed 90 contracts under four rounds of NELP. At present, exploration in 81 blocks is in progress.

Producing areas with ONGC and OIL: ONGC and OIL have 239 and 22 Petroleum Mining Leases (PMLs) respectively for production of oil and gas. PMLs also allow exploration in the area along with production.

PSCs for discovered fields: The Government has signed 4 PSCs for medium size fields and 24 PSCs for small size fields for production of oil and gas.

Performance of Upstream Sector

The recently released Integrated Energy Policy (IEP), (GOI, 2006c) better explains the performance of upstream sector of the industry when it points out that domestic production of crude oil has remained between 30.3 million tonnes and 33.98 million tonnes during 1990-2005. Not only has domestic production stagnated, known oil reserves have also remained in a narrow range with total oil reserves being of the order of 739 million tonnes in 1990-91 and were estimated to be 786 million tonnes in 2004-05. The proved reserve to production (R/P) ratio was 23 in 2004-05. We now import 72 percent of our consumption and our import dependence is growing rapidly. There has been no significant increase in known crude oil reserves during the last decade in spite of large investments in exploration activities. As a result, crude oil production has stagnated and the gap between the demand and domestic availability of crude oil is widening. Import dependence will keep rising, unless dramatic new discoveries are made. This raises serious concerns about India's energy security and our ability to obtain the oil we need and the impact of constrained supply on oil prices and on our economy. All projections show an increase in the gap between the domestic crude oil production and consumption. In fact, according to International Energy Agency (henceforth referred to as IEA) India will be import dependent to the extent of 94 percent by 2030.

Apart from availability of supplies in physical terms, the outgo of foreign exchange in procuring crude oil has been an equally significant issue. The Five Year Plans have consistently raised concerns on the issue of foreign exchange. For instance, the Sixth Plan pointed out, that two thirds of country's earnings of foreign exchange through merchandise exports have to be utilised for oil imports.

Intensifying Exploration

It is surprising that though exploration has been a top most priority in the GOI's agenda over the last four decades, the country is facing these dire consequences of increasing crude oil imports, as far as performance of exploration sector is concerned. For instance, the Third Plan talked about an intensified programme of mineral exploration and development. The Sixth Plan, similarly, called for a greatly intensified effort towards both exploration and development. Similarly, the Seventh Plan pointed out the need for intensifying exploration as well as for extending exploratory activities to inadequately explored and unexplored basins. Further, the Ninth Plan envisaged acceleration of exploration efforts, while the Tenth Plan pointed out that the thrust area is acceleration of exploration efforts especially in deep offshore and frontier areas. Despite these concerns, the country largely remains unexplored, that is more intensive exploration could have been carried out. Time and again analysts have questioned the country's exploration strategy.

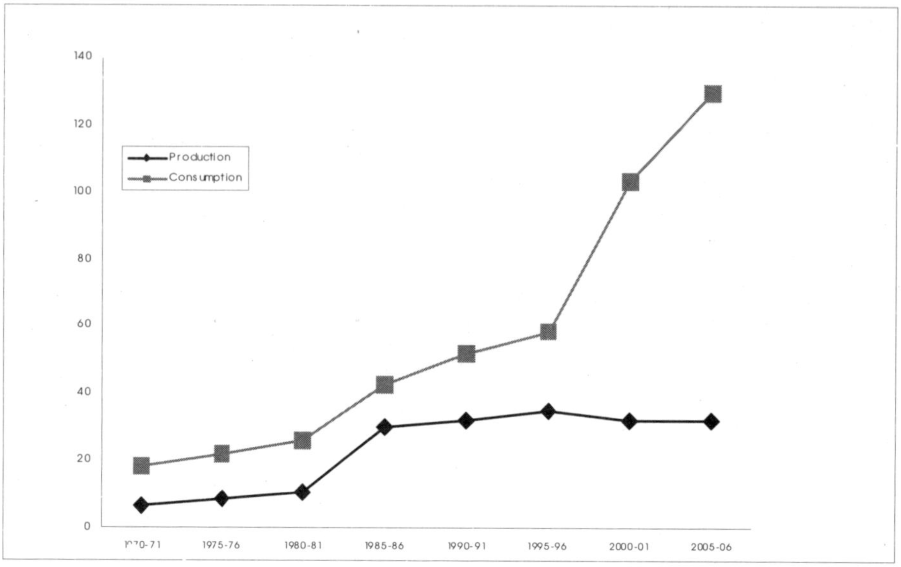

Note: Figures for 2005-06 are Provisional.

Source: GOI (2007a).

Figure 2.6: Crude Oil Production and Consumption (million tonnes)

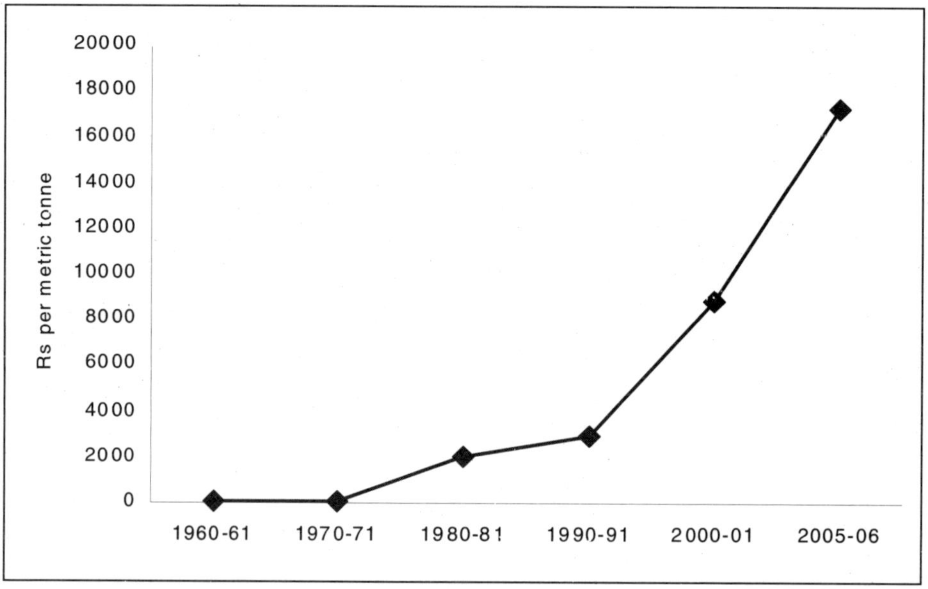

Note: Figures for 2005-06 are Provisional.

Source: GOI (2007a).

Figure 2.7: Unit Value of Crude Imports (per metric tonne)

Whatever are the shortcomings of the implementation strategy, the exploration performance has not been note worthy, it appears.

Table 2.7: Status of Unexplored/Poorly Explored Areas in the Country

Year	*% Unexplored*	*% Poorly explored*
1999-00	41	17
2002-03	32	19
2003-04	30	19
2004-05*	22	22

Note: Figures for 2004-05 are provisional.
Source: GOI (2006d).

Analysts have pointed out that even in fairly explored areas drilling intensity is very low, averaging only 12 wells per 10,000 sq km. No wonder IEP holds that there has been no significant increase in crude oil reserves during the last decade in spite of large investments in exploration activities. Its call for not relying on the possibility of finding oil domestically is indeed a cause of concern. Our proved reserves data shows that supply side interventions, namely, intensive exploration, acquiring equity oil abroad, building strategic storage of crude oil, using bio-fuels among others, have not resulted in any significant increase in the availability of oil. Proved reserves have increased from 3.8 thousand MB at the end of 1985, to around 5.9 thousand MB at the end of 2005.

Currently producing fields also are no different. For instance, the average recovery factor from the producing fields of ONGC has remained stagnant in the range of about 28 percent over the last few years, very low by international standards. Efforts are now being made through secondary recovery methods like the Improved Oil Recovery (IOR) / Enhanced Oil Recovery (henceforth referred to as EOR), so that these can be improved to 35 percent over a 10 year period and to about 40 percent over 15-20 years. Though necessary, these strategies are short-term measures for a problem, which essentially is a long run one. Moreover, these strategies are also not easy to implement. EOR schemes are complex, energy intensive, and also expensive. But if implemented appropriately, they can cut unit costs, lower the decline in production from mature fields from the expected 15 to 4 percent per annum and increase the rate of oil recovery by 15 to 20 percent.

It makes a great deal of economic sense to intensify exploration efforts in the Indian basins, especially in the frontier basins so that their hydrocarbon

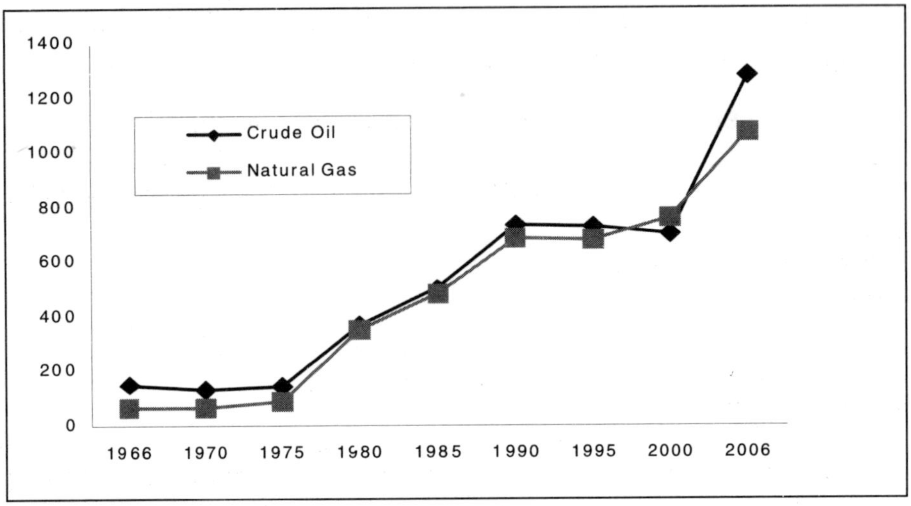

Note: For crude oil million tonnes and for natural gas in Billion cubic metres. Figures as of January 1st and provisional for 2006.
Source: GOI (2007a).

Figure 2.8: Oil and Natural Gas Reserves

potential is fully assessed as early as possible. However, this intervention requires substantial investments. Fortunately, it has already dawned upon our policy makers that efforts of the two NOCs needed to be supplemented through additional investments in the E&P sector from multinationals and Indian companies.

Private Sector Intervention

It was against this background regarding the exploration scenario in the country that GOI started looking for private capital to complement capabilities of our NOCs. It must be pointed out that the importance of private capital has always been duly acknowledged earlier. The Third Plan, for instance, had clearly acknowledged the role of private capital to join the search of oil in India GOI had been inviting private investment in exploration of oil and gas in the country since early 1980s. However, initial efforts to attract private investment were limited to offshore areas only. Till about 1991, GOI had invited around 3 bidding rounds for exploration of cil and gas limited to the offshore area only. These initial efforts to attract private investments did not have the required continuity until 1991. However, since 1991, the GOI began offering exploration blocks on a regular basis, as can be gauged by the fact that between the year 1991 and 1995, the GOI invited six bidding rounds which included both offshore and on land blocks.

In spite of sustained efforts aimed at increasing the indigenous production of oil and gas through the efforts of the private sector, and PSUs, it was felt that much more needed to be done. It was emphasized that despite these good efforts, they were not leading to a substantial increase in the domestic production of crude oil and natural gas. Moreover, constraints were also faced in the sense that there were not enough risk capital investments in the exploration, along with the latest exploration technology and the management practices. For instance, over two-third of the Indian sedimentary basins remained unexplored or poorly explored. Out of the estimated total prognosticated hydrocarbons reserves of 28 billion tonnes, only less than one fourth had been established. The efforts of the NOCs, also needed to be complemented and there was also a need to provide a level playing field as well as competition to the NOCs by giving similar fiscal and contract terms as applicable to private investors.

Given the historically prevalent situation till about 1990s, the GOI reviewed the policy of inviting investment in exploration of oil and gas including the fiscal and contract terms. Given the concerns and clear objectives in mind, the GOI in February 1997 formulated "The New Exploration Licensing Policy" (henceforth referred to as NELP). The main features were:

1. No mandatory state participation through ONGC/OIL or any carried interest of the Government.
2. Blocks to be awarded through open international competitive bidding.
3. ONGC and OIL to compete for obtaining the petroleum exploration licenses (PEL) on a competitive basis instead of the existing system of granting them PELs on nomination basis.
4. ONGC and OIL to get the same fiscal and contract terms as private companies.
5. Freedom to the contractors for marketing of crude oil and gas in the domestic market.
6. Cess to be exempted for production from blocks offered under NELP.
7. Companies to be exempted from payments of import duty on goods imported for petroleum operations.
8. No signature, discovery or production bonuses.

The policy provides a level playing field to private investors by giving the same fiscal and contractual terms as applicable to NOCs. Under NELP, PSCs for 110 exploration blocks have already been signed. In first five rounds of NELP, the expected investment is of the order of U.S. $ 5 billion. Private/JV companies under NELP have made 30 discoveries. It is estimated that oil and gas in-place reserves accretion under NELP is approximately 510 MMTOE from 16 discoveries. Reserve accretions under NELP have upside potential of further increases after appraisal of all the hydrocarbon discoveries.

Table 2.7: Summary of NELP Exploration Blocks

Parameter	*NELP I*	*NELP II*	*NELP III*	*NELP IV*	*NELP V*
No. of blocks offered	48	25	27	24	20
No. of blocks bid for	28	23	24	21	20
No. of bids received	45	44	52	44	69
No. of blocks awarded	25	23	23	21	20
No. of PSCs signed	24	23	23	20	20
Signed on	April 2000	July 2001	Feb. 2003	Feb. 2004	Dec./ Sept. 2005
Area awarded (Sq Km)	1,94,735	2,63,050	2,04,588	1,92,810	1,15,180

Source: GOI (2006f).

Private/Joint venture companies have emerged as significant players in hydrocarbon exploration during Tenth Five Year Plan period. Perhaps for the first time in the history of Oil and gas production in the country, the share of private sector players in the upstream sector is expected to be high, if not dominant during the Eleventh Five Year period. Crude oil production of 211.64 Million metric tonnes (henceforth referred to as MMT) during the Eleventh Five Year Plan period is expected to be about 26 percent higher than the Tenth Five Year Plan. The increase in crude oil production will be mainly due to contributions by private companies. A similar role is expected of the private sector in the natural gas production also during the Eleventh Five Year Plan.

Table 2.8: Crude Oil Production (thousand tonnes)

	1990-91	2000-01	2001-02	2002-03	2003-04	2004-05	2005-06
ONGC	29,513	25,057	24,710	26,005	26,057	26,485	24,404
OIL	2,647	3,286	3,182	2,951	3,002	3,196	3,234
JVC/Private	—	4,083	4,140	4,088	4,314	4,300	4,552

Note: Figures for 2005-06 are provisional.
Source: GOI (2007b).

Table 2.9: Crude Oil Production in Eleventh Plan (million metric tonnes)

	2007-08	*2008-09*	*2009-10*	*2010-011*	*2011-12*	*Total*
ONGC	27.16	28	29	28.53	27.37	140.06
OIL	3.75	4.05	4.73	5.44	5.90	23.87
Pvt/JV	10.57	10.78	9.76	8.75	7.85	47.71
Total	41.18	42.83	43.49	42.72	41.11	211.64

Source: GOI (2006g)

The need to attract investment was considered for the following reasons:

1. Over two-third of the Indian sedimentary basins remained unexplored or poorly explored. Out of the estimated total prognosticated hydrocarbons reserves of 28 billion tonnes, only less than one fourth had been established.
2. The efforts of National Oil Companies (NOCs) needed to be complemented.
3. There was need to attract risk capital investments in exploration, along with latest technology and management practices, and infuse fresh geological ideas.
4. To provide a level playing field as well as competition to the NOCs by giving similar fiscal and contract terms as applicable to private investors.

The broad parameters considered for offering exploration blocks under NELP are as under:

1. Availability of area i.e. no PEL/ML has been issued to NOCs or JVs/ Private Companies.
2. Availability of sufficient geo-scientific data, to attract oil companies.
3. Preliminary inter-ministerial clearances including defence and environmental clearances.

NELP implementation consisted of the following features:

1. Deep water areas were offered for exploration for the first time under NELP.
2. Data packages and information dockets were digitised and given in CD-ROMS/Exa-byte Tapes.
3. The total areas covered under exploration in the four rounds of NELP is about 0.9 million sq. kms. which constitutes about 80% of area presently under exploration in the country.

4. A total of 90 contracts have been signed in the four rounds of NELP.
5. The bidding process leading to award of blocks and signing of contracts have been completed in 3-7 months under NELP as compared to 24-48 months or even more taken prior to NELP rounds.
6. With its combined emphasis on work programme as well as profit sharing in the bid evaluation criteria, NELP has generally attracted rather aggressive work programme commitments and commercial terms for the Government as compared to previous bidding rounds.
7. Emphasis is on higher 3D seismic surveys under NELP, which is expected to improve exploration efficiency and reduce chances of drilling dry wells.

Pricing in the Indian Context

Till late sixties, bulk of the crude that was needed for our requirements was being imported into the country from West Asia. But after Mumbai High was discovered our dependence in terms of crude imports and crude throughput at the refineries started decreasing. Import dependency decreased from 65.7% in 1973-74 to 18.5% in 1984-85. But, thereafter, it started showing an upward trend touching 36.2% in 1990-91 and to 69.2% in 2000-01. Today about 70% of the crude we need is being imported and the indigenous share amounts to just 30% of our requirements. Based on the relative growth in demand and production, it is estimated that oil dependence will be as high as 85 per cent in 2020.

Oil and Natural Gas Corporation Limited (ONGC) and Oil India Ltd. (OIL), the two National Oil Companies (NOCs) and private and joint-venture companies are engaged in the Exploration and Production (E&P) of oil and natural gas in the country. Crude oil production during 2003-04 was 33.37 MMT by ONGC, OIL and private/ joint venture companies. Crude oil production target for 2004-05 was 33.64 MMT. However, actual production during 2004-05 was 29.4 MMT.

Prior to 1981, crude oil prices were fixed on various considerations like import parity, long run marginal cost etc. In 1981, Government revised crude oil pricing departing from OPC concepts. Thereafter, the prices of indigenous crude oil were unchanged till 1992 when the Cabinet Committee on infrastructure reviewed the crude pricing and observed that due to un-remunerative price of indigenous crude oil, ONGC and OIL, the two public sector undertakings under the administrative control of the Ministry of Petroleum and Natural Gas engaged in exploration and production of oil and gas, were unable to generate resources for developing more oil fields and exploration in new areas. The Cabinet Committee recommended that the domestic well head price of crude oil should be so determined as to compensate ONGC and OIL for the cost of production and reasonable return on investment. Thus under APM, the prices of indigenous crude oil were based on cost plus return of 15% post tax on capital employed. Effective 1.4.1998, the crude oil producers had been paid a pre announced increase in percentage (75% for 1998-99, 77.5% for 1999-2000, 80% for 2000-01 and 82.5% for 2001-02) of the international FOB prices on a year-to-year basis subject to a floor of Rs. 1,991/ MT and a ceiling of Rs. 5,570/ MT (Rs. 6,470/MT for March 2002). Post APM, effective 1.4.2002; consequent to dismantling of APM, the prices of indigenous crude oil are determined on the basis of the Crude Oil Sales Agreement (COSA) between the producers and the refineries by benchmarking various indigenous crude oils to equivalent international crude oils.

The import parity price of ONGC crude oil from 2002-03 onwards is inclusive of the following components:

(i) FOB price of respective marker crude adjusted for Gross Product Worth

(ii) Ocean freight

(iii) Ocean Loss

(iv) Insurance

(v) Custom Duty

(vi) NCCD at the rate of Rs 50/T (applicable from 01. March 03)

(vii) Port dues

(viii) Octroi (applicable for Mumbai refineries of HPCL and BPCL only)

As far as OIL is concerned, since 1.4.2002, its crude oil has been bench marked to Nigerian Bonny Light due to its similarity in quality. However, OIL does not receive the full import parity price and instead receives only the FOB price adjusted for Gross Product Worth (GPW) and discount towards Base Sediment and Water (BS&W) plus 50% of pipeline transportation charges in respect of crude oil sales to all refineries except NRL (NRL does not pay any pipeline transportation charges), if the FOB price of crude oil is above US$ 21 per bbl. However, if the crude oil price is below US $21 per bbl, OIL would receive sales tax in addition to FOB price plus 50% of pipeline transportation charges, as stated above. However, the FOB price has always remained above US$21 per bbl since 1.4.2002.

The various components that are considered while determining the pricing of crude oil in terms of the Memorandum of Understanding signed by OIL are as under:

(i) Monthly average of high—low Free on Board (FOB) price of Nigerian Bonny Light as per PLATTS Oilgram.

(ii) Difference in quality between Bonny Light and OIL's crude oil (termed as Gross Product Worth) determined on the basis of product yield and prices on 4 cut basis. The 4 cuts are:

- LPG cut (Propane and Butane derived from Saudi Aramco Contract price Ex. Arab Gulf) up to C4.
- Naphtha (C5-175) FOB, Singapore.
- Gas Oil 0.5% "S" (C-175 – 350) FOB, Singapore and
- Fuel oil 180 CST 2% and LSWR (in equal proportion) (C 350+) FOB, Singapore

(iii) Base, Sediment and Water.

(iv) RBI reference rate for conversion to India Rupees.

Regarding imported crude oil, the pricing is based on the actual cost incurred by various refineries while importing the same and comprises items like FOB cost, freight to India, Insurance, ocean loss, customs duty, wharf age etc. In the international oil market, crude oil is traded based on market related pricing. The absolute price of crude oil is not fixed at the time of finalization of the contract and price prevailing at the time of loading of cargo is taken. For example, crude oil of major exporting countries like Saudi Arabia, Iran, Iraq, Kuwait etc. is sold by National Oil Companies on term basis for one year. However, the price for cargoes loaded in different months is different and dependent on the price prevailing in the month of loading.

Further, since there are more than 100 grades of crude oils produced in the world and all are not actively traded, the methodology of pricing of crude oil is based on one "Reference" or "Marker" crude oil that is actively traded in a particular region. Typically there is a premium or discount over the "Marker" due to quality/locational differences etc.

For high sulphur crude oils imported by India, Oman and Dubai are the Marker crude oils. For most low sulphur crude oils imported by India, Brent is the marker crude oil. Considering the proportion of import of low sulphur and high sulphur crude oil into the country, an indicative Indian Basket price has been devised with weightage of 57% to the average of Oman and Dubai and weightage of 43% to Brent price. Based on the above weightage, price can be worked out on daily, weekly, monthly and yearly basis. It may be pertinent to note that Indian Basket price is not the price of actual imports but only an indicator for reference purpose.

CHAPTER 3

Indian Downstream Industry

Crude oil is the primary input into production of petrol and other refined petroleum products produced in a refinery. The range and quality of refined petroleum products produced by any given refinery depends on the types of crude oil used as feedstock and the configuration of the refinery. The configuration of certain refineries, particularly in North America, is typically oriented towards the production of petrol whereas the configuration of refineries in most of the other regions is typically oriented towards the production of middle distillates such as diesel and aviation fuels. India is an example of the latter case where, historically, we have built our refineries to maximize production of middle distillates. In addition, there are refineries, which are configured towards certain other specialty products such as base oil, naphthenics and bitumen. Over the years, refineries have made investments to be able to better process different types of crude oil. This has enabled them to more easily substitute between different crude oil. Nonetheless, refineries usually are designed to be most productive using a specific range of crude oil. When they substitute other types of crude, their efficiency and productivity could decline (FTC, 2005).

Unlike crude reserves, petroleum refineries are not concentrated in particular regions. Usually they are sited in the consuming areas. It is normally more economical to build refineries close to the market, mainly because this minimises transport and logistical costs. However, environmental restrictions and local resistance do hamper new additions and upgrades in many parts of the world. For example, in OECD and in North America, it is virtually impossible to build a grassroots refinery. The other OECD regions face similar problems. Most of the new refinery capacity additions, thus, have been made in other regions.

Peculiarities

Downstream production, especially refining related activity, is different from the upstream activity, namely, exploration and extraction. In particular, the production and cost structure of this activity is different from upstream activities in that the governance structures of these two activities can be different. There is much less uncertainty and time lag associated with the recovery of sunk costs while the technological and logistic requirements are different and they have a different industry structure.

Production of petroleum products in a refinery entails joint production. Petroleum products are joint products. There are, thus, practical difficulties in determining the cost of a petroleum product. Joint and common costs form about 95 percent of the total expenses of a refinery. In a petroleum refinery, a product cannot be produced without any other different product being produced simultaneously.

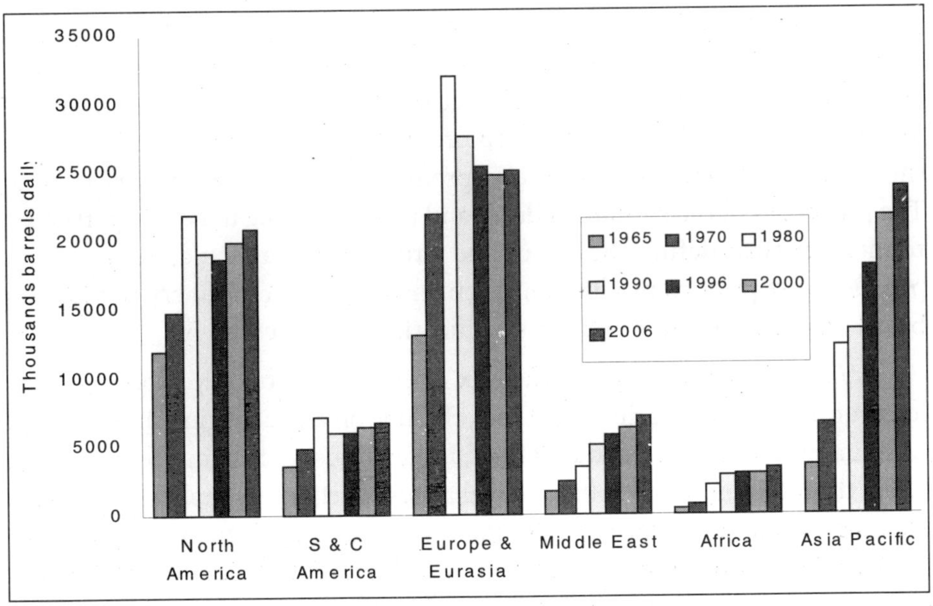

Source: BP (2007) and Historic data sheet.

Figure 3.1: Distribution and Growth in Refining Capacities

Different processes in refineries have a bearing on distribution of joints costs and hence on the pricing of relative products. For a simple old time refinery, which has no cracking process from every barrel of crude oil, it produces a certain fixed amount of petrol, middle distillates and residual. Then the only refining cost is cost per barrel of crude charge, or per barrel of aggregate product output. Each refined product is sold for what it will bring, and there is only one net profit margin, on the whole barrel. There is no refining cost or the profit for the individual products. Some may sell for much more than the value of crude, some for much less. A higher price for one of the products tends to lower the price of others. If middle distillates were in great demand, and the price rose, it would pay to refine more crude oil. Since one could not produce more middle distillates without at the same time producing more petrol and residual, their supply would increase and the price will fall. But this is as far as it pertains to the distillation processes. Once the cracking processes are introduced, the production takes place in variable proportions, enabling, to a limit off course, identification of individual costs. The cracking process in refining has been a paradigm shift from fixed to variable proportions.

Two aspects of refining limit the maneuverability—supply adjustment costs and transportation lags between geographic markets. Supply adjustment costs exist since it is costly for a refinery to deviate from a pre-planned production schedule. Supply adjustment costs arise since refiners must contract in advance for crude oil and optimize refinery operation based on the crude properties. This arises simply because most of the refineries contract for crude oil, several months prior to production, based on the properties of the crude, expected demand for end-products and existing refinery capital. The properties of the chosen crude oil and the processing units at a particular refinery in turn define the set of end products a particular refinery can produce. Just prior to production, a refiner re-optimizes refinery production based on updated prices and the specifications of the crude oil.

While refiners can adjust the mix of end products they produce in the long run, by purchasing different types of crude oil and changing the operation of refinery, significant production adjustment costs exist in the short run, when the crude oil choice is fixed and changes to refinery operation necessitate slowing production. Once the production run begins, a refiner must either alter the operation of production units or blend intermediate streams in a different way to achieve a different mix of end products. A refinery can often only increase the quantity of one high-value end product, such as petrol, by blending a greater proportion of high quality intermediate streams.

The Indian Downstream Market

The demand for petroleum products, particularly transportation fuels and petrochemical feedstocks is increasing throughout the world. Traditional markets such as North America and Europe are experiencing moderate increase in demand where as emerging Asian markets such as India and China are witnessing a rapid surge. This has resulted in a "squeeze" on existing refineries, prompting a fresh technological approach to optimize efficiency and throughput. Major oil companies and technology suppliers/ licensers are investing heavily to revamp their refining technologies in an effort to cater to the needs of the customers.

The Asia-Pacific petroleum markets have seen considerable volatility during the past decade. Dramatic growth in demand has been coupled with periodic down turns the 1997/98 Asian economic crises and the part 2001 slow down. Now the demand is again projected on the high growth path, with China and India leading the way. Despite slower growth in the most industrialized countries in the region, overall Asia-Pacific demand is forecast to increase by nearly 2.5% annually over the next decade. In 10 years global demand is estimated to increase to 29%-up sharply from 20% in 1990. India is the seventh largest and the second most populous country in the world. The country experienced high economic growth in the 90's that has since slowed. However a rebound is expected to return India to the front rank of Asian growth. Despite very low growth over the past few years, petroleum consumption grew by more than 5% annually over the last 10 years. The next decade should see growth pick up against an increase by close to 40% over the forecast period. As with China a large portion of this will consist of light transportation fuels that are more environmentally friendly.

The Ministry of Petroleum and Natural Gas (MoPNG) oversees the entire chain of the oil and gas industries exploration and production of crude oil and natural gas; refining, distribution and marketing of petroleum products and natural gas, and export & imports of crude oil & petroleum products. This report hereafter discusses the current and emerging status of Indian refining industry.

The Consistent Growth

The Indian petroleum industry is one of the oldest in the world, oil having been struck at Makum, near Margherita in upper Assam in 1867, nine years after Col. Drake's discovery in Titusville. India celebrated the centenary of its first refinery (Digboi refinery in upper Assam.) in January, 2002, which continues to be in operation even today. Historical development of refineries in India, since independence is reviewed elsewhere. Over 2.2 mmb/d of refining capacity is installed in India (based on CDU capacity). Of this, 1.02mmb/d is owned by Indian Oil Corporation Ltd. (IOCL) and 0.54 mmb/d is owned by RIL. The rest is distributed amongst Hindustan Petroleum Corporation Ltd. (HPCL), Bharat Petroleum Corporation Ltd. (BPCL) and other companies. It is important to note that India's refining capacity (in terms of CDU capacity) doubled between 1995 and 2001 i.e. from 1.1 mmb/d to 2.3 mmb/d2. It is further projected to reach a level of 2.5 mmb/d by the year 2008. This addition of refining capacity transformed the country from a major importer of middle distillates till 1999, to a net exporter of diesel and other products from 2000 onward, the trend which continues even today as well. Almost one mmb/d of refining capacity came on stream in 1999 alone. This includes the 540 kb/d Reliance refinery at Jamnagar (Gujarat), over 200 kb/d of IOC refineries across different locations, plus additions from HPCL and BPCL. Finally little over 100 kb/d of capacity was added at two IOC plants in 2001.

The above refining capacity additions were planned at a time when oil product demand was growing at rates exceeding 5-6 percent per annum, but by the time the additions materialized, demand growth had diminished to 1-2 percent per annum. This resulted in overall petroleum product surpluses, forcing existing refiners to find export markets for their products. Furthermore, this situation led to the cancellation and delay of some planned refineries, resulted in losses of millions of dollars. As of April 1, 2002 the Indian Oil-refining sector had 10 companies with 18 refineries and combined installed capacity of over 115 MMTPA. Of these 10 companies, RIL is a private sector refinery, MRPL a joint sector entity and the rest public sector enterprises. ONGC is a recent entrant in the refining business and has taken a stake in MRPL.

Keeping both the consumers and producers interest the government of India decided to decontrol the sector in a phased manner. To maintain the viability of public sector refineries in the decontrolled regime, the govt. in September 2000 decided to integrate the pure refining (stand alone) companies with the integrated majors. Post restructuring, in financial year 2001-2002, the share of IOC and BPCL in India's total refining capacity increased up to 41.4% and 15.2% respectively. Refining capacity in the country as on 31st March 2004 was 125.96 MMPTA, with crude throughput during the year around 119 MMPTA. Consumption of petroleum products in 2003-2004 was much lower at 108 MMT and surplus was to be exported. Product exports and imports during 2003-2004 were around 14.6 MMT and 7.87 MMT respectively.

At present, however, there are 19 refineries operating in the country, out of which 17 are PSUs and two private sector ones with a total refining capacity of 149 million metric tonnes per annum (henceforth referred to as MMTPA). Out of the 17 PSUs refineries, seven are owned by IOC, two each by HPCL, BPCL, and ONGC, and one each by NRL and BRPL. The private sector refineries belong to the Reliance Industries Limited (henceforth referred tc as RIL) and Essar Oil Ltd. Historically, the PSUs dominated the downstream sector, similar to the upstream sector. As can be seen the share of private sector in the Indian refining capacity stands at nearly 30 percent. With new refineries already planned by the private sector majors, the share is expected to remain constant. Though private sector share in the refining capacity is increasing, commensurate increase in share of sales of products and market share of oil companies doesn't reflect this as GOI follows a policy of subsidising marketing operations of the PSUs only. This acts as a disadvantage to the private players and hence they curb their operations.

Table 3.1: Indian Refineries, Sources of Crude Oil and Ownership

Refineries	*Location*	*Capacity (MMTPA)*	*Crude Source*	*Ownership*
BPCL Mumbai	Coastal	12.00	Mumbai High + imported	Public
MRPL Mangalore	Coastal	9.69	Mumbai High + Middle East + Sudan	Public
KRL Kochi	Coastal	7.50	Indigenous + imported	Public
CPCL Narimanam	Coastal	1.00	Cauvery basin & PY-3 fields	Public
CPCL Manali	Coastal	9.50	Cauvery basin & PY-3 fields + Mumbai High	Public
HPCL Mumbai	Coastal	5.50	Mumbai High + imported	Public
HPCL Vizag	Coastal	7.50	Indigenous + imported	Public
OCL Haldia	Coastal	6.00	Imported crude (Middle East)	Public
ONGC Tatipaka	Coastal	0.08	KG offshore oil fields	Public
OCL Barauni	On land	6.00	Imported crude (Middle East)	Public
OCL Digboi	On land	0.65	Assam crude	Public
OCL Koyali	On land	13.70	Ankleshwar + imported	Public

(*Contd.*)

Refineries	*Location*	*Capacity (MMTPA)*	*Crude Source*	*Ownership*
OC Guwahati	On land	1.00	Assam crude	Public
OCL Mathura	On land	8.00	Mumbai High + Imported (Nigerian, Middle East etc)	Public
OCL Panipat	On land	12.00	Mumbai High + Imported (Nigerian, Middle East etc)	Public
BRPL Bongaigaon	On land	2.35	Assam crude + Ravva crude	Public
NRL Numaligarh	On land	3.00	Assam oil fields	Public
RIL, Jamnagar	Coastal	33.00	NA	Private
Essar Oil, Vadinar		10.50	NA	Private
Grand total		**148.97**		

Source: GOI (2006h).

It is important to examine the petroleum product markets that these companies operate in. Over last few years, we are witnessing an unprecedented trend, the share of light distillates (petrol, naphtha, LPG among others) between 1995-96 and 2005-06 increased by 67 percent of the total basket as against a drop of 23 percent for middle distillates (kerosene, diesel, ATF, LDO), thus, narrowing the gap. While the share of light distillates in total petroleum products basket was around 18 percent in 1995-96, it increased to 30 percent

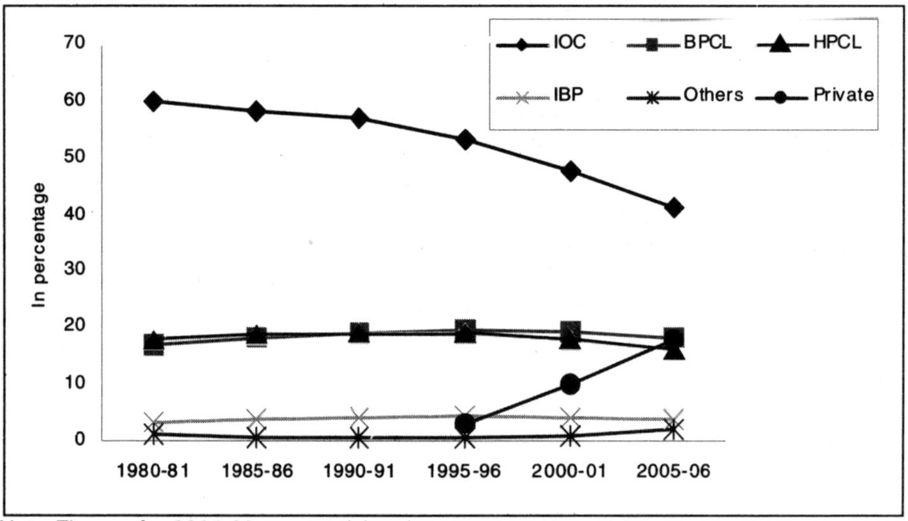

Note: Figures for 2005-06 are provisional.
Source: GOI (2007a).

Figure 3.2: Sale of Products and Market Share of Oil Companies in India (percent)

in 2005-06. This has been largely on account of consumption growth in naphtha, LPG and petrol. During the same period, share of middle distillates decreased from 62 percent of the total to just 48 percent. Among other reasons this could be due to steep increase in light distillates, which increased the total product consumption, slower growth in diesel. Such has been the change in dynamics of product sales that while in 1995-96 diesel constituted around 43 percent of total petroleum product consumption, in 2005-06 it constituted only 36 percent. This is in sharp contrast to the historical dominance of diesel in particular and middle distillates in general in consumption basket.

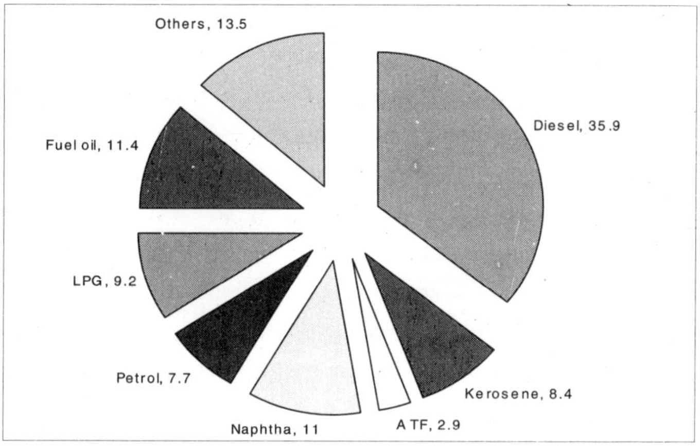

Source: GOI (2006h).

Figure 3.3: Percentage Share (2005-06) in Consumption for Key Products

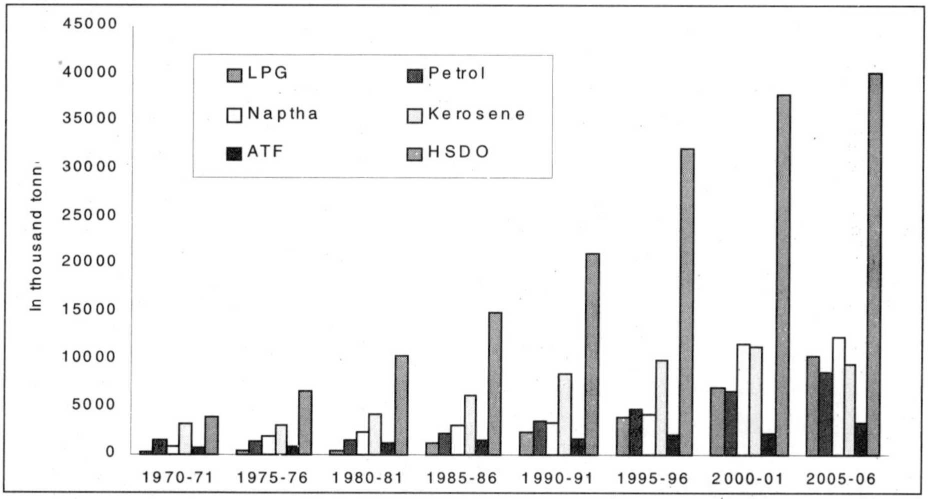

Note: Figures for 2005-06 are provisional.
Source: GOI (2007a).

Figure 3.4: Consumption of Key Products (thousand tonnes)

Petrol, ATF and diesel constitute around 47 percent of the basket and are predominantly used in the transport sector and hence called transportation fuels. Share of these fuels in the total petroleum product basket is increasing. While they constituted around 33 percent of the total petroleum product basket in 1970-71, they made up around 47 percent in 2005-06. However, merely using the total consumption figures of petrol, ATF and diesel as a barometer of their usage in the transportation sector could be misleading.

Unlike petrol and ATF not all diesel is used in transport sector, on an average 56 to 60 percent is accounted for by the transportation sector, which comprises of road transport, aviation, shipping and the railways. But road transport consumption constitutes 90 percent of the total transport consumption. Thus, around 34 million tonnes of petroleum products are directly consumed in this sector. This constitutes more than 30 percent of our total consumption of petroleum products which is an under estimate. For consumption of petrol and diesel in India grew at 7.3 percent and 5.8 percent per annum respectively between 1980-81 and 2004-05 (GOI, 2006c). While the population of India's six major metropolises increased by about 1.9 times during 1981 to 2001, the number of motor vehicles went up by over 7.75 times during the same period (GOI, 2005b). The compounded annual growth rate of private vehicles in the country (cars & two-wheelers) for the period 1991-2004 has been 20 percent, while non-private, namely buses & trucks it has been only around 8 percent (GOI, 2006i). Thus, the share of transportation sector consumption should have increased. But data doesn't reflect this growth.

This anomaly can be explained by the consumption of kerosene in the transportation sector, which goes unaccounted and deflates consumption of diesel and hence consumption in transportation sector. Raha (2005) points out that nearly half of our total consumption of petroleum products is diesel, especially when the rampant adulteration of diesel by kerosene is factored in. In other words, a sizeable quantity of kerosene released through the public distribution system (henceforth referred to as PDS)—estimates range from 30 percent upwards—is actually used as a substitute for diesel. Kerosene adulteration suppresses the sales figures for diesel. NCAER (2005), World Bank (2003) among others have highlighted massive kerosene leakage. World Bank (2003) estimated that half of the subsidized kerosene is diverted to the black market and to other sector such as transport. IEP estimated that only 56 percent of kerosene released by states reaches people as PDS kerosene. A lot of kerosene to be distributed under PDS system is diverted for adulteration with high priced diesel even at the depot levels. Other products, within the petroleum products basket, largely find their uses in industrial applications.

Given the growth in consumption of petroleum products, we are witnessing a consistent decline in demand elasticity of petroleum products. Consumption of petroleum products is largely dependent on economic growth the country achieves, among other things. Progressively, however, as country develops, there seems to be a decoupling of this relationship. One of the major reason for declining elasticity in Indian context has been the higher contribution of services sector compared to past while contribution from manufacturing sector has more or less remained the same.

Table 3.2: Declining Demand Elasticity

	VII Plan	*VIII Plan*	*IX Plan*	*X Plan*
Petroleum, oil, lubricants growth	6.9	6.8	4.9	2.7
GDP growth	6	6.8	5.5	7.8
Demand elasticity	1.15	1	0.89	0.35

Source: GOI (2006f).

The Fuel Quality

A steady evolution in product specifications caused by an endless wave of fresh environmental regulations play a major role in the development of petroleum refining technologies. In the United State and Europe gasoline and diesel specifications have changed radically in the past decades and will continue to do so in future. Currently reducing the sulphur levels of finished product is the dominant objective. Sulphur is "ubiquitous" in petroleum and refineries are now beginning to push the limits technologically on how to handle this issue, as tighter product specifications emerge world wide.

India has also put in a place Auto Fuel Policy prepared by a group of experts and accepted by the government of India for the implementation in the country. The policy provides a clear cut road map for changes in vehicular technology and corresponding fuel quality for the whole country. Measures are also proposed to reduce emission from "in-use", vehicles. It is expected that the implementation of policy would lead to better ambient air quality, which will reflect through improvements in public health and better environment. The salient features of National Auto Fuel Policy include compliance of Bharat Stage II (equivalent to Euro II) norms by all new vehicles (other than 2/3 wheelers) from 1st April 2005 in the whole country and the Euro III equivalent norms in the whole country from 1st April 2010. The 11 major cities would meet Euro III equivalent norms from 1st April 2005 and Euro IV norms from 1st April 2010. In respect of "in-use" vehicles the policy suggest new improved pollution under control checking system, inspection and maintenance system, checking system for catalytic converter and conversion kits for CNG/LPG vehicles. There are further guidelines for compliance of emission norms as well as for buses/ trucks plying on inter-state routes as well. It is estimated that the existing domestic oil refineries, in addition to the investment of Rs10,000 Crores (US million $ 2174) already made to achieve Euro stage II / Bharat Stage II auto fuels specifications would need to incur an additional investment of around Rs 18,000 Crores (US million $ 3913) by the year 2005. Further investment of around Rs 12,000 Crores (US million $ 260) will need to be made during the period 2005-2010. The investment requirement of automobile industry is estimated at around Rs 25,000 Crores (US million $ 543) over this period.

The policy suggests taking into account security of supply and existing logistic prospective that liquid fuels should remain as main auto fuels throughout the country. The policy recommends encouraging use of CNG/LPG in cities affected by higher pollution levels so as to enable vehicles owners to have the choice of fuel and technology combination.

The Deregulation Process

Over the past several years India's oil industry has initiated a number of major reforms with mixed results. The last three years in particularly saw significant events such as down stream oil sector being totally deregulated except continuing subsidy on LPG and kerosene and foreign companies being given marketing rights for transportation fuels, successful discoveries of oil and gas fields within the country and greater focus by oil companies in E&P and gas segment.

In April 2002 the government dissolved its Administered Pricing Mechanism (APM), which resulted in a partial decontrol of domestic prices of petroleum products. In principle, the oil marketing companies,-all of which are government owned are now allowed to revise their sale prices in line with international oil prices. In practice, however they still require the ministry's agreement to do so. In 2002, the process of privatizing state-owned downstream oil companies was initiated. IBP Ltd., a small downstream operator, was the first to be sold, but it was sold to IOCL—the country's largest government-owned downstream company-so this was really a case of one Government Company acquiring another, not privatization. Plans to privatize two other state-owned downstream companies have been put on hold.

An additional factor that has become increasingly important in a fully deregulated scenario is access to distribution and storage infrastructure. A major step in addressing this concern was the creation of Petronet India in 1998. This company has the responsibility to manage distribution and storage infrastructure developed after 1998, under the common-carrier rule, allowing access for all refiners in the country.

In brief, developments in India's privatization process are being watched keenly as the stakes are high for everyone involved. For the government, its future credibility is at stake. For domestic players like Reliance Industries Limited (RIL) and Essar Oil, this is an opportunity to gain access to the retail market. For foreign investors, it is the chance to obtain a slice of the Indian market. Although these changes appear to be dramatic, it must be remembered that the government has no plans yet to cede control of IOC, ONGC and GAIL, which currently dominate the downstream oil, upstream oil and gas sectors, respectively.

After attaining political independence, our planners preferred to adopt the socialistic pattern of the society to attain economic self-reliance. The Second Five Year Plan stated the adoption of socialistic pattern of society as the national objective, as well as the need for planned and rapid development requires that all industries of basic and strategic importance, or in the nature of public utility services, should be in the public sector. Other industries, which are essential and require investment on a scale, which only the state in the present circumstances, could provide, have also to be in the public sector. The state had, therefore, to assume direct responsibility for the future development of industries over a wider area. However, this perception started changing when after four decades of socialism it was realized that PSUs seemed to perform well only when protected through GOI created monopolies, entry reservations, high tariffs, quotas etc.

The major deviation from the then followed policy of socialism started in 1991 when the GOI started deregulating the areas of its operation and subsequently the disinvestment in PSUs was announced. The Industrial policy of the 1991 started the process of de-licensing. The Industrial Policy Statement of July 24th 1991 stated that the GOI would disinvest part of its holdings in selected PSUs but did not place any cap on the extent of disinvestment. Nor did it restrict disinvestment in favour of any particular class of investors. It was acknowledged that deregulation and dismantling of the bureaucratic controls along with the liberalization of trade, technology and capital inflows were some of the far-reaching changes initiated by the GOI under the structural reforms introduced from July 1991. The focus, thus, shifted to ensuring fair business practices, safeguarding consumer interests, and minimizing adverse effects of Industrializations on the environment. No wonder in accordance with these overall objectives of the GOI, the oil industry also needed to be deregulated. Deregulation not only encourages domestic enterprises but it is also considered as an essential ingredient for improving the climate for foreign investment.

Beginning with the early 1990s, a number of policy initiatives were taken by the GOI. For instance, in 1992, lubricating oils were first to be decontrolled when the import of base oil for blending of lubricants was allowed. International majors like Shell, Mobil, Exxon, Caltex took advantage of this and started marketing their lubricants in the country. Again in February 1993, the private sector was allowed to import LPG and kerosene under their own arrangements and sell it at market related prices. No controls on distribution or pricing were exercised. In addition to the products covered under the parallel marketing scheme, imports were allowed for products like the ATF, furnace oil (henceforth referred to as FO), benzene, toluene, and bitumen against "Special Import Licenses". The situation during this early phase of reform was very critical as far as the oil industry was concerned. On one hand, the share of oil and gas in commercial energy consumption was increasing, and on the other hand, domestic resources to meet this shift in consumption were dwindling.

During the last two decades leading to the early 1990s, the value of net imports of crude oil and petroleum products was consistently increasing. In the later part of the Seventh Plan, the import bill on petroleum products was substantial. This was largely on account of stagnation in domestic crude oil production levels. No wonder one of the thrust areas of the Eighth Plan was to restrict oil imports to reasonable levels. The Eighth Plan clearly spelled out the concerns when it pointed out that the import bill of petroleum products continues to be substantial and in fact has increased in later part of the Seventh Plan, as the level of demand satisfaction from indigenously available crude oil has declined from 70 percent in 1985-86 to 56 percent in 1990-91. This is was on account of the stagnation in domestic crude oil production

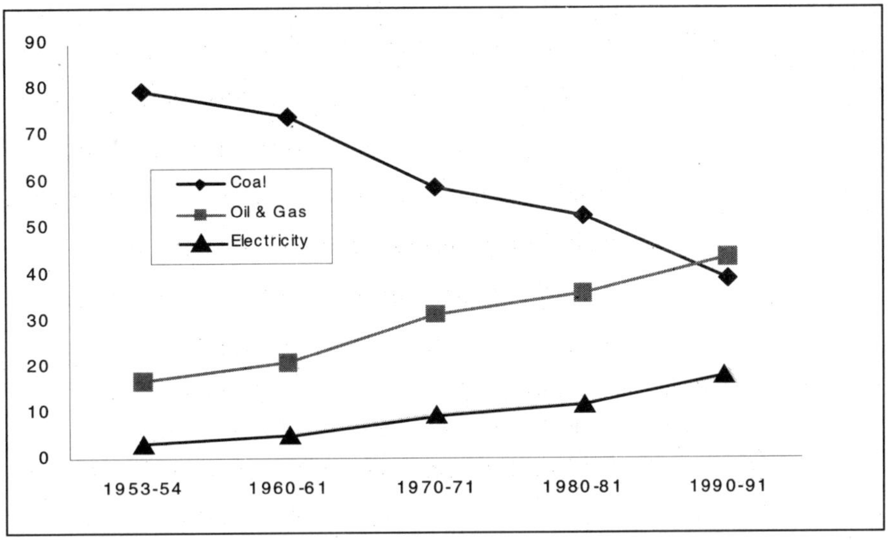

Source: GOI (1992).

Figure 3.5: Share of Different Fuels in Commercial Energy Consumption (percent)

levels. It was envisaged that any further increase in dependence on oil imports, due to an increase in demand, is likely to put severe pressure on foreign exchange reserves and in view of the uncertainty of world oil prices, make the economy more vulnerable. It would, therefore, be necessary to examine the oil intensity and dependence on petroleum products in each sector of the economy and to find ways to contain, and where possible to compress, the demand for the oil products.

Table 3.3: Oil Imports in Relation to Domestic Oil Production and Total Exports

Year	*Value of net imports of crude oil & petroleum products*	*Oil import as % of total exports*	*% of oil demand met through indigenous sources*
1970-71	136	8.6	35.4
1975-76	1242	30.8	35.2
1980-81	5258	78.4	31.8
1985-86	4316	42.1	70.1
1989-90	5622	20.8	61.6
1990-91	9775	30	56.3

Source: GOI (1992).

The Report of the Group on "Hydrocarbon Perspective 2010: Meeting the Challenges" laid the stone for the deregulation of the Indian Hydrocarbon sector. GOI (1995) was expected to carry out an in-depth analysis and make suitable recommendations, which would be inputs for consideration by a Strategic Restructuring Group also called the 'R' Group (GOI, 1996). GOI (1995) among many recommendations recommended that it was necessary to abolish the APM and introduce market determined pricing mechanism wherein the prices of crude oil and petroleum products will be determined by market forces.

GOI (1996) observed that oil industry also need to be liberalized with easier entry for a range of actors that could contribute to its development in keeping with the national objectives. This will include the private sector in India as well as international companies that could do business in this country's hydrocarbon sector. One of the most important perspectives of GOI (1996) was the emphasis on the need to introduce competition, domestic and international, in the hydrocarbon sector, upstream, mid-stream and downstream. Competitive markets and consequential market determined prices would help to mobilize massive resources for investment required and also deploy them effectively.

APM had worked satisfactorily until recently and helped the PSU oil companies to grow under a protective environment. However, APM had become a serious handicap in securing oil supplies for future. In order to achieve the primary objective of securing oil supplies to meet the future growing demand, it would be absolutely necessary to move towards a market-driven price mechanism and to free the petroleum sector from APM. GOI (1996) recommended the gradual phasing out of APM and introduction of a free marketing mechanism. In 1996, the GOI also appointed an Expert Technical Group (henceforth referred to as ETG) to examine the impact on various sector at different levels of duty structure in the face of dismantling of APM. The ETG dealt with phased movement to market determined pricing mechanism and rationalisation of custom tariffs, and excise duty rates in respect of dismantling of APM along with its impact on various other sectors.

The recommendations of GOI (1996) and the ETG paved the way for a phased dismantling of the APM structure. The GOI in November 1997 decided the details of the dismantling programme of the APM and the duty structure for the terminal year i.e. 2001-02. The principal elements of the dismantling programme and the sequence were as follows:

1. Dismantling of the APM in the petroleum sector in phases.
2. Cost-plus formula is to be withdrawn for indigenous crude oil producers, the price receivable by oil producers would be increased to international levels in a phased manner by paying a pre-announced increasing percentage of weighted average free on board (henceforth referred to as F.O.B.) price of actual imports of crude oil during the transition period.
3. The system of retention pricing was to be abolished for all (existing and new) refineries, and pricing of petroleum products at the refinery gate level would move towards import parity, however, refinery gate prices of controlled products, like petrol, diesel, kerosene, LPG and ATF will be fixed at "adjusted import parity" prices for the existing refineries during the transition period, all other products will be sold by the refineries at market driven prices.
4. Consumer prices of major petroleum products would be moved to market prices, price of diesel will be fixed on the principle of import parity pricing up to ex-storage point level with immediate effect, and prices of other major products, like LPG, ATF, kerosene and petrol, would be moved towards principle of import parity in a phased manner and pricing of Paraffin-wax, Bitumen, Naphtha, FO and low sulphur heavy stock (henceforth referred to as LSHS) will be decontrolled.
5. The transition period would be utilized for servicing and amortizing Oil Bonds worth around Rs 18,200 crores, proposed to be issued by the GOI to the oil companies, the price of crude and petroleum products as mentioned above would be fixed by OCC with enhanced autonomous powers.
6. Imports and exports of all petroleum products, except crude (slop crude and crude condensate), NGL, ATF, petrol and diesel would be decanalised during the transition period, however, sourcing and import of crude would be allowed to joint and private sector refineries under actual user licensing policy.
7. Duties on crude and petroleum products would be rationalized in a phased manner.
8. Investments in the refining sector would be encouraged by providing reasonable tariff protection and making marketing rights for transportation fuels, like petrol, diesel and ATF conditional on

owning and operating refineries with an investment of at least Rs 2,000 crores or oil E&P companies producing at least three million tonnes of crude oil annually.

9. Cost-plus formulae for shipping crude oil is withdrawn and the rates would move towards market related rates.
10. Freight subsidy on supplies to far-flung areas would be met through the fiscal budget.
11. A regulatory framework to oversee the functioning of and enforcing a competitive framework in the Hydrocarbon sector would be established.

The decision came into force with effect from April 1st 1998. Accordingly, in the phase, effective April 1998, the APM was dismantled for the upstream and refining sector and a partial deregulation took place for the marketing sector. Subsequently, effective April 2002, the GOI announced complete dismantling of APM.

Table 3.4: The Phased Programme of Reforms

Particulars	*Model*
Year One (1998-99)	
1. Removal of cost plus formula and payment to crude producers as percentage of weighted average FOB price of actual imports	75%
2. Products to be controlled during transition period	Petrol, diesel, kerosene, ATF and LPG
3. Withdrawal of retention margin concept for the refineries and refinery gate prices for controlled products	Adjusted import parity prices to existing refineries and tariff adjusted import parity prices to new refineries
4. Products to be decontrolled	Naphtha, FO, LSHS, Bitumen, Paraffin wax
5. Exim policy	Decanalisation of import/exports of all petroleum products except crude (slop crude and crude condensate), NGL, ATF, petrol and diesel
6. Souring of crude	Souring of crude to be liberalized and import to be allowed for joint and private sector refineries under actual user license
7. Customs duties	Rationalisation done in a phased manner
8. Increase in price of kerosene (PDS)	30% of existing ex-storage point price
Increase in price of LPG (Domestic)	33% of subsidy passed on
9. Freight and other under-recoveries	33% to be passed on, in an equated manner

Particulars	*Model*
10. Shipping of crude oil	Withdrawal of cost plus formula for shipping of crude oil and move towards market related rates
Year 2 (1999-2000)	
1. Payment to crude producers as percentage of weighted average of FOB	77.5%
2. Increase in price of kerosene (PDS)	30% of revised ex-storage point price at the end of year 1
Increase in the price of LPG (Domestic)	A further 33% of subsidy to be passed on
3. Freight and other under-recoveries	A further 33% to be passed on in an equated manner
4. Rationalisation of duties	To continue
Year 3 (2000-01)	
1. Payment to crude producers as percentage of weighted average FOB price	80%
2. ATF	Deregulation of imports and pricing
3. Increase in price of kerosene (PDS)	20% of the revised ex-storage point price at the beginning of the year
Increase in price of LPG (Domestic)	Suitable adjustment in prices to reach subsidy level at 15% of import parity
4. Freight and other under-recoveries	Balance subsidy to be passed on, in an equated manner
Year 4 (2001-02)	
1. Payment to crude producers as percentage of weighted average FOB price	82.5%
2. Increase in the price of kerosene (PDS)	Suitable adjustment in prices to reach subsidy level at 33.33% of the import parity
	Full deregulation
Year 2002 onwards	
	Transfer of subsidy on Kerosene (PDS), LPG (Domestic) and freight subsidy on supplies to far flung areas to the fiscal budget of the GOI

These policy reforms in petroleum sector were reflected in the Ninth Five Year Plan of the country. Thus, given the overall move towards the liberalization process, the Ninth Plan identified certain key thrust areas for the oil and gas sector, namely, formulation of an overseas oil and gas supply policy, deregulation/rationalization of the APM, creation of adequate refining capacity, improvement of product quality, removal of the administrative bottlenecks, setting up of a regulatory mechanism both in upstream and downstream sectors, etc.

Financial Performance

Financial performance of petroleum companies in the controlled era that is till 1998 was governed largely by the APM regime, which provided the players with assured returns on capital employed. The idea was simple: prices of crude and its output were fixed in a manner so as to assure returns to the oil industry, as a whole, in different segments. Things, however, started to change post 1998. In a deregulated era, market forces in many ways determined overall profits of players. Cost structure in refinery made a difference in margins. For example, through better control on costs one could earn more margins. No wonder since 1998 the profitability of Indian stand-alone refineries has been a function of the spread between international product and crude prices (international refining margins), exchange rate movements, duty protection levels, and refinery complexity. While the first three are external factors and therefore "uncontrollable", individual refineries can have significantly differing refining margins and consequently profitability based on its configuration. The complexity level and consequent ability to process "sour" crude has become all the more important given the differential between light and heavy crude in recent times.

The deregulated era in the downstream sector has seen a significant surge in the profitability of companies. Though, this should not be construed as if domestic refineries are operationally more efficient, and that their physical performance has improved. This has largely to do with the pricing policy adopted by GOI for the sector. As a result of which the financial performances of the companies are not related directly to physical performance, given that refineries in India are price takers.

Table 3.5: GRM of Few Domestic Refineries in U.S. $/BBL

	2001-02	*2002-03*	*2003-04*	*2004-05*	*2005-06*
IOC	2	4.1	5.3	6.20	4.60
HPCL-Mumbai	1.81	2.84	4.3	5.60	3.22
HPCL-Vizag	1.67	4.4	4.6	5.06	2.56
BPCL	2.4	3.73	4.64	4.56	1.64
CPCL	1.93	3.86	4.39	5.33	4.37
KRL*	2.4	4.2	4	5.90	3.20
MRPL	2.91	4.2	3.9	5.68	3.66
RIL				8.8	10.3

Note: *Since merged with BPCL.
Source: ICRA (2006) and (2005).

Under APM, production of PSU refineries was coordinated by the OCC keeping in mind regional product demand patterns. Post deregulation, refineries have been free to determine their capacity utilization and yield patterns in accordance with the demand and realization of various petroleum products. As per import parity system followed till June 2006 in the post deregulation era, pricing of products were being calculated in the country on the basis of international price of the product, which is a notional cost that is not an incurred one. Retail selling prices of petroleum products have been built upon this notional price at which petroleum products would have been imported into the country and not on the basis of the actual ex-refinery price of these products produce by Indian refineries. The basic ex-storage selling prices of petrol and diesel have been uniform at all refinery locations throughout the country and as per the existing arrangement between the OMCs and refineries, this basic price at refinery level on import parity basis is revised on a fortnightly basis depending upon prevalent international prices.

What has been happening is that the actual cost of refining and the refinery margin within the country was not being taken into account in the pricing of products. During 2001-02 to 2003-04, as an example, there has been a consistent rise in refinery margins and consistent reduction in refining costs in respect of all refineries. But despite having reduced refining costs in the country, the final prices of products were being arrived at taking into account a whole lot of notional costs, which had been boosting the refinery margins. For example, customs duty paid on petroleum products doesn't go to GOI, as we are not physically importing petrol and diesel. But these are included in the price build-up as we follow import parity pricing for petroleum products. Similar is the case with ocean freight, insurance etc. Though, refinery margins looks healthy for the domestic refineries this is actually not reflected in the overall profitability of the companies. For instance, a look at the profit after tax for oil PSUs explains the picture. Though refinery margin have shown improvement, the profit after tax has shown a declining trend due to the under-recoveries in the marketing segment of the company. Thus, though, the refinery division of an integrated company or stand-alone refineries made profits, the marketing division of the same company or a stand-alone marketing company made losses. This has affected the overall profitability of the whole company.

This vexed policy on pricing, wherein the refinery division of a company makes profits and marketing division of the same company suffers losses has made the reform process in marketing sector almost a non-starter. For

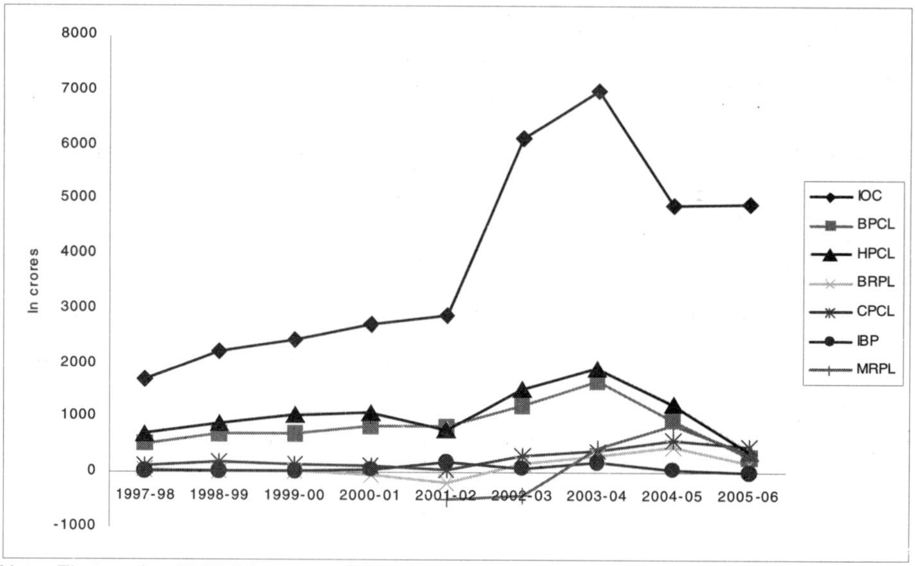

Note: Figures for 2005-06 are provisional.
Source: GOI (2007a).

Figure 3.6: Lower Profitability (crores)

instance, 5 years after allowing private players to market fuels in the country, private players have hardly shown interest. Private players, who actually have invested in setting up their marketing networks, merely ended up booking losses for their ventures, though they have taken away market shares from the PSUs. Given the current policy framework wherein prices are controlled at the marketing end of the segment, there has been considerable restraint from the private sector retailers. They have complained over making the marketing of fuels an equitable exercise, wherein the GOI also shares the burden of pricing control of the private players.

Marketing reforms initiated by the GOI in the sector has not created a competitive market structure, though they were a rationale for reforms. Under marketing reforms initiated by the GOI through various policy measures over the years, it was expected that private players would emerge and there would be healthy competition in the sector. But it is obvious that issues pertaining to pricing, conditionality for entering the marketing of fuels among others are the holding back reforms in the sector. We are no way near a more competitive framework where new investment can be expected to be made by the private sector, thus, leaving the field once again to PSU companies. Moreover, public sector marketing firms among themselves haven't had any competitive run either, with their market share hardly changing.

In more recent years, a very different kind of model has been developing in the Indian marketing sector. The OMCs are competing among themselves for volumes, interestingly, not by way of price, but by all other non-price based competitive policies. The OMCs have been indiscriminate in their expansion of facilities. This development has taken place due to the commercial freedom granted to OMCs. Now they choose locations on their own, without government intervention, for setting up of retail outlets subject to viabilities. Within last five years the number of retail outlets in the country has increased by 67 percent. With around 18,500 retail outlets five years ago, with no private sector participation, now the figure stands at 31,000 with around 1,700 in private sector. Also throughput per retail outlet was standing at between 250 to 275 kilolitres per month. This throughput has already come down to 140-145 kilolitres per month. Lower pump throughput and consequently lower profitability, along with higher working capital requirements (because of the sharp rise in fuel prices), have adversely affected the viability of the retail business, especially for new entrants. To offset the pressure on margins, some of these outlets have gone in for non-merchandise sales, the profits from which have, however, not been on the expected lines. Besides, the increasing availability of CNG in major cities is also having an impact on the automobile fuel retail business.

These developments are in sharp contrast to the experience across major international markets. In the U.S., due to intense competition, number of petrol stations nationwide has shrunk significantly, from over 202,000 in 1994 to about 167,000 in 2003—a 17 percent decrease (GAO, 2005). In the United Kingdom (henceforth referred to as U.K.) since 2000 traditional oil companies have sold or closed over half of their owned networks. There has been a consistent decline in the market. Interestingly, most of the European market is also what we call, "over pumped", that is more pumps than what are required.

The GOI has, thus, advised oil companies to go slow, on expansion plans in the urban region and concentrate more on the rural areas. Thus, with the opening of the marketing sector, instead of private firms competing with the OMCs, they are competing among themselves, which has not been looked upon well by the GOI. What makes the situation worse for consumers is that prices have not been affected due to intense competition among OMCs. Prices across pumps, across different companies are fixed in a city and, thus, volume based competition in no way benefits the consumers. Given the current developments in sector, the mid-term appraisal of the Tenth Plan cautioned

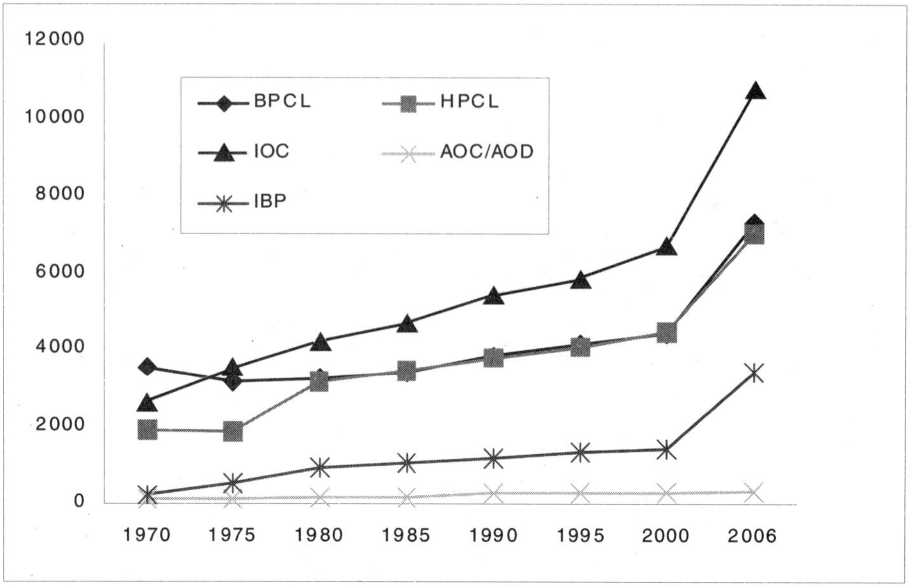

Note: Before nationalisation BPCL and HPCL were in foreign hand.
Figures as of January 1st and for 2006 they are provisional.
Source: GOI (2007a).

Figure 3.7: Sudden Increase in Retail Outlets

when it said, "All the marketing companies are making pre-emptive investments by setting up a number of retail outlets. The viability of these outlets needs to be examined. A sub-optimal pattern appears to be emerging with each company planning to set up a retail network that primarily absorbs its own output. This phenomenon will be addressed once real competition emerges in marketing of petroleum products."

Challenges in Deregulated Era

Though the GOI is slowly loosening its grip on the petroleum sector, there are many challenges that need to be addressed in the deregulated era. As far as the upstream sector is concerned, availability of domestic resources to meet the increased demand for crude oil is the major challenge. The success of our exploration strategy over the years has been questioned time and again. Even the NELP has come in for a lot of criticism, from within the GOI itself. For instance, reports pointed out that despite one of the most liberal exploration licensing regimes, India has failed to attract any oil majors to explore in India. Clearly, the Indian exploration strategy needs to be revisited in the light of changing face of the Indian oil industry, both upstream and downstream. Moreover, with the world crude market becoming unstable, meeting more and more requirements of crude oil through imports raises considerable questions on energy security. Analysts point out that looking at the policy issues for the 21st century India needs a three-pronged strategy for the upstream sector of petroleum industry namely:

1. Intensification of exploration by NOCs in selected basins
2. Upgradation of the large tracts of sedimentary areas in the country to improve the marketability of blocks
3. Attracting technologically superior foreign oil companies to India

Downstream sector raises the question of too much GOI intervention in the sector and resultant problems for the sector. A case in point is the optimal utilization of the North-Eastern refineries. The oil refineries of the North-Eastern region at IOCL, Digboi, IOCL, Guwahati, BRPL, Bongaigaon and NRL, Numaligarh were established to process indigenous low sulphur Assam crude oil. Due to increase in crude processing capacity in the refineries and decline in Assam crude oil availability, there has been a substantial gap between the installed capacity and actual processing of crude oil in these refineries. Presently the NE refineries are processing 6.0 MMTPA crude compared to the installed capacity of 7.0 MMTPA. To increase the processing upto 7 MMTPA, crude availability for these refineries has to be increased by 1 MMTPA. Out of the 6.0 MMTPA crude processed, about 4.5 MMTPA is available from the NE Oil fields and the balance 1.5 MMTPA Ravva crude is processed at BRPL. Moreover, given that BRPL is given the Ravva crude, less and less is made available to HPCL, which in turn has raised concerns over crude processing capacity, sulphur dioxide emissions, GRM and availability of Euro III products. Increasing crude processing is also not one of the right answers given that the NE region is already in a surplus situation. The present production of petroleum products in NE refineries is more than the demand in the region. The balance product is being transported to other parts of the country. Any addition to crude processing in these refineries will lead to transportation of more products to other areas for marketing, which will involve additional cost to the oil companies. Such imbalances inherent in the refining industry, given the joint nature of production, are further compounded by GOI dictates on pricing and other obligations.

Yet another peculiar feature persisting from the early days of the industry is the reliance on middle distillates and the configuration of the Indian refineries. Henderson (1975) critically analyzed the refining capabilities and pointed out that Indian refineries are not complex. They comprised basically atmospheric and vacuum distillation units with varying secondary processing capacity of cracking, reforming and vis-breaking units. Indian refineries set up during the 1960s and 1970s were based on the processing of either indigenous crude oil from Upper Assam or imported crude. These refineries were of low capacities the largest being of approximately 3 MMTPA and were characterized by simple configurations. For instance, the refineries which were designed to process crude from Assam, visbreaking unit was replaced by a delayed coking unit and kerosene treating was essentially an extraction process of removal of aromatics so that smoke point specifications could be met. The conversion levels also were moderate and since environmental stipulations were not at all stringent, high sulphur fuel oil could easily be consumed to meet the internal energy requirements of the refineries.

Things haven't really improved in recent years either. The average light and middle distillates in the U.S. and in Europe is 90 percent, but in India it is still 72.5 percent. The Indian refining industry should be able to meet its crude requirement by being able to process only high sulphur crude, and from it produce 90 percent distillates (light and middle), which is what Reliance presently does. The GOI has realized the problem at hand. For instance, Petroleum Minister very recently pointed out that as a result of the benchmarking exercise of PSU refineries, follow up projects are being implemented to increase their profitability. These projects are likely to be completed in the year 2010, involving a total investment of over Rs. 20,000 crore (GOI, 2006k). Thus, GOI is looking at a two fold action plan. To begin with, refineries would be modified to take 100 percent high sulphur crude oil and de-bottlenecking and installing additional capacities of the CDUs and VDUs. At a later stage, refineries would be working towards installing delayed coker units. Though, this is the right step forward, it appears that Indian refining industry was behind schedule, if refinery investment patterns over the last few year's across the world are any indicator.

A look at the global refinery investment pattern highlights Indian concerns and reveals why we need to move fast towards refining heavier and sourer crude oil. Over the period from 2000 to 2005, there has been an extraordinary growth in process expansion to reduce sulphur levels in products. Moreover, in addition, there has been a phenomenal increase in the ability of a refinery to process heavier and cheaper crude oil through the "coking" process.

Table 3.6: World Refining Investment Patterns (MB/D)

Process	*2000*	*2005*	*Growth*
Crude capacity	81.5	82.4	1.1
Coking	3.7	4.4	18.9
Coking Tons/d	152.4	196.6	29
Cracking, FCC	13.8	14.5	5.1
Hydrocracking	4.0	4.7	17.5
Hydrotreating	36.7	41.3	12.5
Sulphur Tons/d	56.1	71.1	26.7

Source: ICF (2005).

In comparison to more sophisticated refineries in the U.S. and Europe, Indian refineries have less upgrading capacities as well as less ability to handle extra heavy and sour crude oil. All the same, Indian refineries are able to meet the light product requirement and are net exporters of petrol, diesel, naphtha and kerosene. But this has come at a cost because they have to depend upon processing light or medium heavy crude oil, whose prices have been rising. Most of the older refineries which are PSU do not have adequate upgrading capacity to increase the higher valued product nor do they have the capacity to process heavier or sourer crude to take advantage of their lower prices. It is suggested that new refineries should be configured to overcome these problems. Also, in the case of the older refineries, many have catalytic crackers, which were bought more for political reasons rather than economic reasons. Since Indian product demand has a greater percentage of diesel and LDO fraction than petrol, new refineries should have hydrocrackers to maximize the yields of middle distillate products (Shenoy & Gulen, 2005). Increasingly the world crude oil supply is getting heavier and sourer. For India, which is working to be an export hub for petroleum products, the challenge to produce cleaner petroleum product meeting ever-tightening environmental standards will indeed be a significant one. Refiners will, therefore, have to keep adjusting their upgrading capacity so as to be able to match the heavier supply barrel to growing requirement for lighter products with less and less sulphur.

Rationalisation of Taxes

The biggest challenge for the downstream sector of the Oil and gas industry is the rationalisation of taxation structure and pricing of key products, namely petrol, diesel, LPG and kerosene, which constitute more than

60 percent of consumption of petroleum products in the country. Rationalisation of tax structure in petroleum sector has been under consideration for some years. Differential customs duty on crude oil and petroleum products provide effective rate of protection to domestic refineries, which needs to be corrected. Moreover, these duty structures vary across range of products creating further distortions in petroleum market and in markets were petroleum products are inputs. Currently, customs duty on crude oil is 5 percent. There is no customs duty on domestic LPG, PDS kerosene and fertilizers inputs (naphtha and LSHS) thereby putting these products under a regime of negative effective protection. Customs duty on petrol, diesel and other products is 10 percent, which translates to an effective rate of protection as high as 40 percent for these products.

This duty differential provides higher margins for the domestic refining industry. Brown & Wu (2003) point out that these differentials have enabled Indian refiners to enjoy positive margins even at times when the market-driven Singapore margins have been negative. Throughout 2001, Indian refining margins were at least U.S. $ 1.00/BBL and U.S. $ 1.50/BBL higher than Singapore margins for hydroskimming and cracking yields, respectively. This tax policy has far reaching effects. Due to the guaranteed high returns, Indian refiners operate under high utilization rates, which, in turn, worsen the regional product surplus.

Taxes in petroleum sector have always been a contentious issue between the MoPNG and the Ministry of Finance. MoPNG has argued for higher differentials in an effort to support the domestic industry. The Report of the Committee on Pricing and Taxation of Petroleum Products under Chairmanship of Dr. C. Rangarajan, which submitted its report in February 2006 does indeed, makes a case for allowing some effective protection to domestic refineries. Reasons cited were that refining industry is subject to cycles, and that providing some protection and thereby adequate refining margins is necessary for encouraging investment in expansion, and more importantly in modernization of our refineries. The report though did call for reducing effective protection across aboard, especially for petrol and diesel, given the very high level of effective rate of protection.

Taxes are also high on the Indian petroleum sector. The oil industry contributes a substantial amount both to the Central and State exchequer in terms of duties, taxes, royalty, dividends and this share is increasing as far as the central sector is concerned. For, on an average, contribution of the sector to sales tax revenues hovers around 34 percent, for the excise it hovers around 43 percent and as far as customs duty is concerned, it is around 24 percent.

This is not surprising as all over the world, kerosene, petrol and diesel are priced very close to one another in terms of energy content. When it comes out of the refinery, diesel cost about Rs. 23.75, petrol Rs. 23.60, and kerosene Rs. 23.40. However, because of high taxes on these products the price gets distorted so much that the price of kerosene ends up at Rs. 9, diesel Rs. 34, and petrol Rs. 46 or Rs. 47. The price of kerosene in particular is significantly distorted as, on one hand it is a poor man's fuel, and on the other hand, it is a subsidised product. Thus, as taxes on a subsidised product could actually increase the subsidy burden on government, price of kerosene has been kept low.

Table 3.7: Component of Taxes in Retail Prices (percent)

Product	*Central taxes*	*State taxes*	*Total taxes*
Petrol	38	17	55
Diesel	23	11	34
Domestic LPG		11	11
PDS kerosene		4	4

Source: GOI (2006l).

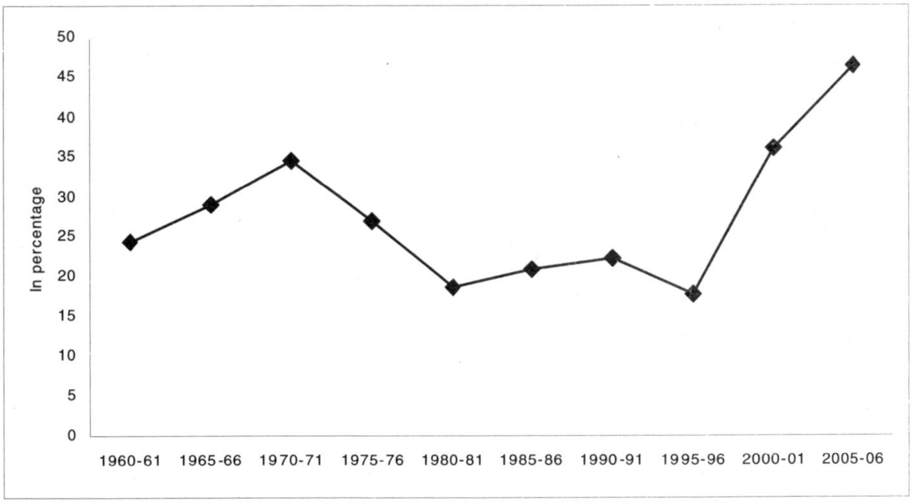

Note: Figures for 2005-06 are provisional.
Source: GOI, 2007a.

Figure 3.8: Central Excise on POL as percent of Total Central Excise

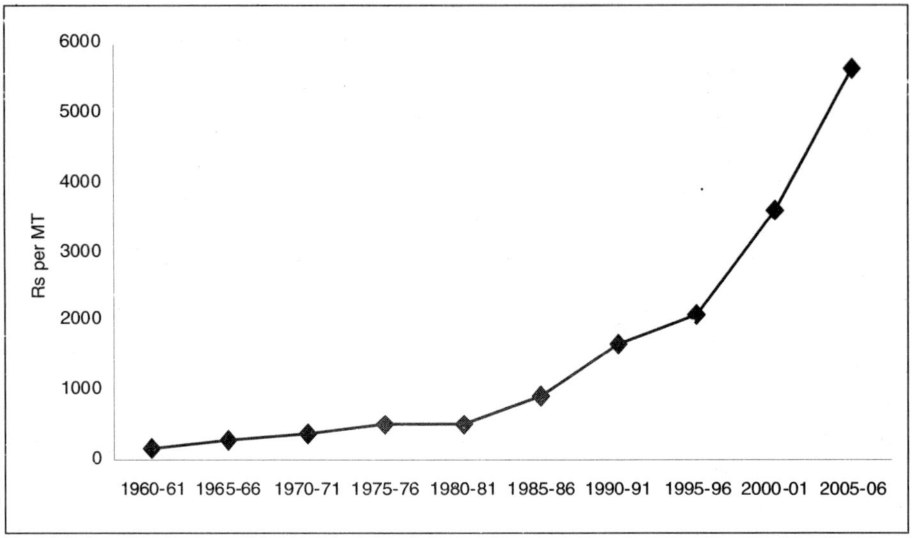

Note: Figures for 2005-06 are provisional
Source: GOI (2007a)

Figure 3.9: Composite Unit Incidence of Central Taxes on Petroleum & Products

There have been no signs of reduction in taxes, which is not surprising. Taxing fuel (Bacon, 2001) is one of the easiest ways to get revenue. Fuel taxes are relatively easy to collect and straightforward, and the consumption of fuels as a group is relatively price inelastic and income elastic, ensuring buoyant revenue as income rises and tax rates are increased. So while petroleum product taxes are important in developed countries, they may be even more important in developing countries. The incidence of central taxes on the petroleum sector has shown a consistent upward trend.

The state governments too maintain high taxes on petroleum sector. As state taxes on petroleum products are mostly ad valorem, there has been a substantial increase in the contribution by the petroleum sector to the state exchequer. Moreover, there is a wide disparity in the rates of taxes across various states. On petrol, the rates vary from a minimum of 20 percent to a maximum of 34 percent. Similarly, in case of diesel, the rates vary from a minimum of 12 percent to a maximum of 37.72 percent. For example, in Andhra Pradesh the sales tax/VAT rates are 33 percent for petrol and 22.25 percent for diesel. In Delhi the figure stands at 18.16 percent and 11.68 percent. This creates disparity in regional prices. The petroleum sector's contribution on sales tax to the State exchequer represents a substantial portion of the State government revenues.

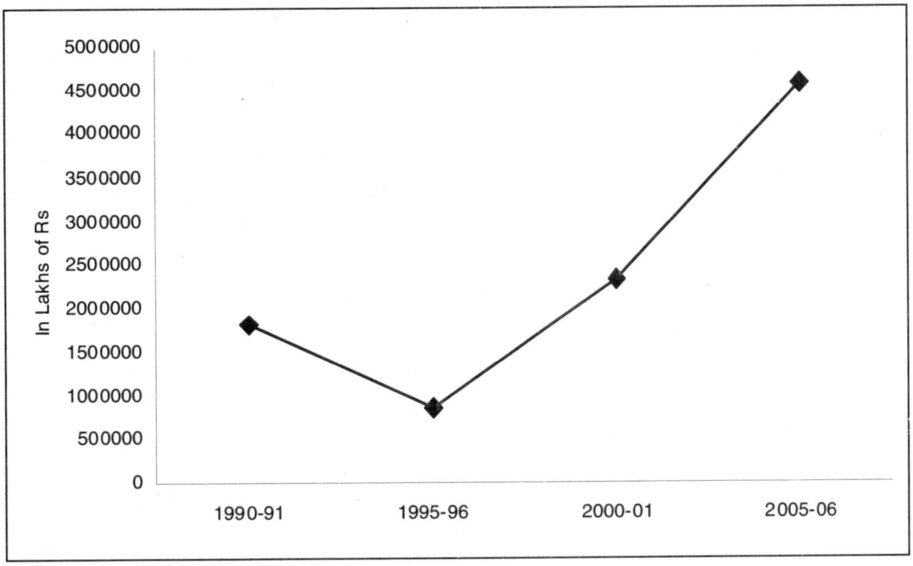

Note: Figures for 2005-06 are provisional
Source: GOI (2007a)

Figure 3.10: Sales Tax Payment from Oil and Gas Industry (lakhs)

Taxation

As part of the overall move towards rationalization of taxation structure in industry, the GOI should also try to correct the historical anomaly as far as the excise duty on petrol and diesel is concerned. Historically, there has been a wide disparity in the excise duty on petrol and diesel in our country. For example, the current excise duty is Rs.14.64 per litre on petrol and Rs.4.97 per litre on diesel. This is contrary to world wide trends where the excise levies on both products are more or less equal. Indeed, in some countries, diesel is costlier than petrol. The contrary trend in our economy leads to inefficient substitution of one fuel for another.

Moreover, the nature of levying taxes also has recently come under scrutiny, given the persistent high oil price regime the sector has been facing over the last few years. Most of the taxes in the petroleum sector are ad-valorem. Thus, high prices only increase the burden of taxation. No wonder GOI (2006l) clearly pointed out that the wisdom of imposing ad-valorem duties during a time of persistent price increases is debatable. Not only do ad-valorem levies exacerbate the burden on the consumer, but they also result in the GOI willy-nilly benefiting through higher tax yields making it vulnerable to the criticism of 'profiting at the expense of consumers'. There is, therefore, need for both softening and smoothing the impact on the consumers of international price variations and for the GOI sacrificing 'windfall gains' in revenue. This clearly suggests the need for shifting from the current mix of specific and ad-valorem levies to a pure specific levy.

The Parliamentary Standing Committee on Petroleum and Natural Gas in their various reports has recommended that a fixed/specific duty should be levied on each petroleum products instead of ad-valorem duty. Moreover, they have also pointed out that sales tax should also be specific instead of ad-valorem. MoPNG in turn has also requested State governments to reduce/ maintain sales tax rates on petrol and diesel at earlier agreed levels, which is 12 percent on diesel and 20 percent petrol.

Over and above the impact of conventional taxes on the sector, in the Indian context as of 2007, irrecoverable levies pose special challenges. Many state governments in India are also levying irrecoverable taxes on crude oil. In Mumbai, the two refineries of HPCL and BPCL pay an octroi of 3 percent on crude oil entering the municipal limits of Mumbai. Similarly, the state governments of Karnataka, UP, Bihar, Assam and Haryana also levy entry tax on crude oil.

Table 3.8: Rate of entry tax on crude oil (percent)

State	*Rate of entry tax on crude oil*
UP	4
Haryana	4
Karnataka, Bihar, Assam	2

Source: GOI (2006l).

As this is an incidence on raw material, it cannot be recovered from product prices, which leads to erosion of the GRM. It also results in a non-level playing field for different refineries and they also become non competitive when they export their products. In addition, all refineries are not marketing companies and inter-state inter company transactions attract Central Sales Tax (henceforth referred to as CST). This cannot be recovered from the customers in the consuming states as this amount to double taxation. However, the incidence of CST can be removed if the movements are rationalized. That the impact of such taxes are high can be gauged from the fact that at a crude price of $ 60 per BBL, it is estimated that the impact of octroi/entry tax on crude oil will be an annual burden of about Rs 2,700 crore during 2006-07.

Though taxes as a percentage of retail prices in India for petrol and diesel are similar to the levels prevailing in the developed countries, they are higher than the rates prevailing in the neighbouring countries where the rates of taxes on petrol and diesel are more moderate. High taxes on petroleum sector are norm across the world except for few countries. GOI though will have to take a conscious policy decision as to whether they want to continue with such high taxes on sector, given the prevailing high prices of oil and its products in the international market? Gwilliam et. al. (2001) points out that one of the principal objectives of setting taxes on transportation fuels is to reduce congestion and reduce air pollution. Thus, seen from this perspective, taxes should be high on goods that cause negative externalities, petroleum products are a good example. For India though, it is a sharp contradiction, for the recommendations of various successive reports from Parliamentary Standing Committee on Petroleum and Natural Gas argue for lowering the taxes on petroleum sector. Even though taxes may seem high in Indian petroleum sector, they are essential. Given also that they are relatively price inelastic, resources can be garnered by the GOI creating least distortions.

Table 3.9: High Taxes in Retail Prices (percent)

Country	*Petrol*	*Diesel*
France	65	47
Germany	66	50
Italy	62	43
Spain	54	37
UK	68	60
Japan	45	34
Canada	33	25
U.S.A.	17	19
Pakistan	42	20
Nepal	31	22
Bangladesh	24	24
Sri Lanka	37	5

Source: GOI (2006l).

Pricing in the Downstream Sector

Regulation of oil prices was first attempted in India when the Valued Stock Account (VSA) procedure was agreed between the Government and Burmah Shell in 1948. In the 1960's, various committees namely the Damle Committee, 1961, Talukdar Committee, 1965 and the Shantilal Shah Committee, 1969 were appointed by the Government to recommend the pricing modalities for petroleum products in India. These committees recommended prices to be determined on principles of import parity. Ceiling selling prices were recommended for various petroleum products. Subsequently, in 1974, the Government appointed an Oil Prices Committee (OPC) headed by K.S. Krishnaswamy. This committee recommended discontinuation of the import parity basis and a shift-over to determination of the prices of major petroleum products on "cost plus basis" which came to be commonly known as the Administered Pricing Mechanism (APM). The regime recommended by OPC was amended by Oil Cost Review Committee (OCRC), 1984 headed by J. S. Iyer wherein the basis of compensating return was amended from a flat rate on the capital employed to 12% post tax return on net-worth and weighted cost of borrowings. The main features of the APM were as follows:

(a) National crude oil producing companies namely ONGC and OIL were allowed operating cost plus 15% post tax return on capital employed for indigenous crude oil production. Capital employed represents the sum total of net fixed assets (gross block of fixed assets less depreciation) and normative working capital.

(b) Oil refineries, pipelines and marketing companies were allowed operating cost and return on capital employed. Capital employed was bifurcated into net-worth and borrowings. Net-worth was taken from the balance sheet as the sum total of equity capital and free reserves. The balance capital employed was considered as borrowings. On the net worth portion, return at 12% post tax was provided whereas the average actual rate of interest was provided on the borrowings.

(c) Subsidisation of consumer prices of certain products like Kerosene for public distribution and Domestic LPG by cross-subsidisation from certain products like Petrol, Aviation Turbine Fuel (ATF), etc., and indigenous crude oil.

(d) Uniform prices of each administered petroleum product at all refinery locations by equalizing all costs like cost of crude oil, freight, margins to oil companies etc.

(e) It ensured stable prices so that the domestic market is insulated from the volatility of prices in the international market.

The above objectives were achieved through the operation of the Oil Pool Account which was used to adjust the variation in various elements of costs. The Government in January, 1995 had appointed a Strategic Planning Group on Restructuring of the Oil Industry ('R' Group) comprising eminent experts from the Public Sector and Private Sector, distinguished energy experts and academicians to make recommendations to meet the policy objectives and initiatives required for restructuring the oil industry. The 'R' Group had recommended the gradual phasing out of APM and introduction of free marketing mechanism due to following reasons:

- APM can not generate sufficient financial resources required for investments in the upstream and down stream sectors.
- Private Capital as well as foreign direct investment would not be forthcoming in view of the inherent regulatory controls imposed by the government.
- APM does not provide strong incentives for investments in technological upgradations or for cost minimization.
- APM has not been completely successful in achieving the primary objective of ensuring a consumer friendly and internationally competitive vibrant petroleum sector capable of global presence to provide energy security to the country.
- Since all costs are reimbursed, there is no incentive to make profitable investments. Therefore, cost plus formula breeds inefficiencies.
- With the entry of the private sector, the cost plus formula will encourage 'gold plating' of the plant and inflate costs which the consumer would have to bear.
- The subsidies and cross subsidies have resulted in wide distortions in the consumer prices and do not reflect economic cost of petroleum products, which are not being passed on to consumers automatically. This in turn has led to inefficient use of precious fuels and large-scale misuse of highly subsidized products.

The Government constituted an Expert Technical Group in June 1996 comprising representatives from various ministries like Finance (DEA),

Planning Commission, BICP etc. to examine the impact on various sectors at different levels of duty structure in case of dismantling of APM. The report of the Expert Technical Group had dealt with phased movement to Market Determined Pricing Mechanism (MDPM) and rationalization of customs tariff and excise duty rates in respect of dismantling of APM along with its impact on various other sectors.

In September, 1997 the Government decided "in principle" to dismantle the APM in a phased manner based on the recommendations of the Strategic Planning Group on Restructuring of the Oil Industry ('R' Group). Thereafter, in November 1997, the Government announced the details of the phased programme for dismantling of APM after taking into account the recommendations of the Expert Technical Group (ETG) which dealt with phased movement to Market Determined Pricing Mechanism. The cost plus approach and a pre determined margin on net worth formula did not encourage oil producers as ONGC and GAIL to invest their internal resources on high risk high reward sedimentary basins, including frontier areas, to develop oil and gas reserves from marginal fields or to introduce enhanced oil recovery techniques that will maximize country's hydrocarbon wealth. In order to sustain the accelerated exploration and production efforts essential future oil security, public sector crude oil producers needed to be freed from Government controlled pricing mechanism so that they can get international prices for their production.

The Government had accordingly initiated the phased programme for dismantling of Administered Pricing Mechanism (APM) from April, 1998 with a view to attract investment in the Petroleum Sector to meet the growing demand, and to promote competition, efficiency and better customer service. Effective 1.4.2002, the APM has been fully dismantled. The oil companies made frequent revisions in the selling prices of petrol and diesel during 2002 and 2003 when the international prices were fairly stable. However, the years 2004 and 2005 have witnessed sharp and spiraling increase in International prices of crude oil and petroleum products. The impact of such phenomenal price increase in the International market is bound to have major impact on Indian Oil Industry which is heavily dependent on imports for crude procurement. To insulate the end consumers, it was decided that the share of burden should be equitably divided between various stakeholders i.e. Government, Oil Companies and consumers. Moderate increases in retail prices coupled with customs and excise duty reductions on Petrol, diesel, PDS kerosene and domestic LPG have been carried out.

Pricing Methodology

Crude oil, both indigenous and imported, are refined into various petroleum products viz. motor spirit, naphtha, light diesel (light distillates), aviation fuel, kerosene, high speed diesel (middle distillates) furnace oil, bitumen, waxes, etc. (heavy distillates). The demand for petroleum products is rising rapidly in the country. During the 9th Plan (1997-2002), consumption of petroleum products grew by 4.9 per cent. The consumption of products is estimated to reach 120.4 MMT by the terminal year of the 10th Plan, i.e. 2006-07, resulting in a compound annual growth of 3.7 per cent for the Plan period. The pricing of these refined products have gone through various phases. Moving from Valued Stock Account system to import parity pricing and then to retention pricing, the industry has now entered another era of complete deregulation with a shift to market determined pricing mechanism.

Though the process of deregulation of the prices of petroleum products started in 1998, five commodities viz. petrol, diesel, domestic LPG, PDS kerosene and aviation fuel continued to be controlled commodities. ATF was later decontrolled w.e.f. 1.4.2001. But until 31st March, 2002, there was Administered Pricing Mechanism for the other four commodities. Ever since APM was completely dismantled, oil companies were allowed the leeway to sell their products at market determined prices guided by the concept of import parity. Consequently, retail prices in the domestic market tend to fluctuate in tandem with global price movements. This means, in the post-APM era starting from 1.4.2002, Oil Marketing Companies (OMCs) have been given the right to determine the selling prices of petrol and diesel (except PDS kerosene and domestic LPG which are subsidized) based on Import Parity Mechanism, after prior consultations with MOP&NG.

Import parity price means the price that the actual importer would pay for the imported product. The various components of import parity price of petroleum products are given below:

(a) Free on Board Price (FOB) as quoted in Arab Gulf Market and reported by Platt and Argus,

(b) Premium/discount as published in Platt and Argus,

(c) Ocean freight from mid port in the Arab Gulf to Indian Ports,

(d) Insurance,

(e) Exchange rate,

(f) Custom Duty,

(g) Ocean Loss,

(h) Wharfage and Port charges.

The retail selling prices of petroleum products are built upon this notional price at which these products would have been imported into the country and not on the basis of the actual ex-refinery price of these products. The retail selling price of petrol/diesel for the consumers is thus calculated by adding freight up to depots, marketing cost and margin, state specific irrecoverable levies, excise duty, delivery charges from depot to retail pump outlet, sales tax and other local levies and dealers commission to this basic price at refinery level on import parity basis.

The basic ex-storage selling prices of petrol and diesel are uniform at all refinery locations throughout the country and as per the existing arrangement between the oil marketing companies and refineries, this basic price at refinery level on import parity basis is revised on fortnightly basis depending upon the prevalent international prices.

The marketing costs and margins, dealers' commission, delivery charges within free delivery zones are also uniform. The prices at various locations will vary depending upon the distance from the refinery, rate of sales tax and other local levies.

In case of Kerosene (PDS) and LPG (Domestic) the Government has decided that the subsidies on these products will be on a specified flat rate basis for each Depot/ Bottling Plant and will be met from the fiscal budget. After providing for the aforesaid subsidy, the retail prices would then vary as per changes in the international oil prices.

Decontrolled Era; Petrol, Diesel, SKO and LPG

Initially from 1.4.2002 till about end of December, 2003, the Companies used to set the prices of petrol and diesel every fortnight and they were doing so because the crude market and the petroleum market were relatively stable. But during this period, any hike in retail selling price of PDS Kerosene and domestic LPG had been spared by oil marketing companies. In 2004, the oil prices started rising in the international market. Although the oil marketing companies were granted freedom to fix retail selling prices on fortnightly basis, the prices were being revised after informal clearance from MOP&NG and there was no price revision of petrol and diesel from the period 1.1.2004 to

15.6.2004 although the ruling prices in the international market were abnormally high during this period. Same was the case with SKO and LPG. But w.e.f. 16.6.2004 finally moderate increases to the extent of Rs. 2 per litre on petrol and Re 1 per litre on diesel were made coupled with excise duty changes. Retail selling price of LPG (packed domestic) too was raised by Rs. 20 but kerosene was again spared of any hike.

Government worked out a new methodology with effect from 1st August, 2004 allowing OMCs limited freedom to revise the price of MS/ HSD within a price band. The concept of price band was based on the principles of rolling average prices of these products in the international markets. Accordingly, oil companies were permitted to carry out autonomous adjustments in prices within a band of +/– 10% of the mean of rolling average C&F prices of last 12 months and last quarter, i.e. three months.

In case of breach of this band, the OMCs have to approach the Ministry of Finance through MOP&NG to modulate the excise duty rates so that the spiraling prices prevailing in the international markets do not cause undue hardships to the consumers. The year 2004-05 witnessed unprecedented high oil prices in the international market. As compared to the average Indian basket crude price of US$ 27.98/ barrel during 2003-04, the average price during 2004-05 (April, 2004–January, 2005) was US $37.87 /barrel. During February and first fortnight of March, 2005, these prices were stated to be US $ 42.67/ barrel and US $ 48.98/ barrel respectively. To contain the impact of increase in international prices of petroleum products on domestic prices, the Government reduced excise duty on petrol from 30% to 26% and on diesel from 14% to 11% effective 16.6.2004. The duty was further reduced on petrol from 26% to 23% and on diesel from 11% to 8% with effect from 19.8.2004. The Government has also reduced customs duty on petrol and diesel from 20% to 15% with effect from 19.8.2004. On 16.06.2004, excise duty on LPG (Domestic) was reduced from 16 per cent to 8 per cent. On 19.08.2004, excise duty on PDS Kerosene was reduced from 16 per cent to 12 per cent.

However, the international prices went up further during the month of October, 2004. With the under-recoveries on petrol and diesel estimated to be around Rs. 3000 crores for the period April-October, 2004, further increases were announced effective 5.11.2004. Retail selling price of petrol was fixed in line with the import parity price. The retail price of petrol was further revised downwards in line with international prices effective 16.11.04. However, the increase in the diesel retail price was pegged at 50% of the level of increase required on the basis of import parity and no further increase was made in the diesel price on 16.11.2004.

The retail selling price of LPG (Packed Domestic) was revised by the oil marketing companies effective 16th June, 2004 and again on 5th November, 2004 by Rs. 20 per cylinder each time, in view of the abnormally high prices of crude oil and petroleum products in the international market. But the oil marketing companies did not hike the retail selling price of PDS kerosene oil marketing companies since April, 2002.

Even as the country entered the deregulated phase of petroleum sector, world crude oil market entered a phase of sustained high prices. Particularly from 2003 onwards there has been an unprecedented, sharp and spiraling increase in international oil prices, a period just after Indian oil and gas sector was deregulated. Around early 2006 both the prices of crude and prices of sensitive petroleum products were close to their highest levels at around $63.23 per BBL for Indian basket of crude. Impact of this global price trend on the domestic situation has been two fold. First, the burden of subsidy on PDS kerosene and domestic LPG ballooned to unprecedented levels – the current burden of subsidies is Rs. 15,000 crores on account of PDS kerosene and Rs. 11,000 crores on account of domestic LPG. Second, GOI took back control of price setting for petrol and diesel, and restrained the 'pass-through' of the international prices to domestic consumers. GOI, thus, started to decide the prices of petrol and diesel for Indian companies. This, as we would subsequently see in more details in the following Chapter, was always not in interests of companies.

The Rangarajan report tried to address issues pertaining to various aspects of pricing and taxation of petroleum products with a view to stabilizing/rationalizing their prices, financial position of oil companies, conservation of petroleum products, and establishing a transparent mechanism for autonomous adjustments of prices by the Oil companies. While many of recommendations of GOI (2006l) were accepted, some are still under serious consideration of GOI.

General Principles of Tax Theory

A fundamental principle of tax theory is that taxes should, as a rule, be levied on final consumption goods rather than on intermediate goods. If, however, not all consumption goods are taxable, it may be optimal to levy

Table 3.10: Status of Recommendations of Rangarajan Committee

Recommendations	*Benefit*	*Status of Implementation*
Pricing Petrol and Diesel		
Shift to trade parity formula for determining refinery gate as well as retail prices	Lower refinery gate price and marketing losses	Implemented
GOI to keep arms length from price determination and to allow flexibility to oil companies to fix the retail price under the proposed formula	Autonomy to OMCs on retail price fixing	Exists on paper, actual implementation uncertain
Reduce effective protection by lowering the customs duty on petrol and diesel to 7.5%	Lower refinery gate price and marketing losses	Implemented
Address the under-recoveries to refineries due to irrecoverable taxes	Higher GRM to refineries	Not yet implemented
Pricing LPG (domestic) and kerosene (PDS)		
Restrict provision of subsidized kerosene to BPL families	Lower marketing losses to OMCs	Pilot scheme launched. Delay in nation-wide launch likely
Raise the price of LPG (domestic) by Rs. 75/cylinder. Beyond this one-time increase, retail prices to be gradually raised to market rates	Lower marketing losses to OMCs	Not yet implemented
Discontinue the practice of asking ONGC/GAIL/OIL to provide upstream assistance, instead collect their contribution by raising the OIDB Cess from the present level of Rs. 1,800/MT to Rs. 4,800/MT	More transparency in upstream assistance	Not yet implemented
GOI meeting the balance cost of subsidy from Budget	Onus on GOI if it wants to provide subsidy	Not yet implemented
Restructuring of excise levy		
Excise levies on petrol & diesel to be made at specific rates instead of ad valorem rates	Cushion to OMCs and consumers in a rising oil price environment	Not yet implemented

Source: ICRA (2006).

taxes on intermediate goods that are inputs to the untaxed consumption goods. A complementary principle is the well-known inverse elasticity rule. Assuming that a number of conditions are met (identical consumers; perfect competition; no externalities associated with the goods; no substitution in demand between commodities; all goods taxable), then, according to this rule, the tax rates on consumer goods should be so set as to be inversely proportional to the goods own-price elasticities of demand, to minimize the overall loss of welfare. The generalized Ramsey rule extends these principles to allow for substitution among commodities.

Application of this principle in its pure form is likely to be distributionally perverse, since the demand for most basic necessities (such as staple foods) is inelastic, while that for nonessential goods is likely to be more elastic. If the basic distribution of income is viewed as inequitable, an extended, distributionally based version of the Ramsey rule can be used. That is, taxes should be structured not to produce the same proportional change in demand for all goods but to have a greater impact on the goods that make up a relatively larger share of the budgets of higher-income households than on the goods that are more important for low-income households.

Tax rates on goods that have external costs should be adjusted upward to reduce their consumption to a social optimum. Where commodity taxes are not needed for other purposes, "Pigovian" taxes should be applied in such a way that the tax on the item creating the negative externality is proportional to the marginal social damage (so-called Pigovian tax rates). In the more realistic case in which the government needs to impose taxes for general revenue collection as well as to correct the externality, the incremental tax adjustment for dealing with the externality of a good should be applied to that good only; there is no reason to control the consumption of the good by adjusting tax rates for its complements or substitutes independent of their own polluting characteristics. The additional revenue collected can be used to adjust general tax rates downward.

Tax rates on automotive fuels vary markedly from country to country, ranging from heavy subsidies for all fuels in Nigeria and Iran to high taxes in Europe. Most developing countries tax gasoline—considered consumption good of the rich—more heavily than diesel (an intermediate good) or kerosene, a consumption good of the poor. Taxes on transport fuels typically seek to satisfy multiple objectives, including:

1. Raising government revenue for general (non-transport) expenditure purposes.

2. Efficiently allocating resources to and within the transport sector.
3. Financing road provision and maintenance.
4. Reducing congestion.
5. Reducing the environmental externalities of road transport.
6. Redistributing income.

It is not possible to achieve all these objectives simultaneously through fuel tax policies alone. Most governments complement fuel taxation with other policy instruments—in particular, to correct for externalities. The challenge of meeting the various objectives is especially difficult in low-income countries, where fewer policy instruments are available. In determining the levels and structure of fuel taxation, important compromises have to be made between the effects on government revenue generation, income distribution, the efficient use of roads, and environmental pollution. In so doing, attention must be accorded to the relative importance of each objective; the efficiency of fuel taxation as an instrument for achieving the objectives; and the magnitude of any perverse effects in relation to other aims. The general principles of optimal commodity tax theory, which focus on minimizing the loss of welfare to consumers in raising a given sum of money for the government through commodity taxation, provide useful guidance for evaluating these compromises. Although other (non tax) instruments are important, recent work shows that they are much more effective if supported by appropriate tax and pricing policies.

Setting Taxes on Transport Fuels

Diesel is the most efficient of all vehicular fuels, and diesel vehicles in a given vehicle category generally have lower fuel costs than others, although they are more expensive to purchase. For heavy-duty vehicles such as buses and trucks, the tradeoff usually favours the use of diesel. For light-duty vehicles, the payback period for the purchase price differential decreases with increasing annual kilometers traveled, making diesel the fuel of choice for high-mileage vehicles. Vehicles fueled by compressed natural gas (CNG) and liquefied petroleum gas (LPG), two of the cleanest fuels, are more expensive to purchase; only if these fuels are sufficiently lower in price than other fuels will vehicles using them be economically viable. In setting fuel taxes, the goals of such taxation, and the tradeoffs among them, need to be considered.

Raising Revenues

Fuel taxation is important for generating government revenue, particularly in low-income countries with poorly developed direct taxation systems. In these countries, taxes on hydrocarbons can account for as much as one-fifth of all tax revenue. Fuel taxes are also a reliable revenue source because fuel has a low overall elasticity of demand, and the tax can be collected cheaply. Furthermore, fuel taxation can have attractive distributional characteristics. The main danger—that the tax can be inflationary because of its pervasive impact on a wide range of basic consumption goods—applies to most forms of indirect taxation. It should be kept in mind that, where inter fuel substitution is technically possible (as between diesel and gasoline for light- and-medium duty vehicles), widely different tax rates are likely to distort transport fuel demand in favour of the fuels with lower taxes, thus decreasing tax revenue for the government unless overall tax rates are raised for all fuels.

Promoting Efficient Use of Resources

Avoiding economic distortions is particularly important in poor economies. In this respect, the first of the general principles of taxation suggests that fuel taxation should be concentrated on gasoline, which is used predominantly by private cars as consumption good, rather than on diesel, which is used in large quantities by freight and public transport vehicles as a producer good. However, the realities that not all consumption goods are taxed and that producer goods are associated with transport and environment-related externalities argue against zero taxes on diesel or subsidies to it. A number of factors need to be taken into account in determining the extent to which diesel should be taxed.

Financing Road Maintenance

Many developing countries have poor quality road systems because of under funding of maintenance. A fuel tax, or surcharges on the fuel tax that are designated specifically as road user charges, may be the most obvious and acceptable proxy for direct charging, especially when the revenues are transferred directly to a user-managed road fund. Fuel taxes, however, have certain shortcomings in regard to this objective: they do not reflect accurately the road deterioration caused by different vehicle categories, and they provide inefficient signals on vehicle size and weight. Even within the automotive diesel fleet a tax on diesel needs to be supplemented by some charge on vehicle axle loadings, preferably levied on the basis of distance traveled. In principle, users ought to pay the long-run marginal costs of road use, including the costs of capital. For this reason, recent studies have suggested a roads component within a fuel tax up to US$1 per gallon if no other direct charges are being levied.

Reducing Congestion

A fuel tax is not efficient as a charge for congestion because variations in congestion over time and space are only weakly reflected in variations in fuel consumption. Moreover, the fuel tax is usually determined by, and accrues to, the central government, whereas control of urban congestion is a municipal responsibility.

Reducing Air Pollution

The transport sector contributes up to 25 percent of worldwide greenhouse gas emissions. The transport-related pollutants of greatest concern in developing countries, however, are health threatening emissions of fine particles and lead (from the combustion of leaded gasoline). Fuel taxes are not very efficient in reducing externalities from emissions (except for the greenhouse gas carbon dioxide, emissions of which are directly linked to fuel consumption). Emissions and their environmental externalities depend not only on fuel choice but also on vehicle technology, vehicle maintenance, the vehicle-driving pattern, and the location and time of emissions. Some examples of the effects of these factors are illustrative: (a) although diesel is generally the "dirtiest" transport fuel, "clean diesel" technology can be nearly as clean as CNG; (b) poorly maintained vehicles generally have much higher emissions; and (c) emissions occurring only in densely populated areas harm public health disproportionately. The high degree of differentiation of environmental damages from the same fuels across various users, technologies, and locations limits the effectiveness of fuel taxes for controlling air pollution.

Redistributing Income

Many developing countries have very unequal income distribution and weak systems for direct taxation. Given the concentration of car ownership and use in the upper-income groups, a high incidence of taxation on gasoline makes for a very progressive tax. By the same token, where the impact of taxation on diesel has been studied, it has been found to be mildly regressive—

that is, the total expenditures of poor households rise more in percentage terms than those of the rich when the price of diesel is increased. This is one reason why a number of governments rely primarily on a high tax on gasoline to raise revenues from oil products. Based on the above assessment and issues, World Bank lists critical guidelines for taxing:

More precisely targeted alternatives to fuel taxes should be considered wherever possible, in view of the limitations of fuel taxes in achieving multiple objectives. A number of these objectives require fine-tuning on the basis of location- and situation-specific conditions, which cannot be accomplished through taxes set at the national or state level.

Environmental externalities should be corrected for by taxing polluting goods, not by subsidizing nonpolluting alternatives.

There is a strong case for setting the gasoline tax above the general tax rate on commodities. Rich households spend a higher proportion of their budgets on gasoline than do poor households; gasoline vehicles give rise to a number of externalities; and emissions from gasoline engines may affect poor households more than rich households.

There is also a strong case for a diesel tax. Although some diesel is used as an intermediate good, the taxation of even this segment of the market is justified if it is the principal way of charging heavy vehicles for wear and tear on the road and if the final goods (for which diesel is an input) are not necessarily taxed. Given diesel's high long-run substitutability for gasoline in light-duty vehicles and its strongly negative externalities in urban areas, the tax rate on automotive diesel should be set so as to raise the price toward that of gasoline. The only counterargument is the mildly regressive impact of raising the price of diesel.

Tax policies for petroleum fuels should take careful account of, and minimize, the possibilities for socially undesirable interfuel substitution, such as the dieselization of light-duty vehicles.

Chapter 4

Natural Gas Economics

Natural gas is significantly different from other fossil fuels because of its low energy density and its gaseous state. Unlike oil and coal, natural gas cannot be inexpensively stored in large quantities, and sophisticated and expensive infrastructure is required to deliver gas to the end-user. Hence, gas transportation costs are very high. In general, transportation represents 50% of the total final consumer price, compared to 5-10% in the case of oil. Additionally, gas transportation and distribution systems involve large economies of scale and are relatively inflexible; once the infrastructure is built, it cannot be used for other purposes. For these reasons, small-scale gas markets are difficult to develop.

Unlike oil and coal, there is no world gas market: 85% of the gas consumed in the world today is produced locally, and gas trade occurs largely on a regional scale. Thus, there is no world standard for gas pricing or marker price, such as WTI or Brent for crude oil. Small and remote gas discoveries are often hard to commercialise. As a result, there is a large amount of "stranded gas" in the world. The most significant difference is that, while investment in oil and coal production can be made independently from the conclusion of sales contracts, relying on selling the product on the world market, investment in gas production cannot proceed without long-term commitments between prospective producers and consumers.

Although gas and electricity are both grid-bound industries, they have significant differences. The main difference is that gas is only produced where it is found, while electricity, except for hydropower, can be produced anywhere. Thus, transportation plays a different role for gas compared to electricity. Another difference is that, with a few exceptions, alternative fuels can always be substituted for gas, which is not the case for electricity. Thus, gas pricing must take due account of the competitiveness of gas versus other fuels.

The gas industry works like a chain linking the wellhead and processing plant to the transmission network, to the distribution network, and, finally, to the consumer. Each physical link corresponds to a commercial relationship. Each link is dependent on every other link, and the overall strength of the chain depends on its weakest link. As the whole network is vulnerable to disruption, firm and long-term relationships—in the form of "take-or-pay" contracts or vertical integration—are the most common.

The gas industry is very capital-intensive: huge up-front investments are required to produce, transport, store and distribute gas. At normal temperature and pressure, natural gas is about a thousand times more voluminous than oil for the same energy content. Even under high pressure, the energy density of natural gas is about one-tenth that of oil: this means that an oil pipeline can transport about ten times as much energy as a gas pipeline of the same diameter. Thus, transportation costs makes up a greater share of the final price of gas than is the case for other fuels.

The co-ordination of investments along the gas chain is crucial. In many cases, gas resources are far from potential demand centres and require long-distance transportation. Field development and pipeline construction have no value unless a market infrastructure such as gas-fired power plants and local distribution networks is created simultaneously.

The development of natural gas markets is a long process. It took 50 years for the share of gas in the world's energy mix to increase from 2% in 1900 to 10% in 1950. During that period, more than 90% of the gas was consumed in the United States where, despite huge local resources and strong potential demand, the emergence of a gas market faced major challenges. In Western Europe, natural gas was not consumed until after World War II and reached only 20 bcm in 1965. Four decades later, European gas industries and markets are still in varying degrees of development. The world gas market is still under going a shift with its resultant global implications.

The last, but perhaps most important, point is that, unlike oil and coal, the development of natural gas is driven by demand, rather than by production, more precisely by a demand that can justify financing for the investment required all along the gas chain. Resources and infrastructure alone are not sufficient; the market for end-uses must be developed. Moreover, unlike electricity, gas must compete with other energy sources. For example, in the residential and commercial sectors, gas competes with electricity, liquefied petroleum gas (LPG) and heating oil. In the industrial sector, gas competes with coal and oil for use in steam boilers. In the production of electricity, gas competes with coal, oil, nuclear, hydro, biomass and other renewables.

Gas production uses non-renewable natural resources that are part of a country's national assets. Gas transportation and distribution require a fixed infrastructure that uses public land and public streets. All gas activities have important health, safety and environmental consequences. Furthermore, gas distribution and, in some cases, transmission has the character of a natural monopoly. In addition, the power sector, which is a main driver for the development of gas markets, requires clear government policy in order to perform effectively and provide the revenue needed to sustain the gas sector. For the above reasons, the state—either the central government or the local municipalities—has an important role to play. In the past, in most countries the state managed gas activities directly, through state-owned companies. This, however, has changed. The current trend is to let commercial players handle the commercial activities of the gas industry as much as possible. Nevertheless, the role of the government remains essential in establishing a clear policy, regulatory and fiscal framework for the gas industry. This framework should stimulate investment, protect consumer interests and provide a fair revenue for the state. This is particularly important at the early stage of gas-market development.

Natural gas is becoming one of the most important sources of the world energy supply. The increasing importance of natural gas to modern economics raises new concerns regarding the security of gas supplies and the potential formation of a gas cartel very similar to OPEC.

The Natural Gas Market

Europe and Eurasia with consumption of 1146.3 BCM of natural gas was the biggest market, with the North American market consuming around 770.3 BCM of natural gas in 2006. Together these two markets constitute more than

Table 4.1: World Primary Energy Demand in Reference Scenario

	1980	*2000*	*2005*	*2015*	*2030*
Coal	1786	2292	2892	3988	4994
Oil	3106	3647	4000	4720	5585
Gas	1237	2089	2354	3044	3948
Nuclear	186	675	721	804	854
Hydro	147	226	251	327	416
Biomass and Waste	753	1041	1149	1334	1615
Other Renewables	12	53	61	145	308

70 per cent of the total world natural gas consumption market. Thus developments in these markets are key to understand the developments in world natural gas markets. Interestingly enough these two markets also happen to be the largest importer of natural gas through pipelines, with Japan been the largest importer of natural gas through LNG.

Over the recent past, production and imports in the US have not been growing at the same rate as consumption. Traditionally, Canada has been North America's major exporter of gas. However, as growth in indigenous production and export potential from Canada is showing some potential limitations, there appears to be strong pressure for growth on LNG imports, either directly or indirectly (e.g. through Mexico). These pressures for growth have had an upward effect on prices, which has attracted a large volume of spot/short-term LNG in the recent past from a wide range of countries, including cargoes from as far as Malaysia.

The EU market, on the other hand, is going through an important phase of structural change, an important characteristic of which is the market liberalisation resulting from the implementation of the two gas directives as well as the application of competition rules to gas markets. Around 42 per cent of the natural gas consumed in the EU is produced within the region, in particular in the United Kingdom, the Netherlands and Denmark, as well as in Italy, Hungary, Austria, Poland and Germany. This means that the EU currently imports around 58 per cent of its gas needs, and this proportion is growing.

Vulnerable Concentrations

It is often argued that gas resources are more varied and dispersed than oil and therefore sufficient concentration does not exist for the effective creation of a gas cartel. Statistics however tell a different story. If we look at gas reserves, 3 countries with largest reserve hold close to 56 per cent of the world gas reserves, as opposed to 43 per cent for oil. An analysis of trade statistics also shows a perturbing tendency. Just one country Russia accounted for close to 28 per cent of total natural gas trade by pipelines. Talking in terms of LNG doesn't change the picture significantly. Given the characteristics of trade, gas markets will fundamentally be different from the oil market, in that the vulnerability of supply disruption is higher vis-à-vis oil. Over long-term it is expected that gas exports may eventually become concentrated in the hands of just a few major producers, given the distribution of this resource. These trends of increased vulnerability will only get worsen as the world uses more gas as a source of energy.

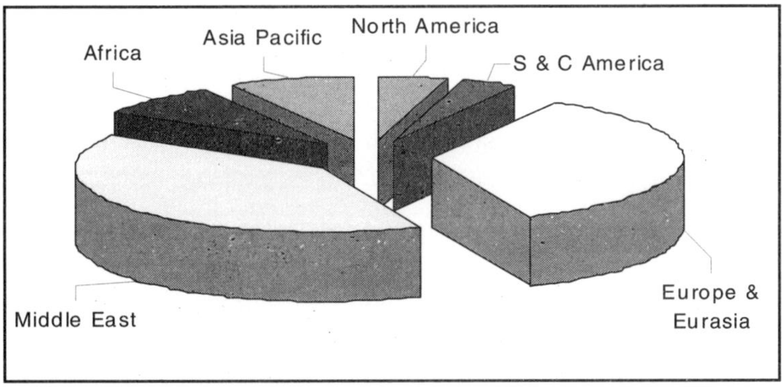

Note: Figures are for Year Beginning, 2007.
Source: *BP Statistical Review of World Energy,* 2007.

Figure 4.1: Distribution of Natural Gas Reserves at the Beginning of 2007

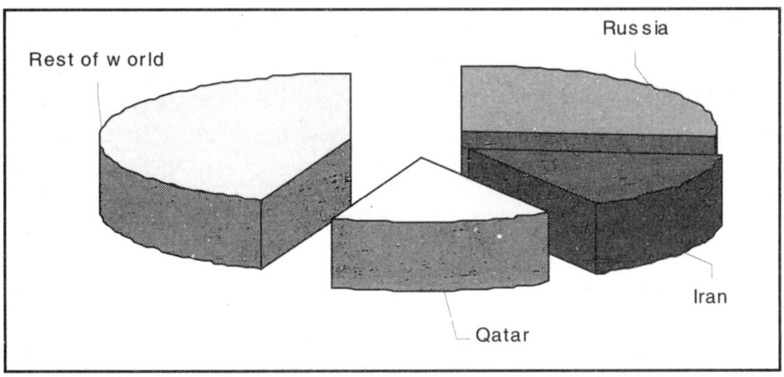

Note: Figures are for Year Beginning, 2007.
Source: *BP Statistical Review of World Energy,* 2007.

Figure 4.2: Vulnerable Shares

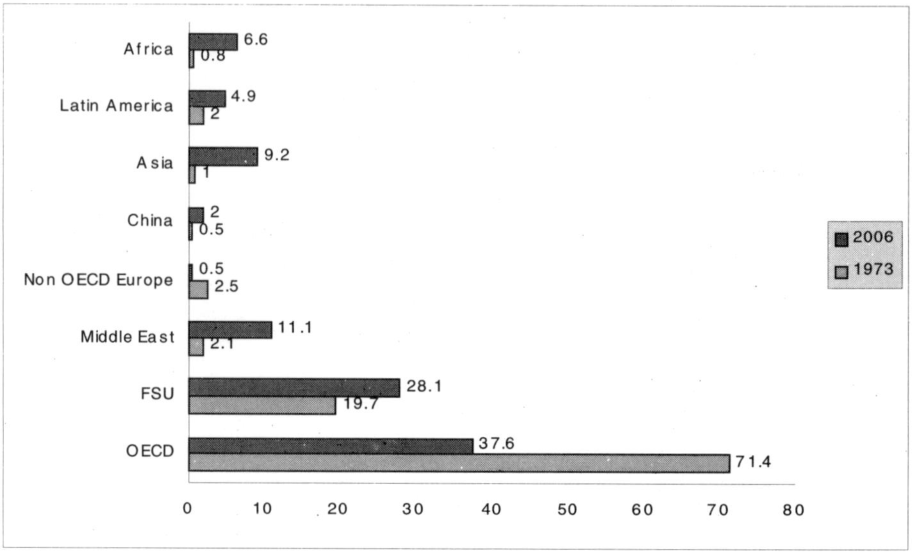

Note: Figures are for Year Beginning, 2007.
Source: *BP Statistical Review of World Energy,* 2007.

Figure 4.3: Regional Share of Natural Gas Production

Cartelization of Supply

Given the distribution of reserves, production and consumption of natural gas, recent moves by Russia to restrict the flow of gas, among others have brought back the fears of Gas-OPEC. This is reinforced by the formation of The Gas Exporting Countries Forum (GECF) in 2001. The aim of the forum is to foster the concept of mutuality of interests by favouring dialogue between producers, between producers and consumers and between governments and energy-related industries, to provide a platform to promote study and exchange of views and to promote a stable and transparent energy market. There are still conflicting views on the potential market power of this forum and the possible influence that it may have on the future natural gas development market. Though, various members of this forum have time and again pointed out that they will not form a gas cartel. But given the recent pronouncements from the powers to be have only furthered the apprehensions of this forum.

Demand and Supply Curves for Natural Gas

In the short run, the demand curve for gas in a given market will be determined by the following factors:

- The importance of seasonal heating load, which in turn is largely a function of residential and small commercial short-term demand. The position of the demand curve is generally driven by the weather.
- The seasonality of demand for gas in power generation and the degree to which seasonal gas and electricity demand peaks coincide, depending on the use of electricity for heating and cooling.
- Demand from shippers for gas to put into storage (which is in turn a function of storage capacity), prevailing storage levels, actual price levels and expectations concerning future price levels.
- Capability of end users to switch at short notice between different fuels and the prices of those competing fuels. Most end users are essentially captive in the short-term.

In most countries, almost all residential customers and the majority of commercial and small industrial customers do not maintain dual-firing equipment to enable rapid switching away from or to gas. Any demand response by these customers to a price change usually lags by several years. Some large customers, however, may be able to switch fuels at very short notice thanks to dual-firing or, in the case of power generators, by switching to alternative non-gas fired plant. The extent to which end users as a whole are able to switch fuels quickly helps to determine the slope of the demand curve; the price of competing fuels affects the position of the curve.

The shape of the supply curve, on the other hand, is determined by the production policy of producers (notably their willingness to shut in production and bring forward or delay maintenance programmes for economic reasons) and the willingness of holders of gas in storage to release it to the market at different price levels. Generally, the supply curve will be steep, since production becomes insensitive to price as output reaches the maximum sustainable level; at low levels of output, the curve will tend to become flat as producers shut wells rather than sell at very low prices. The willingness to sell at different prices is largely a function of expected price movements and storage levels. The position of the gas curve may change according to total short-term productive capacity. The commissioning of a new gas field or the stocking of gas through the low demand season shifts the supply curve downwards.

Demand for Energy as a Derived Demand

Demand for energy is derived from wishes to use energy to obtain desired services. It is not derived from preferences for the energy commodity itself. Energy demand depends primarily on demand for desired services, availability and properties of energy conversion technologies and costs of energy and technologies used for conversion. For example, consumers use gasoline to fuel an automobile or other motorized vehicle, converting gasoline to mechanical energy for motive power. The amount of gasoline used is proportional to the miles the auto is driven and inversely proportionate to the efficiency by which gasoline is converted to useful mechanical energy, measured as miles per gallon (Mpg) of gasoline of the automobile. Demand for gasoline is thus derived from choices about distances vehicles are driven and their energy conversion efficiencies. Similarly, electricity is purchased by consumers only to perform functions using electricity. Typical electricity uses include lighting, refrigeration, space heating, air conditioning, clothes washing, drying, dish washing, water heating, operating electronic equipment such as computers or televisions. Electrical energy is converted to mechanical energy (motors in refrigerators, air-conditioning units, vacuum cleaners), thermal energy (space heating, clothes dryers, water heating), or radiation (lighting, television, computer monitors.)

Electricity demand is derived from demand for the underlying services—comfortable space, refrigeration, cleaning, entertainment, information processing. In each case, efficiency of energy conversion equipment also determines energy demand. Typically, energy conversion equipment is long-lived—automobiles, air-conditioning units, refrigerators, televisions, computer systems, furnaces. Consumers or firms can usually choose among alternatives with various conversion efficiencies; such choices significantly influence energy demand. To the extent that consumers and firms purchase these units with an understanding of their conversion efficiencies, expectations of future energy prices can influence choices of particular equipment. For example, high natural gas prices can motivate consumers to invest in home insulation.

In general, increased energy prices reduce demand by reducing use of energy services and motivating selection of higher conversion efficiency equipment. For example, gasoline prices influence demand through vehicle miles and fuel efficiency of vehicles. Vehicle miles is influenced by cost per mile of driving, including per mile gasoline costs, equal to the ratio Pg/Mpg (where Pg is the gasoline price), and other costs. Increased gasoline prices lead consumers to purchase more fuel-efficient cars. Both factors imply that increased gasoline prices reduce gasoline demand, with the vehicle miles adjusting relatively quickly and vehicular fuel efficiency adjusting slowly as vehicles enter the fleet. Except for firms selling energy resources or energy commodities, the same issues are important for industrial and commercial use of energy.

Demand Substitution Among Energy Commodities

Some energy services can be provided by several different energy commodities. Homes could be heated using electricity, natural gas, oil, or wood, since each can be converted to thermal energy. Cooking could use electricity, natural gas, propane, wood, or charcoal. Thus, energy commodities are typically economic substitutes for one another: the demand for a particular energy commodity is an increasing function of prices of other energy commodities. This substitutability of energy is made possible by and is limited by the available set of energy conversion technologies. Typically one conversion technology can be used only for one particular energy commodity. For home heating, a natural gas furnace cannot use oil, electricity, or wood. Because conversion equipment typically is very long lived, substitution among energy commodities occurs only slowly, and then when new equipment is purchased. Short-run substitution usually can occur only if several energy conversion technologies are simultaneously available for use by particular consumers, e.g., homes that have a central natural gas heating system plus portable electric space heating units. Thus, usually various energy commodities can be viewed as imperfect substitutes for one another, with much greater substitutability in the long-run than in the short-run. The degree of substitutability can be sharply altered by development of new conversion alternatives. For example, automobiles historically were fueled only by gasoline or diesel fuel, but technologies currently being developed would allow autos to be powered by electricity, natural gas, propane, hydrogen, or other energy commodities. Once such conversion technologies are successfully commercialized, gasoline and other energy commodities will become highly substitutable in transportation.

An Essential Good?

In economics, an essential good is one for which the demand remains positive no matter how high its price becomes. In the theoretical limit, for prices unboundedly high, consumers would allocate all of their income to purchases of the essential good. Energy is often described as an essential good because human activity would be impossible absent use of energy: living requires food embodying chemical energy. Although energy is essential to humans, neither particular energy commodities nor any purchased energy commodities are essential goods. Particular energy commodities are not essential because consumers can convert one form of energy into another. Even the aggregate of all purchased energy cannot be viewed as an essential good. Experience from low-energy research facilities shows that an extremely energy efficient home needs relatively little energy. Solar energy could generate electricity or heat water. Travel could be limited to walking or riding bicycles. Solar-generated electricity or wood fires could be used for cooking. For high enough prices of purchased energy, demand for purchased energy by consumers could be reduced to zero. Thus, purchased energy is not an essential good.

Drivers of Natural Gas Demand

Demand for natural gas is influenced by several factors, including the availability of locally produced gas and alternative sources of energy, the cost of gas relative to alternative fuels, and environmental policies promoting the substitution of gas for other more polluting fuels.

Gas has some advantages and disadvantages compared with other fuels. The main disadvantage is that at normal pressure gas is about a thousand times more voluminous than oil for the same energy content. Because of this low energy density, the specific costs of gas transportation and storage are much higher than for oil. Thus, transportation is a crucial and expensive link in the gas chain; its cost can easily account for 50% of the end-user gas price. Transporting gas between point of production to the end consumer—either by high-pressure pipelines or, after liquefaction, by ship—typically involves large investments with a high degree of inflexibility and significant economies of scale. Hence, geographical factors, such as the distance between the production site and the main consumption area, and the concentration of demand, are critical to gas market development.

On the other hand, compared with other fossil fuels, natural gas has advantages which make it attractive for certain uses despite the high transportation costs. Gas burns cleanlier than other fossil fuels, generating no ashes or sulphur emissions, and it is easier to handle, allowing much more precise and uniform combustion. Gas also contains less carbon per unit of energy output than oil or coal; thus its combustion releases less CO2. Furthermore, technological advances have substantially raised the thermal efficiency of gas-fired power generation compared with fuel oil and coal, making natural gas, under most circumstances, a more competitive fuel for base-load power generation.

Transport costs and climatic conditions also help explain why and where gas markets first developed. By and large, the countries with the earliest and largest use of gas (e.g. US, FSU, Argentina, UK, continental Europe) are countries with cold temperatures in winter and where significant gas resources were found close to large urban agglomerations. The extensive use of gas in the residential, commercial and public sectors—combined with gas use in industry—provided the basis for the early development of gas transportation and distribution networks. Often in these countries, there already existed distribution networks for manufactured gas (city gas), which could be quickly converted to transport natural gas. Gas-fired generation developed later, driven mainly by environmental concerns and economics as gas was substituted for more polluting coal or displaced costly oil imports.

Gas Market Models

Economies exhibit a broad range of gas market models, reflecting a variety of economic circumstances and levels of development. Some gas markets are essentially monopolistic, with the production and transportation of gas controlled by a single entity. Other gas markets are highly competitive, with many producers vying for customers over a transportation network to which all suppliers may gain access on similar terms. Many gas markets are somewhere between these two extremes, often with a single wholesale buyer choosing among competing producers but with some or all final gas consumers obliged to purchase gas from the monopoly wholesale buyer. This chapter outlines the different market types and their theoretical advantages and drawbacks.

In describing gas markets, it is important to focus on their links with electric power markets. In many economies, a large share of natural gas is used to produce electric power and a large share of electric power is generated from natural gas. The degree of competition in gas markets may affect the ability of power producers to secure gas at competitive prices, which in turn may affect the extent to which gas rather than other fuels is used to generate electricity. Conversely, the degree of competition in electricity markets may affect the extent to which electric power suppliers take advantage of opportunities for competitive procurement of gas and the extent to which efficiency improvements due to gas market reform are passed through to energy consumers. Broadly speaking, there are three basic types of gas market structure, with substantial variation:

(1) Vertically Integrated Monopoly (single entity controls production and transportation)
(2) Wholesale Competition (transport entity buys gas from competing wholesale suppliers)
(3) Customer Choice (final customers obtain gas from competing retail suppliers)

The Vertically Integrated Monopoly Model

In the vertically integrated monopoly model, a single entity produces gas, transmits it to consuming areas, and distributes it locally. The entity may be the government itself, operating through one or more state-owned firms, or a private firm or consortium with a government license. It may be integrated horizontally as well as vertically, with an economy-wide franchise for gas delivery. In economies with greater geographic extent, there may be more than one vertically integrated monopoly, each with its own geographic service territory. Alternatively, there may be a single entity that produces and transmits gas, from which separate entities, each with a monopoly franchise in a different geographic service territory, purchase gas for distribution to consumers.

If a vertically integrated monopoly controls both production and transportation of gas, there is rarely wholesale competition among producers. In theory, the monopoly might buy some gas from producers abroad if its own supplies were extremely expensive or inadequate to serve demand. But the monopoly will ensure that all of its own production is transported and sold before that of any foreign competitor. In gas-exporting economies, where production is more than adequate to meet demand, competitive wholesale procurement by the monopoly is especially unlikely. At the same time, regardless of whether the distribution function is economy-wide or divided among several geographic franchises, a vertically integrated monopoly provides no opportunity for retail competition among suppliers to final customers. Large industrial firms and electricity generators, who can buy gas directly from the transmission network, have but one production-transmission entity from which to buy. Smaller customers, who must obtain their gas over a local distribution grid, are obliged to buy their gas from the single distributor in their area.

Insofar as economies are net gas importers, a vertically integrated monopoly is unlikely to prevail. In economies that import all or most of their gas, whether by pipeline or through LNG facilities, production must occur primarily in the countries from which gas is imported. It follows that production and transport of gas cannot be vertically integrated within the importing economy. Where a relatively small share of gas needs is imported, there may still be substantial integration of supply and transport within the importing economy. In such cases, the vertically integrated monopoly can minimise its costs by procuring gas imports from competing suppliers abroad. But since the monopoly has no internal competitors, it may not take full advantage of this opportunity.

Particularly in economies where gas markets are at an early stage of development, the integration of production and transport may make it easier to obtain capital for new gas projects. For example, it may be possible to identify a large industrial or power industry customer to absorb all or most of the gas from a newly discovered gas field. In such a case, the gas production facilities and associated pipelines may be easier to finance because there is an identified revenue stream. Meanwhile, the factories or power plants using the gas may be easier to finance because they have a clearly identified fuel source under a price formula that is specified by contract.

The most obvious disadvantage of the vertically integrated monopoly model is that there is little incentive for the monopoly to minimise costs. Without competitors, productive inefficiencies can go unchecked, raising costs substantially. Where the monopoly is government-owned, there may be political pressure to retain staff in excess of what is technically required to produce and transport gas. Because there is only a single gas supplier, excess costs arising from productive inefficiencies can be readily passed on to consumers, who have nowhere else to turn for their gas.

Alternatively, the government may decide to set domestic gas prices below gas prices in export markets, resulting in lost state revenues from abroad and inefficient gas use at home. Without proper regulation, a private vertically integrated monopoly tends to restrict gas output and raise gas prices above the cost of production (including the cost of capital). In this case, some potential gas customers will be compelled to use other fuels instead, so gas demand and markets will not develop to the extent that they would in a competitive environment. Such allocative inefficiency may have major costs to the economy if alternatives to gas are much more expensive. If the alternative fuels are imported, there will also be a deleterious impact on the balance of trade.

Power Market Linkages

Where the gas market has a vertically integrated monopoly, the electric power market may also have a vertically integrated monopoly or may have wholesale competition with a single buyer. Potential problems of productive and allocative inefficiency will then be present in both markets. Insofar as the electric power monopoly or single buyer depends on gas-fuelled generation, elevated gas prices that result from inefficiencies in the gas market can be passed on to electricity consumers in the form of higher electricity rates. Since consumers have only one power source and electricity has no substitutes in many uses, the power monopoly or single buyer can absorb higher gas prices in rates with little damage to profits. Alternatively, if the power monopoly or single buyer gets a subsidised price from the gas monopoly, it may pass on less than the full cost savings to consumers.

The Wholesale Competition Model

In the wholesale competition model, competing entities produce gas but each geographic area has a single entity that buys and transmits gas and a single entity that distributes gas to consumers. There may be a single buyer that purchases, transmits and distributes gas throughout the economy. Alternatively, there may be regional buyers that purchase, transmit and distribute gas in different geographic service territories. Or a single buyer may purchase and transmit gas throughout the economy while regional distributors with franchised service territories sell gas to final consumers.

The extent of wholesale competition may vary according to several factors. One key factor is the adequacy of transportation infrastructure. Where there is plenty of capacity in pipelines and LNG terminals, there is room for many different foreign or domestic producers to compete. Where capacity is constrained, the space for competition may likewise be limited. Another key factor affecting wholesale competition is the buyer's corporate structure. Where the buyer is organised for profit, there will be gains to both public and private shareholders from keeping costs down and a corresponding incentive to procure gas from the least-cost suppliers. Where the buyer is not organised for profit, the incentive to buy gas from the least-cost competitor may be weak.

Because the distributor of gas in each area is also the sole gas retailer in that area, the wholesale competition model does not allow retail competition among suppliers to final customers. Just as in the case of a vertically integrated monopoly, large industrial firms and power generators who take gas directly from the transmission grid have only one entity from which to buy. And smaller customers, who obtain gas from a local distribution grid, must buy from the single distributor in their area.

The main advantage of the wholesale competition model is that there is an opportunity to limit costs by procuring gas from the least-cost producers. Knowing that the buyer has a choice among many competitors, each producer will have an incentive to offer the buyer an attractive price. The buyer can then choose the least-cost sources of supply, which are presumably those that can produce and deliver gas to the economy most efficiently. As indicated above, this advantage may accrue to the extent that transportation infrastructure can accommodate different suppliers and insofar as buyers are organised for profit with an incentive to keep costs down. The clearest disadvantage of the wholesale competition model is that there is little pressure from consumers for the single buyer of gas and the single distributor of gas to minimise costs.

Where the buyer and distributor are organised for profit, they will have an incentive to procure gas from the least-cost suppliers, to ensure that pipelines and LNG facilities are adequate to accommodate competing suppliers, and to operate transmission and distribution infrastructure in an efficient manner. But the quality of management may vary, and the single buyer and distributor of gas in each area may have varying degrees of success in keeping costs down. With only a single supplier in each area, excess costs from productive inefficiencies can be passed on to consumers. Unless the cost of gas becomes so high that consumers turn to alternative fuels, the supplier's excess costs and inefficiencies will remain in place unchecked by competition.

Power Market Linkages

Where natural gas is a major fuel for electricity generation, having only a single supplier of gas is likely to limit efficiency or impede competition in the electric power market. If there is also only a single supplier of electricity, any inefficiencies on the part of the gas producer or supplier can be readily absorbed by the single electricity supplier and passed on to consumers in electricity rates, so there is little market pressure for the inefficiencies to be addressed. If the electricity market should happen to be open to competition, both traditional electric utilities and independent power producers will be obliged to purchase gas from the same supplier, probably at about the same cost. In this case, it will be relatively difficult for IPPs to undercut utility supply costs and compete.

Economies wishing to move from the vertically integrated monopoly model toward the wholesale competition model would need to separate the gas production from gas transmission and distribution. This might involve the sale of gas production facilities to one or more competitors, with monopolies remaining in control of transmission and distribution. Key issues would then include the period over which production assets are to be divested, the bidding system by which prices for the assets are set, and the number of different entities to which production facilities are sold to ensure competition among producers when divestiture is complete.

The Customer Choice Model

In the customer choice model, competing entities produce gas and supply gas to consumers. Typically, since the gas pipeline network is a natural monopoly that would be wasteful to duplicate, the network in each area is controlled by a single regulated gas transmission company and a single regulated distribution company, although several entities may compete to transport gas through LNG facilities. But competing producers and suppliers have equal access to pipelines and LNG facilities, on non-discriminatory terms. Customers can therefore shop among competing gas suppliers and select the one that provides gas at lowest cost.

The degree to which customer choice is provided may vary. Particularly in the earlier stages of reform efforts, retail choice of suppliers may be limited to large industrial firms and electric utilities, which can obtain gas directly from high-pressure pipelines and LNG terminals. At later stages of reform, retail choice may be extended to small residential and commercial customers who receive their gas over distribution networks. Where transmission and distribution are regulated by separate entities, competing suppliers may first gain access to regional transmission grids and large customers, only later gaining access to local distribution grids and small customers.

Customer choice is best provided if transmission and distribution are unbundled from production and retail supply. Monopoly transmission and distribution services need to be regulated to ensure that they are fairly priced and equally available to all competing suppliers. If a monopoly transmission or distribution entity also controls a significant share of production or supply, it will have incentives to discriminate against competing producers or suppliers in determining who gains access to pipelines and LNG terminals, even if the law requires that access be provided on equal terms to all. In this case, it is relatively difficult for regulators to ensure that access to transport infrastructure is non-discriminatory, and a large regulatory staff will probably be needed to do so.

On the other hand, if (regulated) gas transmission and distribution services are controlled independently of (competitive) gas production and supply, ensuring fair access to these services is much easier, and the regulatory task is simplified. If independent entities control transmission and distribution, they will have no reason to discriminate in favour of one producer or supplier over another. Hence, infractions of laws requiring non-discriminatory access to these services will be relatively rare, and a small regulatory staff will probably be adequate to deal with them.

The regulatory task will be simplified insofar as the separation, or unbundling, of transmission and distribution services from production and supply is complete. With separation of *accounts*, the weakest form of unbundling, the transmission and distribution divisions of a company may still communicate with the production and supply divisions, so discrimination is still quite possible. With *functional* separation, information firewalls are established between the various divisions, so the opportunity for discrimination is diminished insofar as the firewalls are effective. With *operational* separation, an independent entity operates LNG terminals and gas pipelines, so fair access to these facilities should be assured even if they continue to be owned by gas producers or suppliers. With *ownership* separation, no transmitter or distributor of gas may also produce or supply gas, so there is an added degree of assurance that competing producers and suppliers will be treated on a level playing field.

The customer choice model provides the greatest possible assurance that gas will be supplied in the most efficient way, at the least possible cost, to those that have the greatest need for it. Buyers and sellers are directly linked. Efficient producers will gain market share form inefficient producers because efficient producers can provide gas at a lower price and attract more customers. Producers thus have clear profit incentives to address their inefficiencies, and sufficiently inefficient producers will eventually find themselves without business and knocked out of the marketplace. However, a fully competitive marketplace for gas, like that for any commodity, may result in price volatility from time to time. Particularly if demand is growing rapidly, there may be a period of high prices until new supply can be put in place to meet the increased demand. After production is increased or new infrastructure is built to meet the demand, prices will decline once again. On the other hand, there are market tools, such as futures contracts that provide the right to purchase gas at a fixed price, that market participants can use to limit their exposure to price volatility.

Power Market Linkages

Customer choice and competitive supply in the gas industry are likely to have economic benefits in the electric power industry, particularly insofar as the power industry is also competitive. If electric power is supplied by an integrated monopoly, regulators may compel it to shop for less costly gas supplies and to pass on resulting savings to electricity consumers, but to the extent that cost savings must be passed through, incentives to shop around will be weak. If power is provided by a single buyer, with wholesale competition among various electricity generators, the incentives to buy gas cheaply will be greater, since failure by generators to do so could result in unsuccessful bids to provide power to the buyer; and a portion of the resulting cost savings may again be passed on to consumers. If the power sector has customer choice like the gas sector, there will be further pressure to minimise generating costs by purchasing gas from the least-cost suppliers, as high-cost generators may ultimately find themselves without customers and out of business.

Transitional Issues

Economies wishing to move from the wholesale competition model to the customer choice model will need to separate the retail supply of gas from gas transmission and distribution. They will also need to put laws and regulations in place to ensure that competing producers and suppliers can obtain access to the transmission and distribution grids on equal terms. A key issue is the form that unbundling should take and the corresponding design of the regulatory apparatus. In moving from functional unbundling to operational or ownership unbundling, the economy may reduce the size and complexity of the regulatory apparatus needed to ensure effective competition. Another important issue in moving to the customer choice model is the extent to which smaller gas customers are allowed and encouraged to participate in the market. Large industrial and power industry customers will generally have a profit motive to shop around for the lowest-cost gas suppliers.

Smaller customers, however, may be reluctant to leave the traditional supplier that has served them reliably for many years, even if competitors can supply gas at lower cost. Smaller residential and commercial customers can be encouraged to choose suppliers by making the process of switching suppliers simple, as well as by providing information that makes it easier to compare the price and service offered by different suppliers. Supplier choice by smaller customers will also be encouraged, when building popular support for reform, if the guaranteed "fall-back" rate charged by the traditional supplier is not reduced so far that it is hard for competitors to beat.

Gas Pricing

Adequate pricing of natural gas is key to the successful development of gas markets. Gas has no exclusive markets; hence the ability of gas to penetrate the market depends on its ability to compete with other fuels. The price of gas to final consumers, relative to that of competing fuels, will therefore affect the volume of gas sold and the expected revenues from sales, ultimately determining the viability of any natural gas project. The challenge is to find the right balance between what price the producer wishes to charge and what price the consumer is willing to pay. The pricing of the intermediate stages of the gas chain also needs careful consideration, and each link needs to be priced according to the risks involved.

Each market has its own unique set of alternative fuels, whose supply, demand and transportation characteristics together set the competitive price for gas. Even within a single market, there may be different prices depending on the type of energy service a customer requires. In South America, gas generally competes with hydropower and other fossil fuels in power generation, heavy fuel oil and biomass in industry (or gas oil and LPG when clean fuel is required), and electricity and LPG in the commercial and residential sectors. The main question about pricing is how the price is set: whether it is set freely by the market players or fixed by some state authority. International experience has shown that government-set prices distort the economics of the gas supply chain, and fail to give the market the signals and incentives needed to develop the gas market. Market competition is always more effective than any form of government price-setting. When a decision has been made to develop a gas industry relying on private initiative and market forces, pricing decisions all along the gas chain should be left to market players, and the state's role should be restricted to preventing anti-competitive behaviour that could damage consumer interests and to compensating for environmental and other externalities not accounted for in market prices.

Natural gas pricing is critically important for gas market development. It should encourage both gas consumption, by providing incentives for energy users to switch to gas, and gas production, giving investors a fair and reasonable return. It should also ensure the viability of each link in the gas chain. To a large extent, the size and shape of a country's gas industry is determined by its pricing policy. The setting of prices for all parts of the gas chain should ideally be left to market participants. The state should restrict itself to protecting captive customers against unfair use of market power and to using taxation to reflect externalities and provide incentives for the development of a gas industry.

Pricing of natural gas throughout the chain from the well-head to burner tip is the key to a coherent gas policy. It is the most important and critical factor in emerging gas markets. The ability of gas to penetrate the market depends on its ability to compete with other fuels: coal in power generation, gasoil and LPG as an industrial fuel when clean fuel is required, and manufactured gas and LPG in the residential sector. Price therefore affects the volume of gas sold. End-use pricing is also of crucial importance for infrastructure development, because the revenues from sales to all categories of end-users will decide the viability of any natural gas project. The challenge is to find the right balance between what price the producer wishes to charge and what price the consumer is willing to pay. In addition, the pricing of the intermediate stages of the gas chain also needs careful consideration, and each link should be priced according to the risks involved. Outside of the gas value chain, gas pricing also needs to take into account the government's environmental and social objectives.

The government needs to reposition itself with regard to gas pricing. Each market around the world has its own unique set of supply, demand, transportation and alternative fuel characteristics, which together set the competitive price for gas. Even within a single market, there may be different prices depending on the type of service a customer requires. Market competition is always a more effective control on prices than any form of government price-setting. Governments need to intervene only where inter-fuel competition is unfair because pure market-based pricing does not take into account environmental impacts, or where there is a risk of monopoly power that could damage consumer interests. This could be done by a taxation policy in favour of gas, as in the case of Japan and Korea, or in the form of the regulation of gas distribution activities.

There are essentially two approaches to gas pricing: the cost-based (or cost-plus) approach and the market-based net-back approach. The cost-plus approach prices gas independently from alternative fuels. It encourages gas production, but does not take into account its end-use competitiveness and the final consumers' interests. It could work in countries where gas resources are abundant and cheap to produce. But it does not encourage efficiency improvements and is ineffective in sending accurate market signals to investors to stimulate competition. This explains why the United States and Canada have both abandoned this approach. The net-back approach links gas prices more closely to competing fuels. It guarantees the competitiveness of gas against competitive fuels, protects upstream and midstream investment and encourages fuel switching to gas. International experience demonstrates that net-back pricing is the best approach to gas market development, especially in a country without cheap and abundant gas reserves.

The Pricing Methodologies

Cost-plus Pricing	*Net-back Pricing*
Well-head (regulated) price	Market value of gas based on price of consumer's competing fuel
+ Pipeline mark-up cost	
	– Distributor charges
+ Local distribution mark-up cost	
	– Pipeline transportation charge
= Sales price to consumer	= Net-back price at the well-head

The Cost Plus Methodology

While this approach attempts to encourage gas production, it does not ensure that the resulting cost-recovery price for gas would allow it to be marketed. A cost-plus system which starts with the cost of production and adds all the costs of transportation, load management and distribution is not adequate for all the countries though. Such a system is more appropriate for cases of large and inexpensive gas reserves close to consumption areas. But even there, costs are not that easy to determine as most cost elements are long-term fixed investments, and financing and specific costs are highly dependent on utilisation. Added to that, costs in a non-competitive environment can be easily flawed. This explains why even in gas rich countries such as the United States and Canada this approach has been abandoned due to its ineffectiveness in sending accurate market signals to investors to stimulate competition.

The Market Replacement Value Methodology

The starting point for market-based pricing of natural gas is the determination of its replacement value compared to alternative fuels for each customer. The replacement value of gas is defined as the price of gas at which the end-user incurs the same costs when using gas instead of alternative fuels such as coal and oil products, taking into account differences in heat value, efficiency and costs for the appliances or equipment necessary to use the energy, plus eventually the different costs of resulting pollution. The market replacement value serves as the basis for price negotiations. Prices above the replacement value will make gas difficult to sell, as customers may then prefer to use alternative fuels that cost less for the same result. Usually gas will still be the fuel of choice, even if the quantifiable costs for using gas are as high as those of an alternative, in view of the low pollution and easy handling of gas which are often not reflected in the equation. For freely negotiated prices the replacement value is a benchmark for the parties. For administered prices—which should be restricted to prices to captive customers, who are mainly householders—the concept may serve as a benchmark for the authorities to judge if a distribution company abuses its dominant/monopoly position.

However, further up the gas chain the replacement value is replaced by the net-back value. The net-back value is derived from the weighted replacement value of all customers above the point considered, by subtracting the costs for distribution, transportation and load management, and other costs necessary to bring the gas from the point in question to final consumers with the required load factor transformation to serve those customers.

It should be emphasised that the translation of these concepts into gas prices is best left to contract negotiations between market participants, with the role of the state being to ensure that contracts are respected. In the case of captive customers who will be served by standardized contracts, translation of the replacement value into a gas tariff should be left to the distribution company, depending on its marketing policy, while the public authority could use the replacement value as the benchmark to prevent any market abuse. The replacement value and net-back pricing approach do not provide a rent for the final consumer. Any rent is passed on to the upstream parts of the gas chain.

With the net-back principle, the rent is passed on further up the chain; if this principle is applied, the profits gained by the distribution and transmission and storage service between customers and the point of production would not exceed the usual risk-adjusted profit on their investment and operation costs. This approach is suitable for countries, which do not have large and inexpensive resources to bring to the marketplace. However, as part of this approach, it should be ensured that the extra rent in the upstream sector translates into investment back into the gas industry. Incentives such as extra tax breaks for investing profits into the gas sector could be provided, and the state would need to make sure that no entry barriers exist for new investors so that extra-high profits either attract more competitors upstream or are re-invested into further expansion of the gas sector.

A state administered net-back concept would have an advantage over a cost-plus system in China because it would start with what the consumer might be able to pay without incurring opportunity costs, and give the right signals to upstream investors. It risks, however, covering only half of the gap. It would still not be able to achieve the complex optimisation of volumes and prices, which can only be achieved by free commercial actions. To cover the other half, there need to be free negotiations of prices and other conditions based on a sufficient number of commercial actors. The market replacement value of gas can be derived by determining the lowest price of natural gas against any competing fuel by taking account of the following factors:

- Price and heat content (usually in net calorific value) of the competing fuel;
- The "Premium" (or disadvantages if any) of gas that can be calculated, including higher efficiency of gas compared to other fuels, lower operating costs, lower maintenance and storage costs, and lower investment. In addition, lower costs to meet environmental standards may be factored in. Eventually, an internalisation of environmental externalities, to the extent they are

not reflected in emission or pollution standards, should also be made.

- Other advantages that are not easily expressed in cost figures, including clean combustion properties, flexible and comfortable application and security, and easiness of supply.

Regulating Pricing

In any market economy, there are grounds for the public authorities to set prices only in cases of market failure, e.g. where market power stemming from a natural monopoly, which cannot be contested, is an issue. Where the supply of a good is competitive, it is most efficient to let the market determine the price. *Ex ante* price regulation (i.e. fixing the prices before the project starts) is against the principle of free markets and competition. It can only be justified in very specific cases, like cases of natural monopolies which cannot be contested. Moreover, regulation is potentially costly, both directly (with respect to the administrative burden) and indirectly through possible resultant market distortions, since regulation can never perfectly replicate efficient market outcomes. Consequently, governments usually seek ways of introducing competition into those parts of the industry where a competitive market can be established. It is vital that gas compete freely and effectively with other fuels, primarily coal and oil, and that pipelines be built freely, subject only to health-safety-environment (HSE) regulation, but not to economic regulation. This will require the removal of price distortions in all fuel markets.

An activity is a natural monopoly when its subdivision would lead to higher unit cost (subadditivity criterion). When looking at this criterion, the element of contestability must be considered. Short-distance transportation may fulfill the criterion of sub-additivity, but in view of the relatively small share of transportation costs in the overall value of gas, the disadvantage of foregoing economies of scale by building a second pipeline may not deter an investor. In addition, from an economic point of view the issue of building parallel pipelines should also be considered from a dynamic perspective. It may be much better for the development of competition to build sub-optimal parallel pipelines than to wait for lengthy regulatory processes. In any case, the possibility of building parallel pipelines is a very crucial element to make gas transportation competitive. The natural monopoly characteristics of high-pressure gas transportation may differ from case to case. In a case like Canada, where huge volumes of gas are transported from the production sites in Alberta to the eastern parts of Canada and the US, the market size for transportation is a multiple of the maximum possible pipeline size, the conditions for a natural monopoly are not met.

Practically all grids have a natural monopoly character, as do gas distribution systems. In addition, they are usually based on using municipal property, namely the municipal streets, which requires a concession, which is often given as an exclusive concession, so that a legal monopoly comes on top of the natural monopoly. In addition, exclusive rights over local distribution in the early stages of development of the industry are usually necessary to give confidence to potential investors that they will be able to recover their capital. Where there is a single gas supplier to a particular enduser, regulating prices can prevent that supplier from charging excessively high tariffs.

However, gas is always subject to competitive pressures from alternative fuels. Unlike electricity, gas can be replaced by other forms of energy in most uses, although the costs of permanent switching capacity may be high. Industrial consumers in particular may be able to switch to coal or heavy fuel oil relatively easily, as do power generators either by switching the input fuels or by optimizing the use of power plants *via* the electric grid. In this case, the need for tariff regulation will be determined by the extent to which the gas company exploits its market power and makes abnormally high profits. Where the costs of gas supply are high, and the costs of switching to alternative fuels are relatively low, there may be very little scope for the gas supplier to extract monopoly rent or profits. In this case, the cost of regulation may outweigh any potential benefit, and it may be better to leave the gas company to negotiate prices freely with its customers.

Oil and Gas Price Linkages

Economic theory suggests that natural gas and crude oil prices should be related because natural gas and crude oil are substitutes in consumption and also complements, as well as rivals, in production. In general, the observed pattern of crude oil and natural gas prices tend to support this theory. However, there have been periods in which natural gas and crude oil prices have appeared to move independently of each other. Furthermore, over the past 5 years, periods when natural gas prices have appeared to decouple from crude oil prices have been occurring with increasing frequency with natural gas prices rising above its historical relationship with crude oil prices in 2001, 2003, and again in 2005.

Since the beginning of the natural gas era in Europe, importers and exporters have based the trade on long-term contracts with an average duration of 20–25 years. In the mid-1980s, three price principles were identified by the IEA:

> [these] have been applied or proposed at various times by various parties to the pricing of wholesale gas supplies to West European transmission companies. These principles may be summarised as suggesting that gas should be priced either:
>
> - So as to be at or near parity with crude oil export prices, or
> - So as to be competitive with the final consumer's alternative non-gas fuels, or
> - So as to reflect historic costs of gas production.

The second principle—that the price of gas should generally be competitive with the prices of alternative (non-gas) fuels—has been the most widely applied in Western Europe and this became known as the 'market value principle'. In addition, pricing was in a process of change in the mid-1980s because of the volatility of oil prices. It was during this period that three-year price reviews were introduced into the majority of Continental European gas contracts.

The market value principle developed after the oil price increases of 1973–74 when the relative value of fuels competing with gas in the energy market became subject to major fluctuations. A documented example where the market value principle was used were the negotiations between (Dutch company) Gasunie and its customers in 1983/84 and this has been the basis of Continental European gas pricing since then. However, the origins of the principle can be traced back to Dutch Minister of Economics J.W. de Pous in the early 1960s.

The rationale for oil-linked gas pricing is that natural gas and oil are substitutable in both the short and the longer term. Price formulae were designed to ensure that the customer base continued to burn gas rather than returning to oil products since the majority of customers had switched from oil products to gas and, given a price incentive, retained the ability to switch back. If customers switched back to oil in large numbers, this would not only deprive gas importers of their market, but force them to incur take-or-pay penalties in their contracts with exporters. To argue that gas prices should continue to be indexed to oil products, it must be possible to demonstrate that:

- In the short-term, customers have the capability and incentive to switch existing plant from gas to oil and back again in response to price signals;
- In the long-term, customers building new plant (or replacing fuel burning equipment in old plant) will choose to install fuel burning equipment which is principally oil-fired, or equipment which is principally gas-fired but with the option of burning gas or oil products, or a plant with the capacity to switch between the two fuels.

In the short-term, for example, there is very little empirical evidence regarding the ability of existing gas customers to switch from gas to oil products and back again within a few days or weeks. It is not clear whether the data are collected—and in some respects whether they can be collected—on any independently verifiable and comprehensive basis. A major problem is that ?theoretical switching capacity', i.e. estimating the number of customers who could physically switch from gas to oil products if given appropriate commercial incentives, may not be a good approximation to ?real switching capacity' i.e. customers who are actually equipped to burn oil products instead of gas at short notice. In some countries there are environmental constraints which require customers to obtain special permission to emit high levels of sulphur and NOx associated with oil products.

The main reasons for the reduction of switching capacity from gas to oil products are practical:

- The need to maintain oil tanks in good condition with an adequate level of stocks, and arrangements for those tanks to be refilled regularly in order to maintain oil burning capacity for more than a few days;
- The need to maintain the pipework between the tanks and the fuel-burning equipment;
- The need to maintain fuel oil-burning equipment in good working order, including the ability to change and clean burners on a regular basis;
- The need to train staff to use oil products, which is significantly more arduous and labour-intensive than the use of gas.

The costs involved in keeping oil-burning equipment and storage in good working order (including the arrangements to ensure continued availability of oil products) and the inconvenience involved in switching, are strong disincentives for many customers to retain this option. Combining these problems with progressive tightening of emission limits on the burning of fossil fuels, it seems likely that the incentive to phase out fuel switching capability, either as a conscious decision or by default, will become increasingly strong.

In the longer term, justification for the continued linkage of gas to oil prices must rest on the proposition that customers building new plant will choose to build new oilfired plant or plant with the ability to switch to oil products on a significant scale for a protracted period of time. Such a proposition appears increasingly untenable. New gas burning plants—especially CCGT stations—are designed to burn gas only; burning oil in these plants not only causes them to run significantly less efficiently, requiring more fuel to be burned for the same output, but may increase maintenance costs and shorten the life of the turbines. No new oil-fired power plants are being built in Europe. Indeed with the exception of southern Europe where this type of plant is being phased out (and mainly replaced by gas) little oil-fired plant remains in operation in Europe other than for a few hundred hours of peak load. The argument in the residential, commercial and industrial sectors is similar. With the exception of customers with no access to a gas supply (which means that switching is not an option), it is not credible to suggest that any significant proportion of customers will install new fuel-burning equipment in their homes, businesses or industrial plants which will allow them to switch between gas and oil products.

The Demand and Supply Pull

Economic factors link oil and natural gas prices through both supply and demand. Market behavior suggests that past changes in the oil price drove changes in the natural gas price, but the converse did not appear to occur. One reason for the asymmetric relationship is the relative size of each market. The crude oil price is determined on the world market, while natural gas markets, at least for the period of investigation, tend to be regionally segmented. Consequently, the domestic natural gas market is much smaller than the global crude oil market, and events or conditions in the U.S. natural gas market seem unlikely to be able to influence the global price of oil.

Increases in oil prices may affect the natural gas market in several ways.

Demand

An increase in crude oil prices motivates consumers to substitute natural gas for petroleum products in consumption, which increases natural gas demand and hence prices. Oil and natural gas are competitive substitutes primarily in the electric generation and industrial sectors of the economy. According to EIA's 2002 Manufacturing Energy Consumption Survey (MECS), approximately 18 percent of natural gas usage can be switched to petroleum products. The National Petroleum Council (NPC) in its 2003 report estimated that approximately 5 percent of industrial boilers can switch between natural gas and petroleum fuels. Other analysts estimate that up to 20 percent of power generation capacity is dual-fired, although in practice it is assumed that the relevant percentage is considerably less.

However, fuel-switching is not limited to dual-fired units. Some degree of additional fuel switching is achieved by dispatching decisions to switch from single-fired boilers of one type to that of another fuel. Although these are limited percentages, the shift in marginal consumption can have a pronounced impact on prices in a tight market.

Supply

Increases in crude oil prices resulting from an increase in crude oil demand may increase natural gas produced as a co-product of oil, which would tend to decrease natural gas prices. Natural gas is found in two basic forms—associated gas and non-associated gas. Associated natural gas is natural gas that occurs in crude oil reservoirs either as free gas (associated) or as gas in solution with crude oil (dissolved gas). Non-associated gas is natural gas that is not in contact with significant quantities of crude oil in the reservoir. In 2004, associated-dissolved gas comprised approximately 2.7 trillion cubic feet (Tcf) or 14 percent of marketed natural gas production in the United States.

An increase in crude oil prices resulting from an increase in crude oil demand may lead to increased costs of natural gas production and development, putting upward pressure on natural gas prices. Natural gas and crude oil operators compete for similar economic resources such as labor and drilling rigs. An increase in the price of oil would lead to higher levels of drilling or production activities as operators explored for and developed oil prospects at a higher rate. The increased activity would bid up the cost of the relevant factors, which will increase the cost of finding and developing natural gas prospects.

An increase in crude oil prices resulting from an increase in crude oil demand may lead to more drilling and development of natural gas projects, which would tend to increase production and decrease natural gas prices. Increased oil prices affect the cash flow available to finance new drilling and project development. Changes in the relative price structure could lead to increases in drilling for one fuel at the expense of the other. However, it is generally expected that increased cash flow would expand supply activities for both natural gas and oil.

Finally, another factor linking the natural gas and crude oil markets is liquefied natural gas (LNG), which permits the transoceanic delivery of natural gas from remote gas-producing countries to large gas-consuming areas such as the Lower 48 States in US. LNG imports to the Lower 48 States may affect the relative economics of crude oil and natural gas to the extent that natural gas consumption occurs at the margin. Most LNG contracts are indexed on oil prices, directly linking natural gas and crude oil prices. While most of these indexed contracts occur primarily in the Pacific Basin, short-term markets for LNG are developing on either side of the Atlantic Basin in the United States and Spain, facilitating interregional gas price competition between the United States and Europe. A "world market" for natural gas likely would reinforce the linkages between natural gas and crude oil prices.

Natural Gas Taxation

Taxation of natural gas and other fuels is a key element of a coherent energy policy, and can play a critical role in stimulating the supply of and demand for natural gas, especially in the early stages of industry development. Taxes are not only the main source of fiscal income, to be spent for the general functions of a state, e.g. to support education, defence, the environment, health, the judiciary system, administration, etc, but can also serve as powerful incentives or penalties to achieve a desired pattern of consumption, especially between substitutable products. Taxes can also be used as instruments to internalise externalities and to convert government policies into economic signals to the market.

Many countries have used favourable taxation of gas as a primary means of supporting market development.

The rapid penetration of gas in the energy balance, such as in Spain and

Turkey, demonstrates the importance of price competitiveness. In both countries, lower taxes on gas sales than on competing fuel oil played a major role in making gas competitive against other fuels and stimulating rapid fuel switching (and also giving the sellers more revenue for investment). For example, in Spain Gas consumption has increased rapidly since the 1970s, reaching 12% of total primary energy supply by 2000. Originally only LNG was consumed, but this is now supplemented by piped gas from Norway and Algeria. The Spanish government has promoted the uptake of natural gas in industry through explicit oil-related pricing and lower taxes on gas (no excise tax) than on oil products (e.g. an excise tax of 40% is levied for light fuel oil). Gas has been consistently much cheaper on a heat equivalent basis than gasoil, and broadly in line with heavy fuel oil prices in recent years. The non-price advantages of gas over fuel oil mean that gas is usually the preferred fuel when an oil or coal boiler is replaced, or for new boilers or direct heat applications.

Again in Turkey for example, natural gas supply (by pipeline and LNG) began in 1992 and reached 16% of TPES in 2000. Gas to industry is priced in relation to heavy fuel oil and is taxed lower than oil products and coal.

Using taxes to implement government policy by influencing commercial decisions by private actors is legitimate as long as the framework is clear, does not discriminate between the actors in the market and is not changed retroactively. This use of taxes is especially justified if differences in taxes reflect differences in environmental externalities and costs, which are not accounted for in market-based prices.

Examples of fiscal measures that foster the development of a gas industry by creating additional volume of demand and/or by increasing investments in the gas industry are:

- Reducing taxes on gas use and giving tax incentives to gas consumers for installing gas appliances and equipment;
- Setting lower excise taxes on gas than on competing fuels;
- Providing tax incentives for re-investment of profits into the gas chain;
- Providing tax exemptions for gas-related investments;
- Reducing or removing taxes on imports of pipeline materials and equipment, which can raise significantly the cost of building transmission lines and local distribution networks;
- Replacing volume-based or revenue-based taxes with profit-based

taxes, to encourage the development of less profitable projects (e.g. marginal fields);

- Removing differences in tax treatment between domestic and foreign companies.

Governments wishing to promote investment in their gas industry should also:

- Periodically review their fiscal terms to ensure that they remain internationally
- Competitive and are consistently applied to all industry participants;
- Streamline the tax system and improve the co-ordination between the central government and provincial and local authorities to avoid the cumulation of taxes;
- Improve the transparency of the tax administration.

Close co-operation between the fiscal authorities and the energy policy institutions is essential to design a taxation regime that appropriately reflects the energy policy objectives of the country.

Natural Gas Regulation

Why Regulate the Gas Sector?

According to IEA there are four main areas where the state may want to set a regulatory framework for the gas sector.

(I) Technical and Health, Safety and Environment (HSE) Regulation

In industries like the oil and gas industries, which have a potentially large impact on health, safety and the environment, the state has a clear role in establishing technical standards and monitoring their implementation. Technical regulation must ensure that market participants are technically qualified to undertake the business, and that the infrastructure is built according to appropriate standards to protect the health and safety of workers and customers, and the environment.

(II) Use of Public Land and Public Streets

Gas production, transportation and distribution are linked to a fixed infrastructure that uses public land and public streets. Hence, the government needs to define rules and eventually charge fees and taxes for the use of public land and public streets.

(III) Resource Management and Rent Sharing

Upstream activities involve the use of non-renewable resources which are typically considered as part of the national assets and which generate an economic rent. Hence, governments normally establish rules and compensations regarding resource management and depletion. Risks and rewards need to be shared according to clear rules, by the government and the companies participating in the exploration and extraction. This is generally achieved by granting the companies extraction rights against the payment of royalties or extra petroleum taxes, over and above the normal corporate income tax.

(IV) Market Imperfections and Externalities (Economic Regulation)

In view of the strong market imperfections and externalities that characterise gas markets, economic regulation is needed to give the right incentives to market participants and to protect consumers against the abuse of dominant market power.

The main gas market imperfections and externalities to be addressed by economic regulation are:

Natural monopolies: Grid-based energy supply activities, such as gas distribution and transmission, have traditionally been considered natural monopolies. The supply of a given commodity is a natural monopoly when economies of scale are such that the costs of supply for the total market are lower if there is a single supplier. This is generally the case for gas distribution, as a duplication of the network by a newcomer would, in the vast majority of cases, be a loss-making enterprise and would be economically inefficient. High-pressure transmission pipelines, however, are not necessarily a natural monopoly, although they do involve large economies of scale and high specificity. Indeed, in a sufficiently large market with a large number of suppliers, gas transmission can be a competitive activity, as a given pipeline may be economically challenged by building a parallel pipeline or by a pipeline on an alternative route.22 However, in small or incipient gas markets, the economies of scale of a pipeline are very large compared to the relevant transportation market and the scope for building a second pipeline over the same route or a competing pipeline from a different supply source will be limited. Given these characteristics, prices charged for distribution and, in some cases, transmission services need to be controlled to prevent the monopoly service provider from exploiting the potential for excessive profits. Storage may also display natural monopoly characteristics, though geology and market size may allow storage services to be provided efficiently by the market.

***Anti-competitive behaviour by gas suppliers*:** There may be concerns about the level of market concentration A dominant company may seek to stifle competition through predatory pricing, especially in the early stages of competition in gas wholesaling and retailing. In the transition from a former state-owned monopolistic industry to a competitive model, regulation is also needed to give new market entrants a fair chance against (former) state-owned companies.

***Supply security issues*:** Security of gas supply can be divided into three risk categories: the short-term risk of disruptions to supplies through the failure of markets to balance supply and demand adequately, the long-term risk that inadequate investment will be made to secure future supplies (noting that short-term security ultimately fails if long-term investment fails); and the risk of inadequate diversity of supply sources in the event of a major disruption from a given source.

***Consumer welfare protection*:** Most governments seek to provide protection to household customers, particularly the poor and disadvantaged.

While there is little difference between countries on technical regulation, the approach to economic regulation varies enormously across countries, reflecting differences in policy objectives, political traditions, institutional and structural factors. Regulation varies considerably from a light-handed or hands-off approach to one characterised by detailed and onerous constraints on gas company activities. The light-handed approach, as in Germany and New Zealand, places primary reliance on general competition law and anti-trust institutions to address anti-competitive behaviour in an *ex post* manner. More detailed regulation, as in the United States, Britain and Argentina, reinforces the foundations provided by competition law with explicit mechanisms to control the behaviour of natural monopolies, including pricing and handling of network access as well as financial and operational performance.

The type of regulatory framework needed also differs significantly depending on the maturity of the gas market. The regulatory framework currently in use in North America, Western Europe and in Argentina is adapted to countries with a well-developed gas industry and markets. It may be premature to adopt a similar one in other South American countries with incipient gas markets.

Principles of Regulation

Before getting into the actual issues pertaining to economic regulation, it is important to discuss the general principles of regulation. Regardless of the chosen approach to regulation and detailed regulatory arrangements, a number of general principles should characterise the regulatory system. These include the rule of law, transparency, neutrality, predictability and consistency, accountability and independence:

The *rule of law:* is the foundation of a regulatory system as it ensures the legitimacy of regulation. Decisions of the regulator should be subject to appeal within the judiciary system.

Transparency: is essential for regulatory quality. Transparency involves the capacity of regulated entities to express views on, identify, and understand their obligations under the rule of law. It is an essential part of all phases of the regulatory process—from the initial formulation of regulatory proposals, to the development of draft regulations, through to implementation, enforcement, and review and reform, as well as the overall management of the regulatory system. Public consultation and accessibility are two key instruments for improving transparency.

Neutrality: means that the regulations should be neutral to all market players without favouring one or another group (non-discrimination).

Predictability and consistency: Rulings and judgements issued by the regulatory authority should be consistent and should have a reasonable degree of predictability based on previous rulings in similar cases.

Independence: of the regulator from the regulated companies is a prerequisite for any sound regulatory system. Independence from government and political actors in the implementation of legislated policy may be desirable to ensure long-term stability of regulatory policies. This independence is critical in countries where there is public ownership of gas utilities. Independence also implies that the regulator needs to be provided with the adequate resources, skills and information.

Accountability: Independence of the regulator must not be confused with lack of accountability. Regulatory agencies, like any other public body, must be held accountable for their actions and must be subject to adequate efficiency controls, especially in those areas not directly related to gas (e.g. general management).

Issues to be Addressed by Economic Regulation

Key elements of the regulatory regime, which may differ significantly across countries, include:

1. Access to networks;
2. Controls on price or rate of return for non-competitive segments;
3. Structure of the sector / unbundling requirements;
4. Regulatory responsibility.

Third Party Access Regime

Third Party Access (TPA) is the right of any third party (a producer, a consumer, a shipper or a trader) to access/make use of the transportation and related services of a pipeline company for a charge (tariff). It entails an obligation for the latter to offer such services, although the extent of such rights and obligations may be limited by relevant legislation. TPA therefore differs significantly from voluntary access, which can take place freely without government intervention. If the economies of scale are large and relevant compared to the size of the transportation market, TPA is the usual method for introducing competition in the transportation segment, by making the transportation accessible for newcomers under the same conditions as the incumbent. TPA may apply to either or both gas distribution and transmission. It may also apply to LNG terminals and storage infrastructure.

There are essentially two types of access regime: regulated and negotiated. In a regulated TPA regime, public authorities (usually the regulator) impose explicit rules on how pipeline companies handle requests for access to the network, and set operational and financial conditions for the use of the system. Under negotiated TPA, on the other hand, market players are free to negotiate the terms and conditions of access. The government may nonetheless play a role in ensuring that negotiated access is effective. For example, it may require the industry to prepare a formal code, setting out essential commercial terms and conditions, including grounds for refusing access. It also normally provides an arbitration mechanism in the event of dispute. TPA, negotiated or regulated may be backed up with requirements for unbundling and information disclosure. Countries may choose one regime for transmission and another for distribution.

The access regimes in North America and Britain are best characterised as regulated TPA. Countries of Continental Europe are just starting to introduce TPA following the adoption of the EU Gas Directive in 1998. The Directive mandates TPA but leaves the choice to each country to decide whether to implement regulated or negotiated TPA. Most countries have opted for regulated TPA.

While TPA works well for existing networks where the investment is in large part amortised, there is an important caveat related to new pipelines. The investor in a pipeline will obviously take some risk, which should either be reflected in his having the exclusive right to use his own investment (at least for some time) or by a risk addition to the tariffs for those using an already existing pipeline to compensate for the risk taken by the original investor. Otherwise, investors might be deterred from investing in new pipelines because of the asymmetry of risk and reward. An alternative way to introduce some competition in the transportation segment while taking into account the need to protect the interest of the original investor is through an open season scheme. Under this scheme, any pipeline project has to be published and interested companies can join the pipeline consortium before construction starts and will get a reserved portion of the pipeline capacity. The pipeline is usually built with some extra capacity, which will be subject to TPA.

In emerging gas markets, when the focus is to provide strong incentives for investments in new infrastructure, it would seem appropriate for governments to offer a degree of protection to investors in high-pressure transmission pipeline, local distribution networks, storage facilities and LNG terminals. Transmission, LNG or distribution companies should not be legally obliged to offer transportation or regasification services to third parties (at least for a given period), although the companies would be free to negotiate such services if they wish. The EU Gas Directive, for example, establishes derogations to TPA requirements for those countries, or areas of countries, which qualify as an emergent market. Derogation may be granted for up to ten years after the first gas supply in the country or in the area.25 The introduction of a TPA regime to encourage gas-to-gas competition should nonetheless remain a longer-term objective, and the government should make its intention and timetable for introducing TPA clear to investors.

The question is different for access to existing infrastructure, especially that of state-owned or formerly state-owned companies. Here the infrastructure was usually not built at an investor's own risk, but was supported by state financing. The arguments developed above for new pipeline infrastructure do not hold in this case, and given the dominant position of state-owned companies or formerly state-owned companies it is usually necessary to ensure TPA to existing infrastructure to allow entry of new market players.

In any case, wherever possible, enabling competition in building new pipelines should be a priority. If a new pipeline can be built economically, there is *a priori* no reason why the incumbent gas pipeline operator should build it, rather than another operator.

To enable competition, the government should not give preference to state companies in assessing applications to develop new transmission pipeline projects. It should also remove the *de facto* monopoly rights over gas transmission that state-owned companies currently enjoy. This would enhance incentives for companies to lower costs and improve the quality of service.

In South America, Argentina has chosen regulated TPA for both transmission and distribution, while Brazil has opted for negotiated TPA for transmission only. An example of a pipeline built under an open season scheme is the GasAndes pipeline linking Argentina and Chile. The consortium includes gas producers, a gas distribution company and a power generator. The expansion of the Bolivia-Brazil pipeline is also planned to be done under an open season scheme, with limitations for the owner of the existing capacity.

Rate Controls

Regulation does not only have to address the rules for TPA, but also the issue of remuneration for the capacity used by a third party. Most countries maintain some form of explicit price controls, either on bundled gas supply or on unbundled transmission, distribution and storage services. These controls are justified by the potential for a natural monopoly company to earn substantial economic rent and the lack of incentives for the monopolistic enterprise to operate efficiently. Such controls may be based explicitly on a calculation by the regulator or other government authority of an appropriate rate of return for the pipeline company.

Where competition has been established in gas supply, price controls only apply to the transmission and distribution business. While the costs of new pipelines are relatively clear-cut and the book value is usually close to the replacement value, the issue is more complicated for older pipelines, especially if they have been devalued by high inflation. In that case, the book value is much lower than the replacement value, and tariff setting will either pass on an undue benefit to a newcomer—if based on book value—or it will create a large profit for the pipeline owner—if based on a replacement value.

Controls on bundled gas-supply prices may be retained provisionally for the dominant supplier until competition has become well established, as in the British residential sector. Some countries, such as Germany, do not explicitly or directly control or regulate prices on the grounds that inter-fuel competition effectively limits the prices that gas companies can charge throughout the gas chain. In New Zealand, there are no explicit ceilings on price or rate of return, but the government may impose price controls on gas companies found to be abusing dominant market position.

In Argentina, the regulator sets maximum tariffs ("price caps") for transportation and distribution on the basis of the cost of providing the service plus a reasonable rate of return on investment. Transmission and distribution companies are free to offer lower tariffs to their clients. However, to ensure transparency and non-discriminatory treatment, they are required to publish their tariffs for different services and customer categories. The price caps are adjusted for inflation every six months and reviewed by the regulator every five years, taking into account efficiency improvements and investments.

The Structure and Unbundling Requirements

The other main issue governments have to address is the structure of the sector, i.e. to what extent vertical and horizontal integration and cross-ownership along the gas chain or with other sectors, e.g. the electricity sector, should be allowed. No single answer or model fits all situations. The appropriate choice for a country will depend on its specific circumstances, in particular on the degree of maturity and the overall size of the market, and on whether the country is a producer or importer of gas. As noted earlier, a key challenge with TPA is to secure non-discriminatory treatment of access seekers and in particular to ensure that an integrated transport company does not discriminate in favour of its own gas supply business. When the owner of the gas pipeline also has interests in production and distribution, it has the ability and the economic incentive to restrict competition in both activities by denying or restricting access to the pipeline to other producers, or by raising the price or lowering the quality of the services it provides to other companies in comparison to those it provides to its own gas supply business. The diversification of upstream activities, as well as true consumer choice, can realistically work only when all producers can have nondiscriminatory access to pipeline transmission to sell their gas.

Unbundling, i.e. the separation of a vertically integrated company's transportation business from gas supply and trading activities, may avoid self-dealing or other forms of discriminatory behaviour. Unbundling also aims at ensuring that costs are correctly allocated to a gas company's different activities, thereby limiting the scope for cross subsidization and facilitating the task of regulating transmission and distribution tariffs. Unbundling can take different forms. From the weakest to the strongest requirement, these are:

Accounting separation: i.e. the requirement for the integrated company to prepare separate accounts for its upstream, midstream and downstream activities. The company should charge itself the same prices for transport services as it does others and should identify prices for the commodity, for transport and for ancillary services.

Management or functional separation: i.e. the requirement for companies involved in various segment of the gas industry to set up separate, distinct divisions or subsidiaries.

Operational separation: Operation of, and decisions about, investments in the transport system are the responsibility of an entity that is fully independent of the gas merchant; ownership of the transmission grid remains with the gas merchant.

Divestiture or ownership separation: gas sales and transport are separated into distinct legal entities with different management, control, and operations; and there is no significant cross-ownership.

Ownership separation solves most concerns because it eliminates both the incentive and the ability to discriminate. It also ensures that each company focuses on its core activity, and allows costs to be better allocated to specific functions. Restrictions to cross-ownership, which have been used in the gas and electricity sectors in several countries, such as Argentina and the United Kingdom, has been shown to be effective in ensuring a level playing field in marketing gas and electricity to local distribution companies.

The "weaker" forms of unbundling reduce, to different extents, the ability to discriminate and may be easier to adopt in some countries, but they do not eliminate the incentive to engage in discriminatory behaviour as effectively as ownership separation. Additional measures to ensure non-discrimination, such as the establishment of "Chinese walls", may be required.

One problem with ownership separation is that it may lead to inefficient investment decisions. Vertical integration offers economies of scope, helps investment synchronisation along the gas chain, minimises transaction costs and reduces the risks associated with the weakness of contractual enforceability. For these reasons, during the early stage of gas market development, when investment in the development of gas reserves and infrastructure is closely tied to specific markets being established, a vertically integrated structure is perhaps the most appropriate. Setting limitations on vertical integration and cross-ownership at this stage could reduce investment and slow the development of the gas market.

Prior to reforms, all countries in South America had high degrees of vertical integration: either one company was responsible for all activities along the gas chain or, in some cases, two companies existed, with transmission being bundled with either the upstream or the distribution segment. Today the situation is far more varied. In Argentina, the law expressly prohibits vertical integration and severely limits cross-ownership along the gas chain. No single player may hold a controlling stake in a company operating in another segment of the gas chain. Transport companies may neither purchase nor sell gas. The same is true in Bolivia, except for projects and operations in remote areas and activities involving the development of new domestic markets, which would not be financially viable in case of vertical disintegration. Colombian law, too, calls for a total separation of gas production, transmission and distribution activities, but implementation is gradual.

At the opposite end of the spectrum is Chile, which does not expressly prohibit vertical integration. Indeed, the state-company ENAP carries out production, transportation and distribution in the southern tip of the country where gas reserves are located. Even in the case of gas imported from Argentina, private consortia, with substantial cross-ownership, carry out transmission and distribution. Brazil and Venezuela opted for functional separation, requiring vertically integrated oil and gas companies to set up separate, distinct divisions or subsidiaries to carry out transmission and distribution activities. There are no limits to cross-ownership and indeed both Petrobras and PDVSA have fully-owned subsidiaries which own and operate their transmission assets.

The Regulatory Responsibility

The regulatory framework that has been described above needs appropriate regulatory institutions to manage it. In most countries around the world, a specialist agency or authority is responsible for implementing the regulatory framework. The authorities' objectives and *modus operandi* are laid down in legislation. Responsibility may be vested in an individual, as in Britain, or in a commission made up of a small number of individuals: five in the United States and Mexico, and three in Italy. Among IEA countries, only New Zealand and Germany have no sector-specific authority and rely *ex-post* on anti-trust authorities to investigate allegations of anti-competitive behaviour under general competition law. Despite significant differences in the approach to regulation, a number of general principles are commonly regarded as desirable in regulatory practice.

Most South American countries now have a regulatory agency dealing with natural gas. In Argentina, it is the *Ente Nacional de Gas* (Enargas), in Bolivia the *Superintendencia de Hidrocarburos*, in Colombia the *Comisión de Regulación de Energía y Gas Combustible* (CREG) and in Venezuela the *Ente Nacional del Gas* (Enagas). In Brazil, upstream oil and gas regulation is carried out at federal level by the *Agência Nacional do Petróleo* (ANP). Downstream regulation, however, is the responsibility of the states, most of which have now created state regulatory agencies, often covering several service industries as well as gas distribution.[28] In Chile, regulatory responsibilities for gas are carried out by the *Comisión Nacional de Energía* (CNE), which also has a policymaking role.

In a growing number of IEA countries, responsibility for regulating the gas and electricity industries is combined in a single body to keep pace with the trend of convergence between gas and electricity industries, as gas-fired power generation plays a growing role in a new gas market and there are clear synergies in the joint supply of gas and electricity to the end consumer. This trend has not yet reached South America.

South American governments will need to decide whether the pace of development of competition in both gas and electricity markets (and the dependence of the gas sector's development on the power sector) warrants the creation of a single agency covering both sectors, or whether to keep two separate agencies (putting in place appropriate co-ordination mechanisms). Independence from electricity regulation may be important, at least in the beginning, to ensure that the specificities of the natural gas sector are properly taken into account. Alternatively, if a joint electricity/gas body is set up, it is important to ensure that it has the appropriate expertise to deal with gas.

A policy directed towards gas market operations and safeguarding public interests is an urgent concern. In complex and dedicated networks such as gas systems, essential facilities are involved, through which controlling parties can obstruct any serious competition by other (potential) suppliers, while exploiting its monopolistic position *vis-à-vis* consumers. At the same time, natural gas projects are delicate ventures as a consequence of their high sunk costs, long repayment periods and vulnerability to variations in supply and demand. In brief, the paradigmatic underpinnings of gas industry regulation, since the end of the 1970s, have undergone a shift from a traditional neo-classical view on the functioning of markets, towards paradigms based on monetarist and public choice theories. The standard neo-classical approach justified state intervention based on the concepts of market failure and public goods, for which welfare maximising decision-making was not to be expected in the gas and power sector.

Traditionally, the natural monopoly character of such services was understood as justification for regulation and public ownership and 'managed' markets (segmentation, concessions and/or exclusive deliveries). Accordingly, the state had to jump in and remedy imperfections and failures, including problems of excessive market power, externalities, lumpy investments, spill-over and so forth. In the US, privately owned utilities were regulated by sector-specific federal and state agencies. In Europe, many utilities had varying degrees of public ownership and/or involvement. The regulators in the US and public ownership in Europe also secured the public interest elements or public values associated with these services, involving issues of safety, security of supply, acceptable prices for specific types of users, objectives of local and sector development, the supply of jobs, and more recently, sustainability and environmental protection.

By the late 1970s and early 1980s, this perspective was replaced by the kind of liberalism associated with the ideas promoted by the governments of Ronald Reagan and Margaret Thatcher. Efficiency, economic reform and political power were sought through tax reductions, 'rolling back the state' and by introducing market-driven competition into the so-called gold-plated industries. Indeed, perfect competition—modelled upon the revised economic textbooks—was to be imposed upon public sectors wherever possible. Gradually, and initially only in a number of Anglo Saxon countries and Chile, free access to consumers and markets, competition in production and retail sectors and privatization were introduced as the basic objectives of structural change in the energy sector. After the adoption of the Single European Market in 1985, these objectives became the points of departure for the European Commission, initially as the key instrument for tearing down the prevailing intra-communal barriers to trade, and later as an objective in its own merit.

Under this paradigm, the conception of a gas supply system as an unbundled liberalised market, with competition in production, services and retail segments, and regulated essential facilities began to emerge. More recently, particularly due to developments in deregulation of utilities in the UK, the Austrian school of economics became involved as an important source of wisdom, providing the basis for dynamic regulation. In contrast with the traditional static equilibrium approach, the Austrian focus is on the dynamic process in competitive markets. As a substitute for competition, price cap regulation (RPI-X) entices operators of regulated essential facilities to bring down their costs, while letting them keep the increased revenues for some time. Yardstick regulation of costs, tariffs, quality, efficient trading and auctioning arrangements are being applied in the gas and electricity industry.

Moreover, a further requirement for 'dynamic' competition and for harnessing its advantages is that new concepts and solutions can be brought into play. Hence, the success of competition is often defined as the number of (new) competitors in the market. Consequently, all new entry is seen as beneficial and accordingly, incumbents must be obliged to sell their products and services as if they were a standalone business, on equal footing with each new entrant. Recently we have been forced to consider a new energy paradigm, due to pressures of, first, the need to modernise and expand the current energy supply systems, and second, the need to adapt the energy system in response to the consequences of global warming by reducing carbon dioxide emissions. These pressures can be perceived as market failures of the (by and large) liberalized international gas/energy market, and as a consequence of externalities, high transaction costs and geopolitics.

The market-based system also promoted a short-term focus on market efficiency, with longer-term security of delivery and supply issues not easily incorporated into companies' market strategies. Helm suggests that these problems could be resolved by: a) the (failing) market, causing very high costs and volatile prices; b) the development of new market-based regulatory concepts; or c) vertical and horizontal integration to reduce the uncertainties of incomplete contracting and asymmetric information. Helm thus explicitly invokes an alternative perspective on economic coordination, the New Institutional Economics (NIE), based on the concept of transaction costs.

The traditional economic theories, referred to above, consider the structure of markets as a crucial driver for the conduct of firms and eventual economic performance. The configuration and relative size of the firm itself was seen merely as a means to acquire economies of scale and scope through vertical and horizontal integration, to the end of achieving market power in up- or downstream markets. The institutional, transaction cost approach takes a broader perspective with regards to the rationale of vertical integration. It considers the shape of firms and the associated structure of markets as alternative arrangements of internal and market governance, to deal with risks involved in transacting.

The adequacy of particular arrangements is seen as dependent on the attributes of individual transactions between buyers and sellers of goods or services in a specific market and how these affect the overall cost of a transaction. Transaction costs include the direct costs of writing, monitoring and enforcing contracts, plus the costs associated with the risk of ex ante investments having an ex post performance that is lower than anticipated, as a consequence of contractual hazards of various types and of the costs associated with internal organisation of the transactions. As stated by Joskow, "The inefficiencies of particular interest are those that arise as a consequence of ex post bargaining, haggling, pricing and production decisions, especially those that arise as the relationship must adapt to changes in supply and demand conditions over time, though inefficiencies in ex ante investments are also relevant." The preferable arrangement of governance structures are those that best fit the character of the transactions involved and the broader context in which these take place. Main characteristics involve, on the one hand, the extent to which parties to a transaction are locked-in, as a consequence of asset specificity. On the other, attributes such as uncertainty, product complexity and information asymmetries also come into play. With respect to asset specificity in the gas industry:

- It can be argued that a large portion of investments are site-specific, often linking up buyers and the seller in tight relationships over the use of the asset;

- Physical asset specificity may also be relevant, particularly when considering the relation between suppliers and end-users, who have invested in boilers and appliances to burn gas of a specific type and composition, or investments in, for example, gas storage or treatment capacity;
- Dedicated assets involve investment by a gas supplier in a remote field to sell a significant amount of gas to a particular (set of) customer(s) at a specific level of revenues, justifying the investment;
- The realisation of lower sales or lower prices would imply an ex post hazard, not anticipated in the investment decision ex ante.

In essence, the idea is that by selecting the right form of governance, whether for a spot-market, a specific contract or a vertically integrated structure, the parties to a transaction will be able to modify the costs of the transaction and exposure to ex ante risks. When, ex ante, it is considered that these costs are not manageable at an acceptable level, the transaction or investment will never likely not materialise, with no additional volumes of natural gas reaching the market. With respect to gas markets, therefore, a leading question would be to what extent the regional/local governance regimes in place reflect the characteristics of the several types of transactions arising within the regional gas markets. It may emerge that the efficient development of markets of a different nature, maturity and risk profile may require different structures of governance, instead of one single market design geared towards a fully competitive market.

Regarding the regulatory perspective, the question seems to arise as to how this new institutional paradigm can to a greater degree contribute to future gas market regulation. Currently, much of the regulator's toolkit and the framework for competition policy are based on the former paradigm of 'full unbundling' and maximum entry in competitive segments. Nevertheless, in the daily practice of regulation, elements of the transaction cost-based approach are already incorporated, such as the conditional allowance of exemptions and large-scale mergers. Moreover, the New Institutional (or transaction cost) Economics, also underscores abuse of market power as a strategy, which depending on the circumstances should be tackled by regulatory intervention.

Generally, regulatory literature seems more advanced in incorporating elements of the transaction cost approach, as will be briefly outlined below.

What conclusions should be drawn from these developments? The observations suggest the need for a careful New Institutional reassessment of coordination mechanisms, which are considered to be less beneficial for consumers under 'structure-conduct-performance' approaches. This, of course, should also involve an analysis of their potential market distortion, as there may exist a trade-off between the stability provided by a dominant position and the potential for abuse. A further question would be whether there exists a trade-off between the various components of a governance structure, such as the degree of integration or unbundling, the regulated or 'free' determination of contract prices and tariffs, destination clauses and regulated access to markets, take-or-pay provisions, etc. Is it necessary to arrive at particular 'packages' of measures of governance? Is it possible that a 'workable' balance between the required investments, the anticipated profits and risk and the costs of governance can be struck, while preferably maintaining a credible pressure of the dynamically competitive market?

Regulatory Reforms

The use of gas is expanding rapidly in most economies, particularly for electric power generation. Combined cycle gas turbines provide an economical and highly efficient means of producing electricity with low emissions of atmospheric pollutants and modest emissions of carbon dioxide. As a result, natural gas has often become the fuel of choice for meeting growing electricity needs.

Although most regions continue to be supplied mainly with the indigenously produced gas, the share of gas supply that is traded between regions grows sharply, from 13 per cent in 2005 to 22 per cent in 2030. This thus calls for more competitive markets internationally and nationally.

World over many countries are moving towards more competitive natural gas markets. Well functioning energy markets that ensure secure energy supplies at competitive prices are key to achieve growth and consumer welfare. The process of market opening has significantly changed the functioning of the markets, provided new market opportunities, led to the introduction of new products and services. Increasingly countries, sooner or later will have to move towards a more competitive framework.

The European Union has already embarked upon restructuring their gas markets. For instance, introduction of competition in Europe's gas markets is an integral part of European energy policy which is directed at achieving the three closely related objectives of a competitive and efficient energy sector, security of supply and sustainability. In accordance with the European Directives, all member states have opened their electricity and gas markets to competition from 1st July 2007. Though many are still under various stages of implementation, the sectoral trend is unambiguous.

Unbundling operations are an interesting trend that the gas markets are currently witnessing, as part of the regulatory reform process. Economic evidence shows that full ownership unbundling is the most effective means to ensure choice for energy users and encourage investment. This is because separate network companies are not influenced by overlapping supply/ generation interests as regards investment decisions. It also avoids overly detailed and complex regulation and disproportionate administrative burdens.

In US the unbundling was initiated way back in 1980s, when large industrial customers and electric utilities were given access to competitively priced natural gas from non-utility gas suppliers, or gas marketers, by state regulators. The customer choice programme of the US is also referred to as unbundling programmes. Under the US customer choice programme, home and small businesses can choose their supplier of natural gas, much as they choose their long-distance telephone provider.

REGULATORY FRAMEWORK KEY FOR MARKET DEVELOPMENT: UNITED STATES

The United States has the oldest and largest gas market in the world. In 2000, gas consumption reached 638 bcm/y. About 84% of this supply is produced domestically, with the balance either imported by pipeline from Canada (15%) or through LNG imports (1%). The share of natural gas in the energy mix was 24%. The industrial sector is the largest consumer of natural gas (42%), followed by the residential and commercial sectors (37%) and electricity generation (13%). The remainder is consumed by the gas industry itself. The US gas market is the most open (at the wholesale level) and mature market in the world. There are thousands of gas producers and millions of consumers. Gas production is concentrated in the south, along the Gulf Coast in Louisiana and Texas, with smaller producing regions in Alaska, the southwest, and central US. Though Texas and Louisiana consume large amounts of gas, most natural gas consumers are located in the northeast, the Midwest, and the Pacific coast, where Canadian imports play an important role. The geographic imbalance between producers and consumers means that large quantities of natural gas must be transported long distances across the country. The US has the most extensive gas pipeline system in the world: 330,000 km in 2000. Natural gas pipelines are privately owned, often by large corporations. Local distribution systems are also privately owned, usually by investors and municipalities. The history of the US gas industry can be divided into the following four eras:

1910-1950: Era of Market Development

The US natural gas market emerged after World War I as a result of the huge gas resources from oil discoveries. It was able to develop because of the existence of large town gas systems and the industrial ability to weld steel pipes making it possible to connect new sources of supply with existing markets despite long distances. The structure was relatively simple. It was characterized by long-term contracts between producers and major consumers, short-distance field-to-city-gate pipelines owned by distributors, and the latter's franchise in exclusive areas under cost-plus state regulation. Nevertheless, economic and regulatory barriers remained, given that the gas industry was not regulated at the federal level but at the state level. This made it difficult to build and operate a pipeline across state borders. In order to overcome this barrier, the US Congress passed the Natural Gas Act in 1938 and established a federal regulatory body, the Federal Power Commission (which later became the Federal Energy Regulatory Commission, FERC) with the power to regulate interstate commerce, construction of pipeline facilities and transportation costs. Regulations were basically designed to ensure reliable supply at reasonable prices.

1950-mid-1970s: Era of Regulation

The 1938 Act was amended by a Supreme Court Decision in 1954, imposing the regulation of prices at well-heads for interstate commerce. Unfortunately, prices were set too low (0.5 \$/MBtu), which discouraged the development of gas resources. At the same time, gas demand was booming in the US economy. This resulted in a supply crisis during the winter of 1976-77 in the mid-west and north-east.

Late 1970s—Early 1980s: Era of Regulatory Failure

The 1978 Natural Gas Policy Act addressed the issue of low gas prices by providing incentives in the form of high prices for production from new gas or unconventional resources. A complex interstate pricing system was introduced which differentiated between expensive gas from newly developed fields and cheap gas from old fields. It also imposed different price ceilings on different gas supplies (up to 29 types of gases!). Since gas prices from new fields were based on costs plus a reasonable rate of return, companies had little incentive to operate efficiently. Gas production boomed, but a number of other problems were caused:

- First, gas prices were artificially raised, on average by a factor of 8 within a decade, which significantly curbed demand.
- Second, the drop in gas demand1, combined with the prohibition of gas use in new industrial boilers and electric power plants by the 1978 "Power Plant and Industrial Fuel Use Act", led to a surplus of gas supply or the so called "US gas bubble".
- Third, pipeline companies—which were allowed to buy gas at well-head, transport it through their own networks and sell it to customers—all contracted long-term take-or pay agreements, and those contracts were based on largely over-estimated future gas demand. The significant drop in gas demand thus caused severe financial difficulties in pipeline companies as they were no longer able to take delivery of the contract quantities and sell them profitably. This led to a crisis of the entire gas industry in the 1980s.

Late 1980s—Present: Era of Adjustment/Restructuring/Deregulation

In the second half of the 1980s and throughout the 1990s, Congress passed new acts deregulating the gas industry and moving towards a more market-oriented approach.

- First, in 1985, the FERC adopted Order No. 436, which introduced open access to interstate pipeline transportation.
- In 1987, Congress repealed the 1978 Power Plant and Industrial Fuel Use Act, and in 1989 well-head prices were scheduled to be fully decontrolled by 1st January 1993 under the Natural Gas Well-head Decontrol Act.
- In 1992, the FERC adopted Order No. 636, which required interstate pipelines to unbundle natural gas sales from pipeline transportation by setting up separate affiliates to handle these

activities. Order No. 636 also enhanced the method for calculating transportation tariffs and introduced a capacity release programme, which forced incumbent companies to release pipeline capacity to competitors. The decontrolling of well-head prices and the two orders (436 and 636) dramatically changed the operation of the gas industry from tight regulation to free competition in the wholesale market, thus introducing the main principles that are now commonly applied in mature markets.

- In 2000, the FERC adopted Order No. 637, which further refined the remaining pipeline regulations and addressed inefficiencies in the capacity release programme.

This policy of market deregulation was a success. Gas production has increased by a dramatic 31% since 1989 when well-head prices were fully decontrolled. After more than ten years of deregulation, the US market is fully liberalised at the wholesale level and is very competitive. Producers, pipeline companies, marketers, distribution companies and large consumers trade natural gas for immediate delivery and forward delivery in a large number of regional markets. Most trading takes place in spot markets at major market centres and hubs on interstate pipelines, the most important being Henry Hub in Louisiana. Based on trade of forward gas at gas hubs, financial markets for gas futures and options, the most widely traded futures use Henry Hub as a reference. Important trading activity also occurs in financial gas markets (futures and options).

The US example demonstrates how the regulatory framework plays a key role in the development of the gas industry: it may contribute to setting free the dynamic forces of competition or on the contrary it may inhibit its development. Regulation must be in line with the state of development of the market. Price-setting is the most difficult issue. The US experience also shows that there is a role for both government and market forces and that their respective roles must be clearly defined. Market forces should be allowed to prevail where competition is present. The correct role for government is to establish a framework to encourage investment in production and infrastructure development and to protect captive customers against the misuse of market power. Where competition exists, the market, rather than the government or regulators, is in the best position to determine price and allocation.

Inter-fuel Competition

Gas is often the preferred fuel for power generation in OECD countries. Gas-fired generation, mainly in combined-cycle gas turbines (CCGT), is projected to meet 76% of their incremental electricity demand between 1997 and 2020. The predominance of natural gas is explained by a number of advantages over other fuels including coal, oil, nuclear power and hydropower:

Lower investment cost: In OECD countries, per kW investment cost of a CCGT plant is only half that of a typical coal-fired plant and is much lower than that of nuclear or hydropower stations. This, combined with the relatively low price and the abundant supply of gas in countries like the US, the UK, and the Netherlands, makes gas the cheapest option for power generation compared to coal and nuclear in such OECD countries.

Higher energy conversion efficiency: CCGT plants can typically achieve 50-55% of nameplate efficiency with the highest level of 60% being tested, whereas the best coal-fired power plant can only achieve an efficiency level in the range of 40-45%.

Lower level of environmental emissions: Replacing a coal-fired generation plant with a gas-fired combined cycle unit can eliminate SO_2 emissions, cut CO_2 emissions by two thirds, cut NOx by 95%, reduce particulate matters by 99% and eliminate solid waste.

Other technical advantages including: (a) Sort lead-time in construction (2-3 years compared to 4-5 years for coal and 6-10 years for nuclear); (b) modularity and low economics of scale, meaning that small units could have the same economic advantages as large units; (c) flexibility for load management as gas-fired units can be used both for base load and peak load, and their ability to start and stop quickly make them excellent means for peak shaving; and (d) smaller requirement for land occupation and cooling water, which, together with their cleanness, allows their installation in densely populated areas.

Fuel Switching: the UK Experience

During the winter of 2005–06, gas prices rose to exceptionally high levels in the UK due to a combination of supply shortfall and lack of storage availability. Some 30 parties obtained temporary permission from the Environment Agency for fuel switching and Grain and Fawley oil-fired power plants were granted derogations from rules capping their generation. The Agency dealt with requests for permanent changes to allow fuel switching from 21 industrial parties and 5 combined cycle gas turbines. The larger the installation, the more investment and manpower are required to maintain the capability to switch fuels. The Peterhead power station in Scotland which, although designed to burn either gas or fuel oil (gas oil and heavy fuel oil), had not used the latter for more than 10 years. Because of the price differential between gas and oil products, the station burned heavy fuel oil for the entire winter and was forced to overcome significant problems with the provision of equipment and supplies of fuel oil, placing significant strains on the staff at the plant.

The result of gas prices at levels which should have meant that any user able to switch from gas to another fuel certainly would have done, was seen mainly in the choice of power station fuels. While gas used in power generation increased slightly during the winter quarters of 2005–06 compared with 2004–05, use of fuel oil nearly doubled (from 0.7mt in 2004–05 to 1.27mt in 2005–06) and coal increased by 15 percent (2.7mt oil equivalent). In the industrial sector the data are confusing; total coal use in industry increased by nearly 60 percent while oil use increased by 15 percent suggesting that some gas load did switch fuels, although this only amounted to relatively small quantities of actual demand of less than half a million tons of oil and around 700GWh of coal.12 What these statistics do not adequately reflect is the closure of industrial plants using gas for feedstock, particularly nitrogen and ammonia producers, and changes in overall economic activity for reasons unrelated to energy prices.

In summary, in response to very substantial price and availability incentives, fuel switching amounted to around 1.5mt of additional oil product demand and around 3.5mt of additional coal demand, most of which can be assumed to have switched from gas. While the UK experience cannot be automatically assumed to apply to Continental European countries, some of the same observations seem likely to be relevant.

Trends in the Natural Gas Markets

Increased Penetration of LNG

The low density of natural gas makes it more costly to contain and transport than either oil or coal. Prior to the development of liquefied natural gas (LNG) technology, the transportation of natural gas was limited to movements that could be served by pipeline. Gas was unable to utilise that mainstay of international oil trade—marine transportation. The development of LNG has changed all that, and with the improvements in technology and costs, gas is rapidly becoming an internationally traded commodity.

Trade movements of LNG have increased consistently over the last few years. For instance, the trade movements have increased from 177.95 BCM in 2004 to about 211.08 BCM in 2006. A number of factors have combined to stimulate the renewed interest in LNG, namely the Combined cycle power generation for growing electric power markets, the effects of technology on cost reduction making previously uneconomic trades attractive, environmental concerns, embrace of gas by previously "gas poor" economies, growing concern for traditional supplies in the face of growth and the "stranded gas" phenomenon.

High natural gas prices will stimulate the construction of new LNG terminal capacity, resulting in a significant increase in LNG import capacity. IEA sees an unprecedented increase in capital spending on new LNG projects between 2005 and 2010 and the biggest increase in capacity ever. A massive 167 million tonnes (226 BCM) per year of new liquefaction capacity is under construction or is planned to come on stream by 2010, involving about $ 73 billion of investment. If all these projects come to fruition, capacity would almost double to 345 Mt/year. Interestingly enough with all the resultant impediments in fruition of various LNG projects, the number of proposed LNG projects continues to grow more rapidly than the number of long distance pipeline projects.

Decreasing Long-term Contracts

The process of liberalization and market integration currently on the way in continental Europe with the ambition to create a functioning internal market for electricity and natural gas is very similar to the developments implemented some 20 years ago in the US and some 10 years ago in the UK. Thus, the developments in these two countries serve as a benchmark for the developments to expect in continental Europe. Empirical evidence on the changing nature of long-term contracts in the US and the UK suggests an inverse relation between gas sector liberalization and contract length. In both countries, long-term contracts between gas producers and wholesale buyers have lost "market share" although long-term contracts do not entirely disappear with market liberalization. Average contract length has shortened significantly from 20-25 years down to approximately 8-15 years.

Decreasing Capital Intensity

Natural gas production is generally carried out in places remote from demand centers. Transportation usually takes place through pipelines or by ship in the form of liquefied natural gas (LNG). As transportation technology improves and economies of scale are reaped upstream, mid-stream and downstream, the capital intensity of the natural gas value-added chain has significantly diminished over the past decades. This is particularly the case for LNG, but it also holds for traditional pipeline technology. In the LNG chain, investment costs per unit of output (million British thermal units, MBtu), has decreased from well above $ 4.50/MBtu in the early 1990s, to about $ 3/MBtu in 2006.

Costs have thus reduced significantly across the chains, for example in liquefaction, shipping and regasification, among others. This decreasing investment intensity leads to a lower risks in the industry, and should thus be expected to have a negative effect on contract duration.

Diminishing Asset Specificity of Investment

Distinct from lower capital costs is the issue of the changing nature of the asset specificity. In the "old days" of the emerging natural gas industry, the emergence of international natural gas trade between large producers (such as Canada or Russia) and consumers (such as the US and Western Europe) required investments in the upstream natural gas fields, pipeline infrastructure, and a downstream distribution network. These investments were often project specific, leading to high asset specificity and, subsequently the well known issues of quasi-rent negotiations, which were often resolved by the use of long-term contracts.

But increasingly the market structures in upstream, midstream and downstream is changing leading to a reduction in asset specificity. For instance, Upstream contracts are no longer field-specific, but related to the overall natural gas exports of a country or a producer. Thus the investments are no longer contract-specific, that is a given field can be used to serve a variety of contracts. The decreasing asset specificity of natural gas trade related investments implies a reduced reliance on long-term contracts to resolve potential hold-up conflicts.

The Indian Context

India is fast emerging as the focal point for the future development of the Asian Natural Gas Market. In recent years, the Indian gas sector has received a progressively growing attention from global companies and has made rapid strides. The rapid growth of the Indian Economy in the Xth Five Year Plan has greatly contributed to the development of the Indian Energy Sector as a whole and provided major triggers for the growth of the gas sector as well. While gas occupies only about 9-10% of the total energy basket, primarily due to supply constraints all these years, the scenario is fast changing.

Gas occupies about 8.5% of the total energy basket of the country. This is much lesser than the world average of 24%. However the scenario is fast changing in the country largely because of the expected increase in the availability of natural gas in the country. The structure of primary energy consumption in India shows that coal (51%) dominates as the major energy source. Hydrocarbon (45%) is the next available energy provider of the nation. Natural gas is fast emerging as an alternative; it meets around 9% of the primary energy needs. Considering the global trend of shift in energy axis from oil to gas, the share of gas in consumption pattern, in the Indian increase gradually in the days to come.

Energy prices are likely to face continued upward pressure, reflecting fundamental changes in demand, supply and geopolitics making significant changes in energy equation. Increase in energy consumption is an index of economic growth. Still, the challenge remains, as India have to support the energy needs for about 1/6 of the global population. Majority of Indian population reside in villages, many of which are quite remote and it is a challenge to cater to their energy needs, be it electricity or supply of petroleum products. The following thrust points, discussed under respective industry segment, merit consideration for the healthy overall development of the oil and gas industry.

The Availability of Gas

Government of India has adopted a multi-pronged strategy to augment gas supplies and bridge the gap between supply and demand for the domestic market. These cover:

- Intensification of domestic E&P activities;
- LNG Imports;

- Exploitation of unconventional sources like Coal Bed Methane (CBM);
- Underground coal gasification;
- Implementation of Natural Gas Hydrate Programme (NGHP) for evaluation of hydrate resources and their possible commercial exploitation; and
- Gas sourcing through transnational gas pipelines.

The E&P activities have been intensified following the New Exploration Licensing Policy. 6 bidding rounds have been successfully undertaken. A total of 162 blocks have been awarded in shallow water, deep waters and onland areas to PSUs, JVs and foreign companies till date. The initial results have been very encouraging, with gas discoveries in Cambay basin, KG offshore and Mahanadi basin. Similarly, significant oil reserves have been discovered in Rajasthan. It is expected that more hydrocarbon discoveries would materialize in the coming years as more and more investment is attracted in E&P activities. Pursuant to LNG coming under 'OGL', a Joint Venture Company, viz., Petronet LNG Limited (PLL), promoted by ONGC, GAIL, IOCL & BPCL, was formed in order to import LNG and to set up an LNG regasification plant at Dahej. PLL has already tied up LNG import with Ras Gas of Qatar for 5 MMTPA. As on date, around 18 MMSCMD of regasified LNG is supplied by PLL out of the import of 5 MMTPA from Qatar. Another 2.5 MMTPA of LNG would be available from Qatar from 2009 onwards. PLL is also sourcing spot cargoes from the international market. PLL has proposed to expand the capacity of LNG terminal at Dahej to 10 MMTPA. The feasibility of importing LNG from other sources, such as Qatar, Iran, Algeria and Australia, etc, is being pursued to meet the requirement of additional gas.

The Xth Plan period saw some significant developments in the Gas supply side scenario. There were indeed some significant milestones. A world-class gas discovery of 8-14 tcf was announced in 2002 in the KG basin on the East Coast of India. This is significant because this was the first major gas discovery in the recent times after the ONGC discoveries of the 1970's which were developed over almost 2 decades. LNG hit the shore of India in early 2004 when the first shipment arrived in India for re-gasification in the Dahej Re-Gasification terminal of PLL. With the advent of LNG and progressive de-regulation of the gas prices, the natural gas sector in India was moving towards certain degree of maturity with better understanding of the pricing mechanisms. Reflecting this, the first spot cargo of LNG brought in by GAIL truly launched India on the global gas map with global suppliers showing serious interest on the Indian Gas Sector. On the infrastructure front, GAIL announced its plans of creating a National Gas Grid, a backbone Inter-state gas transmission infrastructure to provide arterial energy flow across the nation. Further discoveries in 2005/06 on the KG basin have further enhanced the prospects of strong domestic gas supplies in the coming years.

The Infrastructure

Supporting the demand and supply expectations, is the critical imperative for the creation of a strong infrastructure backbone in terms of a National Gas Grid, a network of pipelines across the country connecting multiple sources to every market and paving the way for arterial energy flow in the country. Some of the segments of the pipeline infrastructure is already under implementation. On the supply side, there are two LNG terminals at Dahej and Hazira in Gujarat, which are already operational with a total existing capacity of 7.5 MMTPA. The third terminal in Dabhol with a capacity of 5 MMTPA is under commissioning. There is another terminal at Kochi, which is taking a final shape for implementation.

In terms of Transmission pipelines, there is an existing network of 6300 km including the HVJ network, Dahej-Vijaipur pipeline and other regional networks. During the Xth Plan, pipelines like the DVPL, Kelarus-Malanpur pipeline, Thulendi-Phulpur pipeline got commissioned. In the light of the emergence of multiple sources of gas with multiple specifications and the creation of complex network of pipelines, GAIL took the initiative of implementing a state of the art National Gas Management Centre (NGMC) in Noida in 2005-06, which would the nodal centre for gas supply control across the country and customer level gas balancing. This nodal NGMC is linked to seven Regional centres, which are also operation.

The City gas distribution sector has simultaneously grown with the gas sector growth. From coverage of two cities at the beginning of the Xth Plan, the city coverage has grown to 10 in 2005-06 across the western, northern and southern regions of the country. Currently there is a total city gas distribution network of about 6000 km closer to the transmission network. As far as CNG supplies are concerned, there are 278 stations dispensing CNG in the country and is expected to continuously grow in the coming years.

The Gas Demand

The power and fertilizer sectors have been core consumers of natural gas. These two sectors together consume about 69 per cent of the gas today. The balance goes to industrial units where it replaces mostly liquid fuels. Gas is also supplied to the residential and the commercial sectors in Mumbai, Delhi and a few towns of Gujarat, Assam and Tripura. The Sub Group on Gas Hydrocarbon Vision-2025 also estimated the long-term gas demand. According to this report, as against the requirement of 151 MMSCMD in 2001-02, the domestic gas supply was 70 MMSCMD. The report forecast that in future, the demand supply gap would continue to exist, which will have to be met from imports and increase in domestic production. The HYV projects a demand of 391 MMSCMD by 2025.

Looking at the current demand pattern, the power sector share in gas demand is continuously on the increase in the last five years. Based on the gas consumption levels of 34 bcm IN 2005-06, the share of power sector is about 40% (13.6 bcm; 37.2 MMSCMD). At the same time, the fertilizer sector share has declined from around 35% in 2002-03 to about 29% in 2005-06, while simultaneously the other sectors like City Gas/CNG, Petrochemicals and industrials showing good increase in consumption share. In the Fertilizer sector about 58% of production is based on gas Power Sector, whereas about 11% of total power generation of about 1,26,800 MW is based on gas. The corresponding figures in the Petrochemicals and LPG/Liquid Hydrocarbon sectors are 43% and 31% respectively. This clearly indicates the huge potential for gas consumption in the end use sectors, especially driven by the power sector. While power and Fertilizer would continue to be the anchor markets through the XIth plan period, the industrial and city gas sectors would be the growing market.

Power Sector

Power sector constitutes the single largest chunk of the overall demand for natural gas in India. As per Ministry of Power estimates, while over 10,900 MW generation capacities has been established on gas by 2005-06, if the capacity based on the liquid fuels is also taken into consideration the overall generation capacity of 13,580 MW is presently based on gas & liquid fuels. Bulk of it is on base load and runs on combined cycle operation. During 2006-07 an additional 3225 MW of gas based generation capacity is getting added

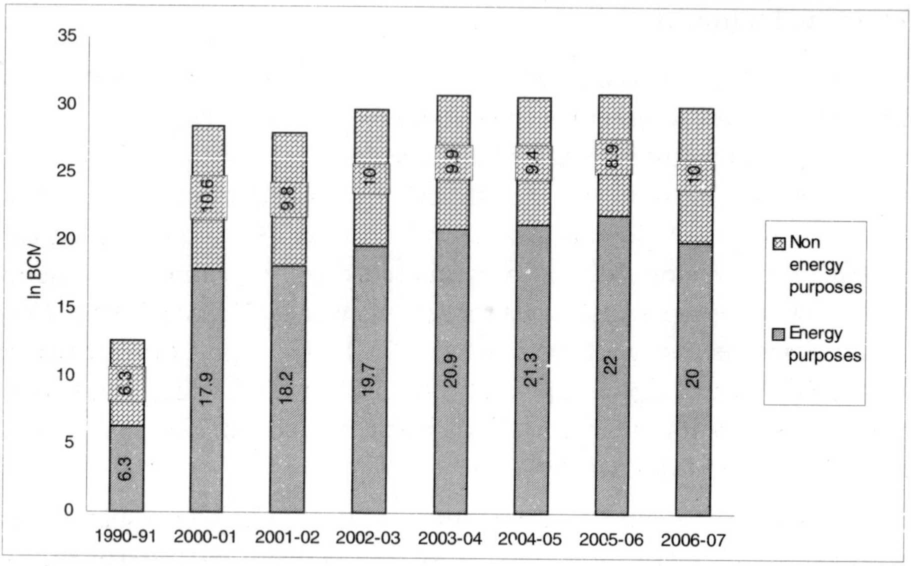

Source: Basic Petroleum Statistics, 2006-07.

Figure 4.4

and availability of gas would be definitely be critical for operating these plants on full load.

The over all natural gas demand for the power sector by the end of X th plan has been estimated by ministry of power as 68.19 MMSCMD, taking into consideration the new capacity addition during the year 2006-07. Depending on the supply position of natural gas the first priority of the sector would be to run existing gas based power plants to achieve the desired PLF of 90%.

Further, depending on the increased availability of gas & prices being reasonable decision to add more capacity based on gas would be taken for the eleventh plan period. It has also been estimated by the Department of Power that during the XIth plan period the addition to existing capacities would be of the order of 70000 MW, out of this 1889 MW of gas based power generation capacity would be definitely added, which would take the gas based generation capacity to 17819 MW during the XIth plan period. Department of Power had also undertaken an exercise to identify gas based projects likely benefits from which could accrue during the XIth plan period and beyond. The estimated capacity for these gas-based power plants is of the order of 31765 MW. Thus the overall new gas based capacity addition identified for future during XIth/XIIth plan periods by the power sector are of the order of 33,655 MW. The magnitude of gas requirement for all these plants would be of the order of 100-120 MMSCMD, when the plants are set-up.

Reasonable Price and Assured availability of long-term would however largely influence the ultimate gas demand in the power sector. Accordingly, gas availability over long-term at reasonable price levels along with stability in the price would be the key factor in the future demand and actual use of natural gas in the power sector.

Gas Demand and Supply Analysis

Gas Demand in India continues to be influenced by the dynamics and cost economics vis-a-vis other fuels pertaining to each of the end use sectors like power and fertilizer sectors primarily.

Power Sector Analysis

The power sector is going to the major sector providing the anchor demand for natural gas. The power Ministry has set in an ambitious target of 70,000 MW for the 5 year period ending 2012, the terminal year of the 11th of Plan. The current thermal power generation is about 90,800 MW, of which 12% (10,900MW) is gas based. As per the Ahluwalia report, the power generation is expected to touch around 157200 MW by 2012 from the current level of about 90800 MW. In short, about 67,000 MW is expected to be added during the period 2006 to 2012. The existing demand for gas as per the current estimates by the Industry and MoPNG in the power sector is about 48-50 MMSCMD in 2005-06 and 70 MMSCMD in 2006-07.

At the current levels, the power sector generation based on gas is about 12% today and projected to increase to 20% by 2032, as per Dr. Kirit Parikh Report 2006. Assuming that the power generation based on gas would increase from 12% to 20% between now and 2032 and taking into consideration the bright prospects for gas supply in the next 5 years, the power generation based on gas is projected to increase faster in the XIth plan period and more slowly in the later period. From a level of 12%, it is assumed that the share would touch about 16% in this period. Keeping *the* above power capacity additions during the XIth plan and percent gas based capacity shares in view, the power sector gas demand is expected to grow at least at the rate of 10% per annum in the XIth plan period based on new generation capacities. Besides, the existing plants also have a potential to switch over from liquid fuels to Gas. In this context, there would be additional gas demand to the tune of 6-8 MMSCMD. Putting them together, the projected gas demand estimates are given below.

Table 4.2

	2007-08	2008-09	2009-10	2010-11	2011-12
Gas demand (mmscmd)	80	88	100	112	125

Fertilizer Sector Analysis

It has been well established that natural gas is the most cost effective fuel vis-a-vis other liquid fuels in the Fertilizer Sector. It is estimated that in the year 2004-05, the gas based fertilizer (urea) production accounts for 66% of the total fertilizer production. Naphtha and FO/LSHS based production accounts for the balance 34%. At the same time, the percent subsidy share of gas-based production is 38% compared to the share of 62% for the liquid feedstock. This is essentially due to the cost effectiveness of gas vs other feedstock. Keeping this in view, Dept of Fertilizers has proposed the case for switch over to 100% natural gas in the fertilizer sector, which is expected to give a push to gas demand in this sector during the XIth Five Year Plan. Based on this premise, the estimated urea demand and the corresponding gas demand for the XIth Plan Period is given below.

Table 4.3

	2007-08	2008-09	2009-10	2010-11	2011-12
Urea demand (lakh tones)	249.51	257.09	264.88	272.92	281.23
Gas demand (mmscmd)	40.82	42.65	52.24	79.36	79.36

Purely looking at it from the point of view of projected gas availability from existing sources for the fertilizer sector, there is an expected progressive decline from the existing sources from about 27 MMSCMD in 2007-08 to a level of about 18 MMSCMD in 2011-12. Given the growth in expected demand in the XIth Plan period for gas in fertilizer sector, the gas shortfall could increase from 20 MMSCMD in 2007-08 to a level of about 60 MMSCMD in 2011-12. In this context, the gas supplies from domestic sources would have to grow fast to meet the increasing demand in this sector

The City Gas Sector

This is another sector, which is going to be potential growth sector. Worldwide, gas distribution is an area, which has grown hand in hand with the gas sector development in terms of supply infrastructure and transmission infrastructure. With the expected growth in the gas supply side and the simultaneous creation of gas inter-state transmission infrastructure in India, this sector is bound to grow in the XIth Plan period. The emphasis on clean environment and the government's keenness to introduce gas distribution infrastructure policy, this sector would get the necessary thrust in the coming years. In line with this, various players, primarily led by GAIL, have drawn up ambitious plans to roll out city gas infrastructure across a number of cities in the country. From the existing coverage of 10 cities, the coverage is expected to grow to 40 cities in the next 5-7 years time frame with a projected investment of about Rs. 9220 crore. With such a level of expansion expected, this sector can be expected to grow at double digit rates in the later part of the XIth plan period. The current estimates of demand in this sector is about 11 MMSCMD in 2006-07 and 12.08 MMSCMD in 2007-08 as per the industry/ government estimates. Assuming a conservative annual growth of 8%, the demand would go to about 12.93 mmscmd, 13.83 mmscmd, 14.8 MMSCMD and 15.83 mmscmd in 2008-09, 09-10, 10-II and 2011-12.

Petrochemicals and other Consumers

The estimated demand as per the current industry estimates in Petrochemicals/Refineries and Internal Consumption (of Gas Industries) sectors is about 25.37 mmscmd in 2005-06. These industries are estimated to grow in line with the economic growth. Hence an annual growth rate of about 7% is assumed during the XIth plan period, which would result in a demand of 33.25 mmscmd by the terminal year of the XIth Plan. Similarly, the sponge iron/steel sector is also expected to grow at the same rate of 7% from the current level of 6 MMSCMD, reaching a level of 7.86 MMSCMD by the terminal year of the XIth plan.

Table 4.4

	2007-08	*2008-09*	*2009-10*	*2010-11*	*2011-12*
Power	80	88	100	112	125
Fertlizers	40.82	42.65	52.24	79.36	79.36
City gas	12.08	12.93	13.83	14.80	15.83
Industrial	15	16.05	17.17	18.38	19.66
Petrochemicals / Other users	25.37	27.15	29.05	31.08	33.25
Sponge Iron/Steel	6	6.42	6.87	7.35	7.86
Total	179.27	193.19	219.16	262.96	280.98

Natural Gas Regulation in the Indian Context

Historically, the government has regulated prices and investments in the Indian oil and gas sector. However, in the past few years, the government has moved towards a market driven economy by withdrawing the restrictions imposed on investments and by decontrolling the prices falling under the Administrative Price Mechanism. The government also mooted a proposal for a common regulatory body for the natural gas and the petroleum sector. The Indian gas market is presently in a transition from an administered control regime to a market driven system. Under the new policy framework in the upstream side, the New Exploration and Licensing policy (NELP) and the Coal Bed Methane (CBM) policy are under operation, and companies are free to market the gas produced from the indigenous blocks (acquired by bidding process) directly in the domestic market at market determined prices. The import of gas through LNG and cross border pipeline gas imports are under Open General License (OGL), and companies are free to market the imported gas at market-determined prices. However, the gas produced by the National E&P companies (ONGC, OIL) from the blocks acquired by them on nomination basis is under administered pricing mechanism. Shortly the domestic gas prices are also expected to progressively move towards a market based pricing system.

With the policy shift towards economic liberalization, globalization and promotion of international competitiveness, the Indian economy promises to become one of the most dynamic economies in the world. In the emerging scenario, foremost is the Indian Petroleum Sector, which is gearing itself to meet the ever-growing and large demands of the economy with world-class product standards and efficiency. Historically, the government has regulated prices and investments in the Indian oil and gas sector. However, in the last few years, the government has moved towards a market driven economy by withdrawing the restrictions imposed on investments and by progressively de-controlling the prices falling under the Administrative Price Mechanism. During the Xth Plan period, India indeed moved towards a market driven gas economy, with controlled prices being applicable only on certain fixed volumes of ONGC/OIL gas being supplied to Power and Fertilizer sectors and small consumers.

As the sector opened up, Government took the initiative to put together a regulatory framework, which took shape during most of the Xth Plan period and finally, the Petroleum and Natural Gas Regulatory Board Act was enacted in early 2006.

The Regulatory Act

Regulatory reforms permit and encourage market forces to enhance competition and produce a more competitive and efficient industry structure. Natural Gas Pipelines and City Gas Distribution lines, being part of the backbone infrastructure of the economy, need a robust regulatory framework in order to curb monopolistic tendencies among the owners while ensuring a fair price to the consumers and fair return to the owner/producers. Thus, the Petroleum Regulatory Board Bill was introduced in the 13th Lok Sabha in May 2002 for the establishment of a Petroleum Regulatory Board to regulate specified activities relating to petroleum, petroleum products and natural gas consequent to deregulation of Petroleum Sector from April 1, 2002. The Bill was later renamed as Petroleum and Natural Gas Regulatory Board Bill. This Bill was deliberated upon by the Standing Committee relating to the Ministry and the official amendments as proposed by Committee were also introduced by the Government in the 14th session of the 13th Lok Sabha in 2003.

This Bill aimed at promoting these objectives by developing a regulatory regime for fair competition in, and orderly growth of, the downstream petroleum and gas sector by providing a level playing field to public and private sector players, resolve inter-entity disputes, and stimulate growth in this sector. After deliberations at the government level and with industry members, the Bill was adopted and passed as the Petroleum and Natural Gas Regulatory Board Act in 2006. The Act provides for a legal framework for the development of the natural gas pipelines and city or local gas distribution networks. Emanating from the act would be the Policy for Development of Natural Gas Pipelines and City or Local Gas Distribution Networks.

The Pipeline Policy

In order to provide a policy framework for the future growth of pipeline infrastructure in the country, the Government has notified the "Policy for Development of Natural Gas Pipelines and City or Local Natural Gas Distribution Networks" on 20 December 2006. The Policy has come into effect from its date of publication in the Gazette of India on 22 December 2006. The salient features of the Policy are as follows:

1. All the natural gas and city or local distribution pipelines will be laid in accordance with the authorization granted by the Regulatory Board under a transparent mechanism. Dedicated pipelines, laid to

supply gas to specific consumers originating from regulated pipelines, will not require the authorization.

2. Regulator shall develop a comprehensive set of technical and safety standards as well as a code for grid connectivity.
3. Progressive unbundling of common carrier transmission activity and gas marketing activity.
4. The designed pipeline capacity to be at least 33 per cent more than the maximum capacity requirement of the proposer and those who tie up for capacity. Such capacity would be made available on an open access and non-discriminatory basis at transportation rates laid down by the Board.
5. The Board may consider different exclusivity periods for setting up of City gas distribution networks and for marketing of gas by the entity developing such networks.
6. Authorization to the proposer may be cancelled with forfeiture of his security deposit, if the conditions of the authorization are not adhered to or the project is delayed beyond the stipulated milestone(s).
7. Once the project is commissioned, the bid bond would convert into a performance bond and would provide the guarantee for satisfactory compliance of the conditions stated in the authorization during the life of the project.
8. The Board will lay down the transportation tariff for the transmission pipeline and city or local natural gas distribution network, as also the manner of determining such tariff.
9. The Government may prepare long tern perspective plan for creating gas pipeline network in consultation with the Board. State Governments. Oil and Gas industry, Gas consuming Industries and other stakeholders. The plan will be kept in view while authorizing/ approving new pipelines.
10. Gas Advisory Board (GAB) shall be constituted by the Government to advise the Government on all matters relating to this policy. The advice of GAB shall not be binding on the Government.
11. To complement and supplement the domestic investment, FDI upto 100% is permitted in laying natural gas pipelines under the automatic approval route.

12. State Governments are required to ensure various statutory and other clearances on a fast track basis.
13. State Governments shall prepare their plans for developing the city or local gas distribution networks, prioritizing the cities or local areas.

Conceptually, a National Gas Grid is a network of inter-connected natural gas transmission pipelines, providing linkage of the various supply sources to the markets in different parts of the country. Such a network of transmission pipelines evolves with the development of supply sources and gas markets. The Gas Grid would evolve with the inclusion of new projects from time to time, depending on the availability of gas and its demand. The Pipeline Policy envisages gas grid connectivity with a view to harmonizing the operations and to provide inter-connectivity to different gas pipelines. For the development of gas sector in India, including establishment of Gas Grid with open market access for all players on a non-discriminatory basis, a comprehensive set of technical requirements and safety standards, as well as a code for gas grid connectivity would be developed by the Board. This would ensure operational compatibility between different gas pipelines. 'Policy for Development of Natural Gas Pipelines and City or Local Natural Gas Distribution Networks' is applicable to natural gas pipelines and city or natural gas distribution networks, except for dedicated pipelines laid to supply gas to specific consumers, provided the same are for their own use and not for resale.

The Notification

The Petroleum and Natural Gas Regulatory Board (PNGRB) has notified the regulations for authorizing entities to lay, build, operate or expand city or local natural gas distribution networks (CGD); determination of network tariff for CGD networks and compression charge for CNG; and exclusivity for CGD networks. The notification of these regulations paves the way for the development of CGD networks in the country. At the time of the constitution of the Board, the Ministry of Petroleum and Natural Gas had transferred a number of applications of different entities pending with them for the development of CGD networks to the Board for necessary action. These entities will need to apply to the Board for authorization for development of CGD networks in line with the procedure specified in the notified regulations.

The regulations authorizing entities to lay, build, operate or expand city or local natural gas distribution networks provide for selection of an entity through an open bidding process for laying, building, operating or expanding a CGD network. The specified procedure is objective and transparent for the development of such networks. The regulations specify the minimum eligibility criteria for an entity to participate in the bidding process. The open bidding is in respect of four parameters with different weightages, viz., lowness of present value of unit network tariff over the economic life of the project (40%); lowness of present value of the compression charge for CNG over the economic life of the project (10%); highness of the present value of inch-kilometer of steel pipelines proposed to be laid during the period of exclusivity in terms of exemption from the purview of the common carrier or contract carrier (20%); and highness of present value of the number of domestic customers proposed to be connected by PNG during the period of exclusivity in terms of an exemption from the purview of common carrier or contract carrier(30%). The regulations specify service conditions and quality of service standards, and the consequences of default and termination of authorization procedure. The regulations also specify the procedure to be followed while dealing with the entities which have been laying, building, operating or expanding CGD network before the appointed day, either authorized by the Central Government or not.

The regulations for determination of network tariff for CGD networks and compression charge for CNG specify the methodology for determination of network tariff and compression charge for CNG for the networks existing before the appointed day which have been either authorized by the Central Government or by the Board under the regulations authorizing entities to lay, build, operate or expand city or local natural gas distribution networks. The tariff will be determined using the discounted cash flow methodology and the rate of return on capital employed shall be 14% post-tax. The gross fixed assets shall be equal to their actual historical cost of acquisition or that normatively assessed by the Board whichever is lower. Similarly, the operating cost shall be on actual basis or based on normative assessment by the Board, whichever is lower. The economic life of the project shall be for 25 years and shall commence from the start-up date of the commencement of physical activities of laying, building or expanding the CGD network.

The regulations for exclusivity for CGD Networks specify the methodology to be used for determining the exclusivity for laying, building or expansion of CGD networks, and exclusivity from the purview of common carrier or contract carrier. The exclusivity for laying, building or expansion of CGD networks shall be for the economic life of the project, which could be considered for further extension by the Board for a block of 10 years at a time, depending on the satisfactory compliance of service obligations and quality of service norms. The exclusivity from the purview of common carrier or contract carrier shall be for a period of five years from the date of authorization for the entities who are selected through the bidding route. As regards the entities which have been laying, building, operating or expending the CGD networks before the appointed day and have been authorized by the Central Government or the Board, the period of exclusivity will be for five years from the date of issue of the letter by the Board for allowing such exclusivity in case the entity has been operating CGD network for less than three years before the appointed day. In case the entity has been operating the CGD network for three years or more before the appointed day, the exclusivity will be for three years.

Pricing in the Indian Context

At present, there are broadly two pricing regimes for gas in the country, i.e., gas priced under APM and non-APM or free market gas. The price of APM gas is set by the Government. As regards non-APM/free market gas, this could also be broadly divided into two categories, namely, imported LNG and gas produced from JV fields. While the price of LNG imported under term contracts is governed by the SPA between the LNG seller and the buyer, the spot cargoes are purchased on mutually agreeable commercial terms. As regards JV gas, its pricing is governed in terms of the PSC provisions. At present, out of the total gas supply of 95 MMSCMD in the country, approximately 55 MMSCMD is APM gas and rest is non APM gas (20 MMSCMD JV gas and 20 MMSCMD RLNG). APM gas, which comes from the existing fields of ONGC and OIL given to them on nomination basis by the Government, is on the decline; while it forms about 60% of the total gas available at present, its share is likely to come down to around 15-20% by 2011-12 while the quantities under RLNG and JV production will go up. The APM regime was introduced in the country to trigger gas demand and ensure that the gas industry takes off faster.

Gas pricing prior to 1997 was decided by the government to fix the prices of natural gas on cost plus methodology and accordingly in 1986 the price of natural gap was fixed at Rs.1400 /MSCM by Government w.e.f. 30-1-1987.

Subsequently, on the recommendation of the committee under the chairpersonship of Dr. Vijay L Kelkar, the price of natural gas was revised to Rs.1,550/MSCM, w.e.f. 1-1-1992, with provision to increase the gas price by Rs. 100/MSCM p.a. up to Rs. 1850/MSCM by 1995.

Based on-recommendations of T.L. Sankar committee, the following pricing mechanism was put into effect from 1st October 1997 vide order no L-12015/3/94-GP dated September 18,1997 issued by Ministry of Petroleum & Natural Gas, Government Of India. The Salient features of the above order on Gas Pricing Mechanism are as follows:

Price of Natural gas is benchmarked to the Import parity price of the following fuel oils—

- Arab Gulf FOBHSFO180 CST, (3.5% Sulphur)
- Cargoes CIF New Basis ARA (1% Sulphur)
- Cargoes FOB Med Basis Italy (1% Sulphur)
- Singapore FOB HSFO 180 CST (3.5% Sulphur)

The 1997 Gas Pricing Order provides that the consumer price for natural gas (the "Consumer Price") is a floating price linked to the basket of international fuel oils (the "International Reference Price") that is determined and fixed quarterly by the Company as per the methodology laid down by the Ministry of Petroleum & Natural Gas. Consumer price of gas at landfall points was benchmarked to the price of above basket of LS/HS Fuel oils as shown in the table below, subject to both a ceiling of Rs.2,850 per MSCM and a floor of Rs.2,150 per MSCM and is linked to a calorific content of 10,000 Kcal. For gas having a lower or higher calorific content, the Consumer Price will decrease or increase proportionately.

Pricing of Gas under Private Sector

Production Sharing Contracts (PSCs) were executed by GOI with Ravva consortium and Panna-Mukta and Tapti (PMT) fields on October 28, 1994 and December 12, 1994 respectively. In terms of PSC for PMT, the ceiling prices are to be revised to 150% of 90% F.O. basket (average of the preceding 18 months), after 7 years from the date of first supply. Thus, the revision was due from June 2004 for Tapti and February 2005 for Panna Mukta. The PMT gas prices have since been revised. While PMT sells 4.8 MMSCMD of gas directly, the balance quantity of about 6 MMSCMD is brought by GAIL, and GAIL paid at the rate of $3.86/MMBTU during 2005-06 and is paying @ $4.75/MMBTU from 1.4.06 based on counter-matching the price offered by prospective consumers in response to the bid floated by the consortium. However, this gas is being supplied by GAIL to power and fertilizers sector consumers along HBJ pipeline at APM price and adjustments are being made through the gas pool account mechanism in terms of the pricing order of 20.6.2005.

In case of Ravva, the revision of ceiling price is due after 5 years from the date of supply and the revised ceiling price is to be negotiated between the Buyer and the Seller in good faith. The price revision for Ravva was due from April 2002. The price revision has been effected with effect from July 2005, and GAIL has been paying @ \$3.50/MMBTU since then. The share of this gas going to APM consumers is being charged by GAIL at APM price, with adjustment through gas pool account mechanism. The total quantity of this gas is around 1 MMSCMD. As regards 0.9 MMSCMD Ravva Satellite gas, it was priced at \$3.3/MMBTU till September 18, 2006. The price has been revised to \$4.3/MMBTU in terms of the provisions of PSC. Since this gas is not under APM allocation, GAIL recovers the full price from the consumers.

As regards the gas from NELP fields, the price of natural gas for sale to consumers shall be in accordance with the PSC provisions. It is to be fixed at arm's length price as per the provisions of PSC under NELP. Prior approval of MoP&NG has to be obtained for the formula or the basis on which the price is fixed.

Pricing of R-LNG

In 1999 for the first time Petronet LNG Ltd, (a JV of GAIL, ONGC, IOCL and BPCL) signed long-term with Ras Laffan Gas, Qatar for supply of 5 MMTPA LNG (equivalent to about 18 MMSCMD). This was first time a Indian company signed long-term contract heralding a new source of gas from outside. Under this contract supplies commenced from February, 2004 and RLNG started following into the market form March, 2004. Even at the time of signing of the GSPA, the issue of pricing was one of the key factors determining the use of RLNG in the Indian market. The price for LNG has been linked to JCC crude oil under an agreed formula. However, the FOB price for the period up to December 2008 has been agreed at a constant price of \$2.53/MMBTU. This price translates to RLNG price of \$3.86/MMBTU ex-Dahej terminal. In order to make the price of RLNG affordable, Indian Empowered Group of Ministers (EGoM) has decided in the meeting held on 11.1.2007 for pooling of prices of 5 MMTPA RLNG presently being imported from Qatar with the price of new RLNG being imported on term contract basis The pool price ex-Dahej of RLNG for various consumers would be about US$4.92/MMBTU.

Recent Policy Developments in Indian Context

The Ministry of Petroleum & Natural Gas revised the natural gas price with effect from June 6, 2006. While the prices for the priority sectors like power and fertilizers remained unchanged at Rs 3,200 per tcm, for CNG distribution and for customers drawing less than 0.05 mmscmd of gas, the price increased from Rs 3,200 per tcm to Rs 3,840 per tcm. With effect from April 2006 the price for all other industrial consumers has been raised from around $3.86/mmbtu (approximately Rs 6,740 per tcm) to $4.75/mmbtu (approximately Rs 8,675 per tcm).

The previous price hike came into effect in July 2005, at that time, CNG and small customers were clubbed with the priority sectors and were offered a concession price of Rs 3,200 per tcm, even as the price for other sectors was increased to Rs 6,740 per tcm. However, the ministry had indicated a gradual alignment of these prices to the market prices over a 5 year period. This 20 per cent hike in prices was the first move in that direction and there was a possibility of further increases for these sectors in the future. The non-priority sectors that include large customers such as petrochemicals, sponge iron and ceramics are the ones worst hit by the price hike. Last year, the prices were hiked by 136 per cent and aligned with the re-gasified LNG prices and the price of gas being sold by the PMT consortium. In 2006 the prices of these sectors had once again increased by 23 per cent and they now align with the current PMT prices, and have been fixed at $4.75/mmbtu with effect from April 2006 for a 2 year period. Natural gas price for the North-east will be 60 per cent of the revised price.

Bibliography

Bacon, Robert (2001): *Petroleum Taxes*, Public Policy for the Private Sector, Note Number 240, World Bank, September, Washington.

BP Statistical Review of World Energy, British Petroleum (Various Issues).

BP Statistical Review of World Energy (2007); June.

Bureau of Transport and Regional Economics (2005): "Is the World running out of oil? A review of the debate," *Bureau of Transport and Regional Economics Working Paper 61*, Department of Transport and Regional Services, Australian Government, Canberra.

Chopra, S.K. (2004): *Towards Sustainable Energy Security in India in the Twenty First Century*, Oxford & IBH Publishing Co. Pvt. Ltd, New Delhi.

Developing China's Natural Gas Market (2002): The Energy Policy Challenges, International Energy Agency.

Energy Economics, James Sweeney, Department of Management Science and Engineering, Stanford University.

Federal Trade Commission (2004): *The Petroleum Industry: Mergers, Structural Change, and Antitrust Enforcement*, Bureau of Economics, United States Federal Trade Commission.

Federal Trade Commission (2005): *Gasoline Price Changes: The Dynamic of Supply, Demand, and Competition*, United States Federal Trade Commission.

General Accounting Office (2004): *Effects of Mergers and Market Concentration in the US Petroleum Industry*, United States General Accounting Office, May, Washington.

General Accounting Office (2005): *Understanding the Factors that Influence the Retail Price of Gasoline*, United States General Accounting Office, May, Washington.

Government of India (1995): *Report of the Study Group, Hydrocarbon Perspective 2010, Meeting the Challenges*, Ministry of Petroleum and Natural Gas, New Delhi..

Government of India (1996): *Report of the Strategic Planning Group on Restructuring of Oil Industries*, Ministry of Petroleum and Natural Gas, New Delhi..

Government of India (1997): *Ministry of Petroleum and Natural Gas Resolution of 21st November*, The Gazette of India: Extraordinary, Government of India, New Delhi..

Government of India (2000): *Report of the Group on Deregulation of Marketing of Controlled Petroleum Products*, Ministry of Petroleum and Natural Gas, New Delhi.

Government of India (2000): *Report of the Group on India Hydrocarbon Vision-2025*, Prime Minister's Office, Government of India, New Delhi.

Government of India (2002): *Disinvestment in Petroleum and Petrochemicals Sector*, Twenty Eighth Report, Standing Committee on Petroleum & Chemicals (2002), Thirteenth Lok Sabha, Lok Sabha Secretariat, April, New Delhi.

Government of India (2002): *Tenth Five Year Plan (2002-07)*, Planning Commission, Government of India, New Delhi.

Government of India (2003): *Demand for Grants*, Thirty Ninth Report of the Standing Committee on Petroleum & Chemicals (2003), Thirteenth Lok Sabha, Lok Sabha Secretariat, April, New Delhi.

Government of India (2003): *Merger and Acquisitions of Oil and Gas Companies*, Forty second Report of the Standing Committee on Petroleum & Chemicals (2003), Thirteenth Lok Sabha, Lok Sabha Secretariat, May, New Delhi.

Government of India (2004): *Central Government Subsidies in India*, Department of Economic Affairs, Ministry of Finance, Government of India, New Delhi.

Government of India (2004): *Marketing Plans of Public Sector Oil Companies and their Implementation*, Third Report of the Standing Committee on Petroleum & Natural Gas (2004-05), Fourteenth Lok Sabha, Lok Sabha Secretariat, December, New Delhi.

Government of India (2005): *Exploration of Oil and Natural Gas including Coal Bed*

Methane, Seventh Report of the Standing Committee on Petroleum & Natural Gas (2004-05), Fourteenth Lok Sabha, Lok Sabha Secretariat, August, New Delhi.

Government of India (2005): *Mid-term appraisal of the Tenth Five Year Plan*, Planning Commission, Government of India, New Delhi.

Government of India (2005): *Pricing of Petroleum Products*, Sixth Report of the Standing Committee on Petroleum & Natural Gas (2004-05), Fourteenth Lok Sabha, Lok Sabha Secretariat, August, New Delhi.

Government of India (2006): "*16 mmtpa refining capacity added along with commissioning of a new grassroot refinery*," Press Information Bureau, Ministry of Petroleum and Natural Gas, December 12, New Delhi.

Government of India (2006): *Activities of Directorate General of Hydrocarbons—A Review*, Twelfth Report of the Standing Committee on Petroleum & Natural Gas (2006-07), Fourteenth Lok Sabha, Lok Sabha Secretariat, May, New Delhi.

Government of India (2006): *Background Material for Economic Editors' Conference 2006*, Ministry of Petroleum & Natural Gas, November 8, New Delhi.

Government of India (2006): *Demand for Grants (2006-07)*, Ninth Report of the Standing Committee on Petroleum & Natural Gas (2005-06), Fourteenth Lok Sabha, Lok Sabha Secretariat, May, New Delhi.

Government of India (2006): *Exploration of Oil and Natural Gas including Coal Bed Methane*, Eleventh Report of the Standing Committee on Petroleum & Natural Gas (2005-06), Fourteenth Lok Sabha, Lok Sabha Secretariat, New Delhi.

Government of India (2006): *Integrated Energy Policy*, Planning Commission, Government of India, August, New Delhi.

Government of India (2006): *Presentation to the Parliamentary Consultative Committee On Refineries*, Ministry of Petroleum and Natural Gas, December 11, New Delhi.

Government of India (2006): *Report of the Committee on Pricing and Taxation of Petroleum Products*, Ministry of Petroleum and Natural Gas, February, New Delhi.

Government of India (2006): *Report of The Sub Group on Marketing of petroleum Products for Eleventh Five Year Plan (2007-12)*, Ministry of Petroleum & Natural Gas, Government of India, New Delhi.

Government of India (2006): *Report of the Working Group on Petroleum and Natural Gas Sector for Eleventh Five Year Plan (2007-2012)*, Ministry of Petroleum and Natural Gas, New Delhi.

Government of India (2006): *Report on Marketing Cost of Petrol and Diesel*, Ministry of Finance, Government of India, New Delhi.

Government of India (2006): *Sub Group Report on Exploration & Production for Eleventh Five Year Plan (2007-12)*, Ministry of Petroleum and Natural Gas, New Delhi.

Government of India (2006): *The Working Group Report on Road Transport for the Eleventh Five Year Plan*, Ministry of Shipping, Road Transport & Highways, New Delhi.

Government of India (2007): "Pricing Policy in CPSEs," *Public Enterprises Survey* 2005-06, Vol 1, New Delhi.

Government of India (2007): *Basic Statistics*, Ministry of Petroleum and Natural Gas, New Delhi, and Various Issues.

Government of India (2007): *Demands for Grants (2006-07)*, Thirteenth Report of the Standing Committee on Petroleum & Natural Gas (2006-07), Fourteenth Lok Sabha, Lok Sabha Secretariat, New Delhi.

Government of India (2007): *Indian Petroleum and Natural Gas Statistics 2005-06*, Economics and Statistics Division, Ministry of Petroleum and Natural Gas, New Delhi.

Gwilliam Ken, Robert Bacon, Masami Kojima, and Kseniya Lvovsky (2001): *Transport Fuel Taxes and Urban Air Quality*, World Bank.

Indian Petroleum & Natural Gas Statistics, Ministry of Petroleum & Natural Gas, Economics and Statistics Division, Government of India (Various Issues).

Marcel, Valérie (2006): *Oil Titans: National Oil Companies in the Middle East* (London and Washington: Brookings Institution Press and Chatham House).

Mehta, Vikram S (2005): "Can Oil majors help?" *Seminar*, November.

Natural Gas Market Reform in the APEC Region, Asia Pacific Energy Research Centre, Japan, 2003.

Raha, Subir (2005): Energy Tomorrow, *Seminar*, November.

Singh, Himmat and Neelam Babar (2005): "The Indian Refining Industry—A Report," Refining Supplement-2, *Hydrocarbon Asia*, January/February, pp.18-26.

South American Gas, Daring to Tap the Bounty, International Energy Agency, 2003.

Stern Jonathan (2007): *Is There A Rationale for the Continuing Link to Oil Product Prices in Continental European Long-Term Gas Contracts?*, Oxford Institute for Energy Studies.

The Role of National Oil Companies in the International Oil Market, CRS Report for Congress, Congressional Research Service, August 2007.

The Use of Profit by the Five Major Oil Companies, CRS Report for Congress, Congressional Research Service, June 2007.

Understanding Today's Crude Oil and Product Markets, Lexecon, 2006.

Villar Jose and Frederick Joutz (2006): *The Relationship between Crude oil and Natural Gas Prices*, Energy Information Administration, October.

World Economic Outlook, International Monetary Fund, Washington, (Various Issues).

World Energy Outlook, International Energy Agency (Various Issues).

Index